Meanderings
of a
Fly Fisherman
Seth Norman

Meanderings
of a
Fly Fisherman

Seth Norman

Illustrations by Roger Cruwys

Wilderness
Adventures
Press

Some of the stories in the present work appeared in slightly different form in the following publications:

"A River of Child," *Gray's Sporting Journal* (February 1996)
"A Tale of Two Rivers," *California Game and Fish* (March 1996)
"Pilgrim's Pike (an Esox Fable)," *Fly Rod and Reel* (October 1995)
"Reflections in Moving Water," *California Fly Fisher* (October 1995)
"The Siamese Avenger," *California Fly Fisher* (June 1995)
"To the Fisher Fishing Alone," *Gray's Sporting Journal* (May 1995, reprint)
"Reading Water on Rangiroa Reef," *Fly Rod & Reel* (January 1995)
"Getting Away," *California Fly Fisher* (January 1995)
"To the Fisher Fishing Alone," *California Fly Fisher* (November 1994)
"The Accidental Trout," *California Fly Fisher* (July 1994)
"Of Grace and a Caddis Case," *Fly Rod & Reel* (July/October 1994)
"Abstaining from Trout," *California Fly Fisher* (March/April 1994)
"A Most Practical Companion," *California Angler* (December 1994)
"Women Who Fish and the Men Who Love Them," *California Angler* (Spring 1994)
"Urban Guerrilla Stripers," *Gray's Sporting Journal* (September 1993)
"Throwing Dace," *Fly Rod & Reel* (October 1993)
"Legends: of Madame X and Cats," *California Fly Fisher* (January-February 1993)
"Destination: September," *California Fly Fisher* (September 1992)

Wilderness Adventures Press books are made to last for generations. They are printed on acid-free paper that will not turn yellow with age. The bindings are sewn, allowing the books to open easily. Our binding boards are covered with 100% cloth. We commission today's top sporting artists to illustrate our books. We believe that our books are the finest sporting books published.

Published by Wilderness Adventures Press
P.O. Box 627
Gallatin Gateway, MT 59730
800-925-3339

10 9 8 7 6 5 4 3 2

Printed in the United States of America

Library of Congress Catalog Card Number: 96-060840

Trade Edition ISBN 1-885106-34-3
Limited Edition of 250 ISBN 1-885106-35-1

Dedicated
to my father,
Maxwell H. Norman:
You knew.

Some of these stories were written as fiction, some as recollection of fact. I based many of the former on real events; the latter are likely distorted by memory, sentiment, anger or affection. Twice I have wildly and fondly portrayed my stalwart friend Terry Breen, which is dangerous because he's now a Deputy District Attorney. Another story contains edged humor about what I later learned might be symptoms of a complex malaise. Once I describe how something happened as exactly as I can remember; a second version takes that truth and tweaks it.

My basic rule was this: When it came to representing real people as honorable and fine as Steve Gore, Private Investigator, I revealed identities. Where I found malice, profound or petty, I disguised the perpetrator, lying outright about names and places and physical features, ensuring anonymity in all cases except those where criminal convictions ensued. If certain issues ever prompt particular questions (have I concealed a weapon while fishing at night in San Francisco Bay?), then I shall seek sanctuary in the Fifth Amendment.

The point is that these are all Stories—writing which essays meaning, not news. In many pieces I try only to entertain. Others invite you on a journey I've taken, for better or worse, and from which I hope you may distill a perspective of some small value, unique to you, perhaps part of your own meander.

Table of Contents

Acknowledgments

This moment has been rather a long time coming, so I have a vast store of appreciation to distribute. Some of this is actually contained in the stories. Not enough.

I'd like to thank my families:

Enid Norman, editor, and as ferociously loyal and nurturing a mother as any wolf cub could want;

My father, Maxwell Norman, who has his moments within, who in his great faith celebrated this book for a decade before his death;

The Morales children: Marc, Cathy, and Eric—long have they owned my heart;

I especially thank Lisa Jungclas, Ph.D., for lighting so much of my way over so many years, tolerating my awful nature, proceeding with humor and courage; then for bringing us The Soph in all her glory; and the whole Jungclas family, for their warmth.

I cannot say enough about the friends who have made me rich: Steve Gore, who taught me much about reading water and life, along with the meaning of "Sterling" as applied to character, and Liz, matching him so well; sly Steve Iacoboni, who would watch out for me, and Mary, who's nicer than he is; Brad Singer, who always knew the meaning of "friend"; Morrie Goldman, who grows wise and kind; Janie Fox-Palmer, who deserves life and does more good with hers than most of us; Terry Breen, partner in a thousand laughs and more arguments—he who held the compass on journeys to hunt Hades and fish the River Styx.

Others who have offered insight and fine companionship: Fred Johnson, may you be well at last; Fred Barnes, one of the Sons, and Jeri; Bob Small and DJ, living well; Tod Norman, Roma and my nephews, too far away, still close; Ernesto, *Mi Gemelo*; gracious Schwartzs, Judy and Claudia; Terry and Steve Murray, for dinners on the deck; Ralph Wood, Frank Piciotta, Al Martin—fishers and friends; the boys at Lubas' wherever you roam; the Bay Wolf staff, whatever you're cooking; Steve

Margulis, Jerome Kass, Jazan Higgins, Marge Nesbit, Helen Cannon, the late Grace Wilson, for encouragement way beyond the call.

>–+–◆>–•–O–•–‹◆–+–‹

To the thousands of mentally ill patients in my classes: it's simply true that I learned more than ever I taught, lessons of spirit.

>–+–◆>–•–O–•–‹◆–+–‹

These editors and teachers have not only encouraged me, but sometimes pushed me headfirst or pulled me handlong toward better writing than I had done: Richard Anderson, heart, soul and both hands of *California Fly Fisher*, for liberty he offers with insight; Carol des Lauriers Cieri, who reads with such joy and generosity of spirit, and who was catalyst to the reaction which brings her name and my words to this page; the late Basil Busacca, for shaping passion with craft "In my class, Seth, God gets a B plus, and only on His better days"; David Foster, iconoclast, of *Gray's Sporting Journal*, champion of difficult stories and real words; David Petzal, *Field & Stream*, who might remember opening a door; Jim Butler, *Fly Rod & Reel*, giving often of his time and kind words; Nick Lyons, a true gentleman I seem both to please and puzzle; Jon Raeside, *East Bay Express*, fighting the good fight when it counted; Burt Carey, Game and Fish Publications, who stole moments to say "Yes!"; Steve Smith, who not only said yes but seized the day; and Chuck and Blanche Johnson, who make the day now.

>–+–◆>–•–O–•–‹◆–+–‹

In the world of flyfishing I have also been lucky, receiving guidance in various efforts from Master André Puyans, Dave Hughes, Pete and Joesette Wooley, Kate and Bill Howe, Doug Lovell, Don Johnson, and Duane Millimen. Uneasy as several of you are sitting together in that sentence, you've all made things better for me.

>–+–◆>–•–O–•–‹◆–+–‹

Last, I owe an enormous debt to the real people I tried to reveal here by the light and in the moments I found them—folks like Sally Merlin, Gary Azevedo, Judy and Steve Carothers, Jeff Owings, Jim Scherer, Bill Newton, Ke-Ke Sulaimen, Dany Leverd, Officer Lee Parker, Donna Smith, Jonathan Allen, Joel Thalheimer, Robert and Apryl Ferris, all the patients I cannot name.

The Warden's Limit

The following is a work of fiction. All characters are fabrications. The places named may be real; some are not. After all, it's been a long time.

Tom's Pond was the first place I saw a fly rod properly fished, and it looked like wicked work. Something about the way Noel waded out so deep, shifting a foot at a time through weed beds soon above his waist. He made such short casts that I knew he'd kept a fish oblivious to his stalk.

Short casts, they were, to a pubescent spin fisherman's mind, 20 feet or so, each one followed by a creeping return. By comparison my own were zingers. I also fished a fly rod, an eight foot Jorgenson glass model to which I'd attached an emerald green, close-faced Johnson Century spin-cast reel, hung below the reel seat with the handle reversed. The outfit was of my own devising and could hurl a quarter ounce bell sinker "From Monday into the weekend," as Noel said, the lead trailing a wisp of four pound test mono like spider silk. On long throws I could feel fibers loading right through the cork, a tension running my arm to the shoulder. Those casts were to "toss-out-the-bobber," what a well-shot arrow is to an infield fly.

I loved to make them, of course, and sometimes they made sense on White Horse, the lake where Noel owned the lodge and I did chores. Especially days when the stock truck dumped its dumb load in the shallow flats near Campground Bay. That would force all the bright rainbows out 50 yards where only I could reach them; and there were afternoons when I'd give away two dozen trout, two or three at a time. "That quiet kid from the store," I heard somebody say, "gave me these fish. Christ, you seen him cast?"

An utterly useless kind of cast for Tom's Pond, the kind I had no interest in making, though even a middling effort would have reached Noel where he waded, most of the way across the two-acre stock tank. From no place on the shore would I find enough water between moss and weed beds to drop a bottom rig without hanging up; nor could I fish a bobber with any reasonable expectation, since the ring of weeds around the bank was twenty feet thick, too wide to surf a trout across if I happened to hook one. No, all my options were poor, save to learn something from watching Noel, who was flyfishing.

That was fine by me. It was, in fact, exactly what I hoped, plus some. The plus was the reason for a certain apprehension, even as Noel waded farther in the falling light, edging out dangerously deep—not just fishing, but hunting as well, seeming to probe the pond into its black heart. Almost up to his armpits, he held the rod way up as he crept in his retrieve, shaking weeds off the line.

I knew lots about those weeds and the denizens therein; that was another small part of the tension. Noel's little brother and I seined similar growth in tanks smaller than Tom's for waterdogs we sold to bass and catfish anglers, and for snakes we sold as feed to bigger snakes at the pet shop in town. I knew that mixed into every net of greens and grasses were seething populations of giant water bugs, which bit; beetles we called water scorpions, which we believed to bite; the odd turtle; snakes of five or six kinds; damsel and dragonfly nymphs; and backswimmers, which do-so bite. The thought of all these swimming around and bumping into Noel's jeans, nibbling in about the ankles of his cheap rubber snow boots, was quite enough to make me shiver.

"You all right?" I called out.

He said nothing, which meant yes.

"Any hits?"

Nothing, which meant no—I could have used a little conversation. I wasn't actually a quiet kid anyway, as almost everybody thought, just shy. "Once you get to know somebody," as Noel would say, "you make every effort to talk them deaf." Besides that, Noel was my agent in this endeavor, and I had a lot riding on him.

I hoped he remembered that. Just as prompt: "It is a big fly, right? You're using the biggest."

"Yes," he murmured. "Now hang on. I think I'm about to—"

>─┼─◆─○─◆┼─<

Bang—there should have been sound, the way Noel's rod snapped down, some noise to fit the lunge and strike. It seemed like there was; and it was just like Noel, also sort of my hero, to call the hit so closely that the fish interrupted him telling me about it. Babe points to the right field bleachers wall. Noel calls his fish.

Which turned out to be the biggest we'd seen all summer, larger than anything that came out of White Horse save for channel cats, a rainbow that sank to three-and-a-half pounds on the postal scale at the store that night, where Noel evaded discussion of where it came from while insisting to curious campers that he "Caught on a fly from wild hairs pulled off the kid's head. Hell no, I'm not kidding."

We had fun with that. But it was all incidental stuff, frosting. What was important was that Noel's big fish was bigger than anything Warden Carter had brought in, or was likely to tonight, the official end of the contest; and that Noel had used the biggest fly of the 36 I'd had tied for his birthday. No matter then, if I was foolish and dead wrong, I had won, standing up—grand with piety, courageously ignorant—against the only real flyfisherman I had met in my life.

>─┼─◆─○─◆┼─<

Warden—Warden Carter. Ironically, the same man was more responsible for Noel's trophy than anybody else, including Noel, for it was Warden who'd stocked Tom's Pond, diverting fish from other destinations—maybe even White Horse—for one of his "private" projects, telling no one, in order "to let the fish grow big."

Only he pretended to believe that he did this for the public good. A fanatic, solitary flyfisherman, everybody called him just "Warden," because that's the way he wanted it, and because he was a sort of man for whom even a last name seemed too personal. Broad and dark, with blue stubble by early afternoon, he lived in a Forest Service cabin without even a dog for company. Sort of lived there: at night you might find him hanging around our store, talking only to Noel at the counter; or more likely prowling some water in his jurisdiction—God help the poacher after closing hour.

An "iconoclast," Noel called him, in a rare burst of big word. I thought something shorter and meaner might fit. Warden made no secret that he liked fish lots better than people, except for Noel, but especially kids. Warden's fondness for my boss was probably the result of Noel saying to Warden's face, in public, things like "When it comes to kids, Warden makes W. C. Fields look like Santy Claus." And, after a Warden diatribe about the antics of boys, "Warden, I guess it isn't so much whether you like children or not, but how you want them cooked."

"You got it," Warden answered then, nodding at Noel with obvious enthusiasm. Then Warden proceeded with his mission: to convert Noel, utterly, to flyfishing.

⊱┄◈┄○┄◈┄⊰

His success on that front, though modest, was another reason Warden deserved trophy credit. It's also where I came in, for while Noel was widely considered the best fisherman around—and hunter, woodsman, boatman; you get the picture—his interest in flyfishing was on the order of "another way to do things." It was one of few character flaws I faulted him for.

I was less cavalier. Somewhere along the line, I'd developed a con-suming, irrational passion for a type of fishing I knew almost nothing about. That Jorgenson fly rod, for example: with reel and line, it was all I'd wanted for the birthday of my eleventh year.

Unhappily enough, two months into 12 now, I understood that tackle alone did not a flyfisher make. All winter my "whipping" casts had played havoc among the lawn shrubs; and I struggled for hours to knot that fat fly line onto a hook—on to, rather than into any eye, since I had none big enough to fit. Even after I'd deigned to read, then mem-orize the booklet that accompanied the rod, I knew little more than "Be sure to observe and talk to experienced flyfishermen, who will cer-tainly be pleased to lend you a hand."

"Not unless he was going to handcuff you," Noel said to that, when I first arrived at White Horse in June. "And I'm damn sure old Jorgensen never met Warden." So I ventured out myself, and, first time, whacked a bat with a back cast, an accident Noel never let me, or any-body else in the Bradshaw Range, ever forget. Pretty soon I put the Century on the rod.

But I'd have taken it off in a minute, if Warden would take me fishing. Or left it behind altogether, if allowed to row his little boat for him while he fished…Why, I'd have sat on a hill with binoculars, if only he let me know where he fished. What would it take, just to get the answers to questions…one night, five or four or—

"My idea of the Devil," Warden told Noel, when I'd begged my boss to pitch my attributes as rower, tackle-bearer, netter-of-fish, "is a teenage boy with a fly rod. Hell is the favorite water of mine where I'll find him, no offense to your help." In spite of this, and because of Noel's urging, I did once screw up enough courage to ask Warden if I'd properly tied a nail knot.

"Go away," he said flatly. "Come back when you're 20."

"I will, sir. But if you could just look, because the book says—"

"*Noel!* Give this kid something to do!"

"He's got it. He's bringing you beer."

"Yeah, and that's illegal. So is *bothering* me." Warden looked at me hard. I had the interesting feeling that—nothing personal, *but*…he really did feel uncomfortable having me around. So I went away.

I came back, though, one Wednesday evening, when Noel was in town getting supplies. He always went in Wednesdays, returning late, but Warden forgot, came looking, then decided to have a solitary beer before heading out to his cabin.

I'd been waiting for such an opportunity. I set down his Schlitz—no glass, his change and, beside that, a five dollar bill.

"Count again," he grumbled, and pushed the money back at me.

"Warden, I'd like to buy five dollars worth of flies."

At the time Noel paid me $40 per month, plus room and board, for six-and-a-half 10-hour days a week. Five dollars was a fair piece of that.

Not Warden's problem, however. This time he pushed the five back at me with the bottom of the bottle, leaving a wet ring around the Lincoln's head. "Huh-uh."

"For Noel's birthday," I added.

He stopped the Schlitz half way to his mouth. "What?"

"Five dollars worth of flies, for Noel, by August 26."

We looked at each other. It might have been the first time he saw me as anything less than an irritating abstraction; then again, it might not. No matter what, I was furthering his end.

"All right," he said. Then, to clarify, "For Noel."

"Right. Can you tell me about how many flies that will be?"
"No," he said, then left with my five.

I didn't much like that answer. In truth, I hadn't the faintest idea how much proper flies cost. We sold none in the store, and the only ones I'd ever seen were the crazy-colored Korean things they sold at Skagg's Drugs, 12 for a buck. So how would I know what was fair? True also, that no one ever called Warden a thief—and after all, he was the Law of a sort. But from what I knew of people, at least of men I admired like Noel and my Dad, there was something wrong with a person who was so disagreeable. Maybe something not to be trusted.

I pondered, deciding eventually that if Warden returned with just three flies, I would have to figure the little things were pricey; then suggest on principle that a fourth was in order—see what happened after that. That's how horses, cars and boats were bought and sold around us, and certainly flies were worth trading as keenly.

So that's about what I did, when Warden came back with 36 flies, nicely displayed in a black cardboard box. Pleasantly surprised, I revealed none of that as I examined each item of my order.

Warden watched me, sucking a Schlitz and appearing annoyed. "Exactly what are you looking for?" he demanded at last.

"Oh, nothing, really."

"Uh-huh. I see."

I continued my perusal. "You know," I said slowly, then stopped.

"What?"

"Well, I'm not sure, but some of these look a little…small." By way of evidence, I picked out a tiny number with delicate gray wings.

"So?"

I considered. "It's just that Noel tries to catch bigger fish, that's all."

Whatever minute respect I might have earned from Warden evaporated, I'm sure. "I see. Uh-huh. How about that." He pursed his lips. "Tell you what, kid…why don't we never mind what you think, and just give these to him? You got your five dollars worth, believe me."

Well, I was 12 and polite as may be expected, I believe. But I was also earning my own way in the world, plus $40 a month; and I was, after all, some kind of long-distance caster. My heroes were men I found reliably well mannered and friendly, often funny, seldom petty or mean. Therefore, if Warden didn't like anybody in the world (except maybe Noel) I wasn't going to take his attitude personally. He intimidated me, sure; but there was something more pressing then, an issue much larger than a little bit of fear—so large in my mind that I actually stepped around the counter to say it, after putting the box down on the counter. With him on the stool, we were just about eye to eye.

"That's what you say," I said evenly, as not to call him a liar. "And there's more flies in there than I thought there would be, so I imagine you're right." I paused, noticing the disgusted expression on his face. "But sir, I want you to know this: these are for Noel, who's my boss and my friend. I'm buying them with my money for his birthday. And maybe I don't know anything about flies, but I do know about Noel, that he likes to catch big fish, because the bigger ones have been around a while, and are smarter. Now, if I'm ignorant for thinking that big fish take big flies...then I've got something to learn." Now I looked at him hard. "And I *will* learn it, sir, someday—I promise you. In the meantime, if 36 is the right number of flies for five dollars, I think they ought to be big ones. Or *you need to tell me why not.*"

I stood and he sat and we looked at each other. I noticed that he was strangling the Schlitz bottle, that his other hand was clenched in a fist with the forefinger sticking out; but he couldn't seem to jack up a word. I waited until I had the queer feeling that he was more at a loss than I was, just then. Suddenly, without knowing why, I felt strong and a little bit sorry. "Anyway," I said at last, "right now, unless you want another beer, I've got to stock the ice box."

⤞⤛⟐⤜⤝

I stocked all right, which filled about twenty minutes of the next five hours of worry. Five hours at least. At 12 I was a champion worrier. Recalling Warden's face, I tried desperately to imagine what was the worst that could happen. Mostly I feared that Warden would simply refuse to sell me any flies at all, big or small. Later, when I got tired, I began to wonder if perhaps he'd tell Noel everything, then claim that I welshed on a debt. And very late that night—was it possible, for him to arrest me? Could wardens do that to kids who demanded bigger flies? If they *really* hated the kid?

The next morning I didn't wake rested. I was still rubbing my eyes when I banged into the store to pour myself a coffee, grunting "Morning, Noel," toward the table where he was, as always early Thursdays, reviewing Wednesday's receipts. He answered "Morning you," in an unusual way.

I glanced over, then stood still. Amidst the piles of yellow and white receipts was a black cardboard box. It was open. I could see the flies from where I stood.

Noel's face had a quizzical expression. He closed the box, held it up, tapped the lid. I did nothing.

"Ah," he said. "If I understand what Warden told me, midnight or so...you should be wishing me an early Happy Birthday, is that right?"

I tried to shrug.

"Ah-*hah*. And—let me get this straight—the bet is...that if in a week I catch a bigger fish than he does—"

"What?"

"—you get a box of flies just like this one. If not, you owe him five bucks."

I had to sit down at the counter, to think about this, slowly and carefully. It only took a minute to be sure that I wasn't going to figure it out. But the prospect—a box of 36 flies—mine. All kinds, all sizes—

It hit me. "But you can only use the big flies, Noel. The biggest ones in the box."

Noel gazed at me for another minute. He looked like he was going to say something, then decided against it. Instead, he nodded. "Right. Of course. We want the biggest fish, don't we?"

>——◆◆——○——◆◆——◄

Which is just what we got from Tom's Pond.

Eventually Noel washed off the last of the weeds, and I wrapped the rainbow for the freezer. The campers went home and the last of the lake regulars left and I still didn't believe that Warden wouldn't show. I was expectant, happily occupied mopping the floor, when Noel waved me over to the counter.

He set out a Schlitz, sweating cold. I looked around.

Noel said "That's for you."

"The heck it is," I said.

"No, really." He raised what was left of his third Miller High Life. "We drink to Warden, wherever he is."

Now I was dumbfounded. "Drink," Noel ordered, so I took a tiny sip, making my usual face. "What's going on?"

He smiled. "You really hate that stuff, don't you? You really do."

"It's terrible. I don't know how people drink it."

Noel shook his head. "Exactly right. That's what I'm saying: that there's no accounting for taste."

I waited. Noel bent over and lifted a big box from behind the counter. It hadn't been there before we left for fishing. He opened it up and flipped out a half dozen sporting magazines from what must have been 50. In almost every one, thin strips of paper marked articles—on flyfishing, it turned out.

I looked at Noel again, who shrugged, reached across to take my Schlitz—"May I"—slugging it even as he popped me a Mountain Dew.

"He's not coming, is he?"

Noel pushed a small cardboard box across the counter. "No. But he left these."

I took the box, held it. "He knew he lost? He just left this?"

"Right."

Thirty-six flies, a selection identical to Noel's. On the lid there was a message in red ballpoint pen ink, all capital letters: "READ THESE MAGAZINES. TEACH YOURSELF AS BEST YOU CAN. GOOD LUCK."

Whatever Warden might have lacked in warmth, he had given more than he bet. And of course, even the bet was a gift.

I still felt very peculiar. Strange, oddly disappointed. At least he could have looked at Noel's fish, told me it was just luck it came to a big fly. "Noel...is there something wrong with him?"

Noel looked thoughtful. "Now there's a question....I don't know. He is the way he is, and Warden William Taylor does not like kids, period. Who knows why not. Maybe something happened. Maybe he would be different, if he could be." Noel indicated the box of magazines, and of flies. "It sure doesn't mean he's all selfish and rotten, does it? And nobody's better at the Warden's job than he is."

"Yeah. I guess."

"But you thought things would change. Hoped it, anyway—that he'd get friendly, you might even go fishing. I know you did, but it's wrong. The man has limits, that's all. He's a good man, with limits. That's all."

I didn't get it, quite. Staring down though, bewildered, I was distracted by the top magazine Noel had pulled out, splayed open now to "Tiny Flies for Trophy Trout."

I had to smile at that.

⊱⊶⊷○⊶⊷⊰

I started reading that night, with that article. I read every single one of the rest, and would report each to Noel, though he never did commit to flyfishing, I forgave him. We saw less of Warden for a while, until the obligatory "thank you" period expired and I could offer him what he wanted from me: to be left alone. He waved, though, if he was in his truck. And when I left for the winter, also forever, I left him a collection of bugs from our bait seines, preserved just the way one of his magazines told me I should.

Thirty years later I still remember the formula and those lessons. For two of those decades I did indeed teach myself, more by accident than design, reading, sometimes reinventing the wheel. I don't recommend that as the only way to learn flyfishing, nor would I discourage anybody from trying that way. All in all, however, the better instruction was Noel's, about gifts and limits. And of course, on the most visceral level—encoded in an old, dark image of Tom's Pond—I'm still certain that bigger flies catch bigger fish, if that's truly what you're after.

The Best Party Ever

So far I'd behaved very well, I thought, mindful of Lisa's edict. "Remember—it's a party. You've fished that pond a hundred times before, and you can fish it next week if you want. But today is a party."

Understand that I'm not anti-social. I particularly enjoy these hosts, who set some sort of standard for using money well: everything about their property is quietly, comfortably beautiful, from the simple elegance of crafted coat hooks to the many long views framed by flowers. The house is a home, the gardens lush with fruit and tomato plants to dwarf Jack's beanstalk. Pleasant twin mongrels wrestle on the lawn while a gelding gallops happily across a sloping paddock. And the pond—

It was a party, all day. Psychologists, mostly, spouses of same, some kids. Not another angler among them, as was easy to tell when evening fell and the barbecue pit hissed on the deck from which I watched bass begin to move, pushing through tulles, swirling in new shadows—

"Remember," said Lisa at my shoulder.

"I didn't peep."

"Don't. And stop looking woeful."

Good food, better wine and I had two hours of light left at the moment our hostess approached me, smiling and smoothing her skirt. "I hate to do this. Please feel free to say no. But I did sort of promise Jaime and Jesse." She laughed. "Well…they would love to go fishing."

I nodded thoughtfully. "Promises are important to children."

"They are."

"You'll explain that to Lisa, when she asks where I've gone?"

"Oh yes. Thank you so much. I do appreciate this."

"My pleasure."

Stay rigged is my Prime Directive, so it was a matter of minutes before I'd fetched spinning outfit, tackle box, nightcrawlers I'd brought just in case, my fly rod. Jaime, seven-year-old son to the estate, carried another rig I'd given to the family some Christmas.

Down through the oak woods, out on the swimming beach beneath a great weeping willow; then into the fiberglass johnboat. By then Jaime was chatting and waving his arms. "I've caught a bluegill already, a huge one! I caught a bass, but he spit it out."

Jesse was strangely quiet. I looked him over. Three or four years older than Jaime, he had light eyes and an unfortunate haircut. His hands pressed together palm to palm, and he was shivering.

"Cold?"

He shook his head once. "No. Only, I can't believe I'm going fishing. I just can't believe it."

No father, I thought.

I've fished with children before. My own adopted trio, kids of friends who drag them across states for a pilgrimage on water. I favor boats for such outings, and bluegill. It's often challenging and sometimes special. I had a sense this outing would be something else.

No father. Or none around: Jesse confirmed this as I rigged rods, warming to the adventure and speaking softly between his younger pal's excited outbursts. "Dad always says he'll take me, but he lives in Los Angeles. So he hasn't, yet. But I think he will."

"Jaime, here you go. Jesse, you'll use mine."

"This one?" He reached for the fly rod.

"No. That kind is sort of complicated."

I showed him how to open the bail on the spinner, a few more basics about baiting and casting. Jaime insisted he "knew how" and promptly flung a nightcrawler off the hook into weeds. "It got off! I need another one! I can't put it on!"

"Hang on, Jaime."

"I'll help him," said Jesse. "I think I can." He did, baiting Jamie's hook just as I'd shown him moments before—before he had ever baited himself.

I watched. When Jesse finished, I handed him the rod. Carefully, silently mouthing the instructions I'd given, he lobbed a little cast. "Like that?"

"Yep," I said, then Jaime zinged another worm into oblivion. "Dang it! They don't hang on!"

I baited Jaime this time, tossing the worm overboard before he could practice hurling. The little bluegill must have been stalking my wristwatch; its jerk on the rod seemed to pop open Jamie's mouth.

"Got one!"

"Jamie's got one!"

"Easy. Stay still—"

"I got one! I—"

Lest we forget that a rod is a lever or that a seven-year-old is stronger than a seven-inch fish: if not for the leash of line this fish might have showed up on the Hubble's lens. Instead, its plunge boatward provoked my third-baseman's instinct. The catch was made secure by the dorsal spine stabbing deep into my thumb.

"Judas—"

"Got him!"

"Way to go, Jaime! And...good catch, sir!"

"*Everybody sit down.*"

"I caught a bluegill!"

"Is that a bluegill? It's a beauty!"

We celebrated with high fives— "What a big hand, sir! Is this your blood? Are you bleeding?"—then I showed them each how to hold the little fish, cradle its belly in wet hands, stroke the green scales. Jamie's cries of joy reached adults on the hill above. Jesse was mesmerized by the fish's dark eye. "He's so alive."

He stayed that way, with explanation.

Jamie's next fish was a bass not so long as his worm. Jaime was disappointed, but Jesse wanted to hold this one, too. "He's a little the same, but different, isn't he? Does this hurt him? He'll be all right, won't he?"

The third fish was another small bluegill, also Jamie's. Jesse praised him as highly as he had for both earlier fish, but I could tell he was worried.

There came a lull after that, while I rowed the johnboat across deeper water. Jesse's back was to me, hunched a little, but when his head turned I saw he was simply soaking in the scene. He inhaled deeply, held the moist air, sighed. "Maybe I won't catch a fish," he murmured, "but it's so pretty here. I never knew it would be so pretty."

Pretty nice kid. And right about the setting. The sun was falling behind the garden hill, glowing orange off the canyon wall opposite; that light also reflected warm from the water, describing tiny gold ribbons where the willow's great limbs trailed across the surface. From above the oak woods came laughter. Closer by on his slope, the gelding watched our progress.

Jaime hooked a bass and lost him. As Jesse re-baited him he cocked an eye at me. I couldn't think of any answer save, "This is the place."

He nodded. "If you say so, sir." Then his gaze fell to the fly rod. "Aren't you going to fish with that one?"

"Oh, probably not."

He considered. "I'll put a worm on for you."

I pointed out the fly, a Micky Finn. He examined the streamer with interest. "I'd sure like to see how you do that," he said. "Just once?"

"I'm getting cold," advised Jaime.

We were drifting into a cove where shallow flats met a deep bank of tulles. I'd always caught bass at the break on our left. To our right, off the flat, was big bluegill water. "Once," I allowed.

After a couple of false casts, I dropped the Finn to the surface. The deer-hair wing floated an instant. That's all it took.

"He *kissed* it!" Jesse cried.

So he had, a bluegill of half a pound. Jesse leaned over as the fish planed in. "Look how fat he is! Why's he so orange? Doesn't he look *just like* the sun did a second ago?"

I'd have stayed out 'til dawn to get Jesse a fish. But Jaime was colder, getting cranky for it; and though Jesse insisted otherwise he was shivering again. So at last I took back the rod, peeled away the worm, then removed the split-shot from his line. "Jesse. Find us the biggest nightcrawler in the box." He did, held it out to me.

"Oh no; you put it on. You're getting expert at baiting."

He liked that. I smiled ."Okay, partner. Are you ready? Because right now we're going to get one together."

He looked a little disappointed when he realized I was going to cast, but the partner role had appeal. "I'm ready," he said hopefully.

"You're sure? Because it's going to be big. A bass—enormous. The biggest."

Now he was grinning back. If he didn't believe, he was enjoying the drama.

"Doesn't have to be the *biggest*," he said.

I laughed, flipped a cast to where the tulles were broken up by a bankside tree. Then I handed him the rod with the reel in free-spool. "When he bites, I want you to let him take it. Just let him have it for a minute."

The big worm drifted down and the line twitched.

"What was that?"

"Jesse. Let him have it."

"That's a fish?"

"Wait. Wait. Wait….Now turn over the bail."

"That's a fish?"

"When the line gets tight—pull!"

No magic: I've fished the pond a score of times, and the best bass was always in this spot. When I saw the rod bow, however, I realized how much the best bass had grown.

"HOLY GOSH!"

"Jesse—"

"Jesse's got one!"

"I got one!"

He looked at me, astonished, then back to where the line entered the water near the stern. He pulled back harder on the rod, felt the fish moving in and, because he couldn't wait, leaned over the gunwale to try and see it. So it was that his face was less than a foot from the surface when three pounds of bass exploded up in a cover-photo shot—gills flaring, body twisting—leaping up higher than Jesse's head, then splashing down with such concussion Jaime screamed.

I was aghast. "Jesse—hold on!"

"OH MY GOSH OH MY GOSH OH—"

"I'm all *wet!*"

"Jesse—" I reached for the rod.

"I'VE GOT HIM."

And he certainly did.

I was still laughing as I rowed us back toward the beach beside the willow. To myself, anyway: it's nice to live a fairy tale once in a while. Jaime was "Hecka-cold" now, annoyed at being soaked; but Jesse looped an arm around him as he sat staring out into a memory only minutes old. I watched him drift the reverie. "Quite a fish, young Jesse. Your first fish was a giant."

He pondered. "Well, you know," he said at last, "it wasn't all mine."

"I figure it was."

"No. Not actually. Not completely. You threw it out—we were partners, like you said…But *partly* mine."

I said "Mostly" and left it at that. Jesse looked about us again, shore to shore—all around this pond in the gathering dark. At last his gaze steadied on the lighted deck far above. We could almost hear words in the conversation.

He nodded as if all of it meant something to him. Putting out his hand, he swept it slowly to indicate hills, sky, willow and water. "This," he said softly, "is the best party ever. This is…the best party of my life." Then, slowly, he mimed a false cast in the air.

Jamie's mother thanked me again. Jesse caught up with me at the car—just in time, too, as Lisa's grim silence was cracking toward comment. When Mom knelt beside my window I saw a wash of other lights glistening in her eyes. "Thank you," she whispered. "You simply have no idea."

I told her the truth, that it was my pleasure. She would have none of that. "No. You just have…no idea."

Maybe, maybe not. "Your son," I said, "I think he's a fisher now. I expect he will be all his life; you might thank me less later on."

She laughed shortly, made a sad reference to her ex's good intentions. "We're not local, so I know Jesse won't see you again. Still…" She shrugged, stood, and with a small smile, looked hard at Lisa. "And thank you, also. For the loan."

That helped. Half an hour into the drive home I got, "You're forgiven." Then, a minute after that, "But you missed a wonderful party."

And I was in trouble again, because I laughed.

6X Redemption

I do not consider myself a purist, but I only flyfish these days. The commitment to long rods—a transition from twenty-five years of fishing every which way—was less conscious than convulsive, part of a change in how I approach the world and make my living, the kind of writing I do, and the last image I see every night before I fall asleep. It's difficult to understand the nature of such a sea change; and I don't presume that telling the story will reveal anything of universal value. Then again, there are probably other people who, sometime, will find themselves moving at a pace or in a direction that ought to give them pause.

⊱─◈─○─◈─⊰

The largest case of police corruption in northern California history sent me hurtling through the Central Valley on an August night, rods rattling in the back of my ancient RV, as grasshopper bodies exploded on the windshield. It wasn't insect carnage that kept me wiping my palms on my thighs, nor was it fear. The unhappy fact was that I believed even then that we—the good guys, Serpico-style sources like Officers Lee Parker and Jonathan Allen and dispatcher Donna Smith, Steve Gore, the investigator friend who brought me into the story, the publisher who would soon print 17,000 words about rapacious thugs in the Oakland Housing Authority Police—we were going to lose. Even with "60 Minutes" filming as I drove, their inquiries prompting, within

hours, indictments from a Grand Jury that had failed to produce anything for six months—

—we, all or some of us, *were going to lose.*

Perhaps I thought this because I had sold out a little and so could not
quite celebrate. Instead, time to go fishing—*to go*, somewhere, fast and
far, *fishing*; so I leaned into the dashboard, trying not to flinch when the
big bugs crashed and smeared.

"Where?" an editor had asked a few hours before I left. Not my own
editor, but another employed by the biggest local newspaper. He'd tried
to break the story himself and failed. Within a month he would quit for
a teaching position.

"I don't know. Fishing."

"Don't leave an address. You don't know how bad these guys are."

Maybe, maybe not. I knew that for years their MO was to sweep
onto a site with eight or nine cars, a hell-bent sergeant directing a mass
assault on too-often innocent victims. The sergeant favored black
leather gloves for such outings, and a matching black leather sap. He
employed the latter when he had a suspect handcuffed in the back seat
of his cruiser; that was his style, metier, and, according to one officer,
"his sexual thing."

Assassination, however, was a different game, and alleged attempts to
intimidate or kill officers opposed to these two had already failed. Lee
Parker alone believed he'd survived three shooting tries. A bomb had
blown up another officer's pickup with the man's father inside. Placed
too far back below the seat, it failed even to injure. A third officer said
he'd had his wheels break off from lug bolts cut almost through, on a
freeway ramp, before he'd picked up speed.

Inept or unlucky, all these. But that was beside the point: I was just a
cipher, and my name wasn't near the top of anybody's list. Still—

"North," I said. "Oregon. Washington."

"That's fine," he said. Then, "Good luck." We'd never met save by
phone, and we've never spoken since.

My butcher had rhapsodized about the Williamson River, drawn me
maps, even given me a pair of big leech flies to fish. Eight hours, he said
the trip would take, but Viola—my RV, the only vehicle I've ever

named—drags about 1200 pounds on each of four cylinders. We don't reach speed limits often; so, a hundred miles up I-5, about midnight, I pulled off at a rest stop.

Which was crowded, almost full. Lots of sleepers, like I would be. Nearly a dozen migrant workers piled under ramadas, wrapped in blankets or sleeping in their clothes. I was about to lie down when a lean guy with a blond beard walked up to my window. "S'cuse me, man. You got any spare change for gas? My ol' lady and me, we—"

>—•>—O—<•—<

I didn't listen to the rest. I have a particular dislike for certain kinds of vagrants. Unlike most reactionaries, or liberals for that matter, I know these types well—I worked two years on the streets case-managing the criminally convicted mentally ill. Much of my effort was aimed at protecting clients from sane, sociopathic, "homeless" predators, nomads without souls.

Harsh? No: harsh is when a schizophrenic client staggers into your office, beaten, robbed of his Social Security check and, for sport, force-fed a month's prescription of Prolixin, his tongue thrusting wildly out of his mouth, eyes agog with terror and a cacophony of voices. Harsh is a 19-year-old girl in her first breakdown who wanders into People's Park in Berkeley late at night, into the company of parasites supported by handouts, more than half addicts, alcoholics and small-time criminals. They live for such opportunities.

Nowadays, and for the last fifteen years, I'd meet her when they are done, on a locked ward. *She* will have the sympathy, compassion and pity that I hold back from hard-luck whiners like this one. So why did I give him a couple bucks? To feel better about other things.

"Thanks, man."

I didn't feel better. Instead, I watched him walk off toward a gray van with Arkansas plates. On the back door I could read part of a badly lettered sign "Vietnam Vet" something something. Not a chance: the guy wasn't 35 years old. Neither was the gaunt woman or second dirty blond man who met him there.

The trio talked. I watched them look over at Viola. My beggar walked back toward me. This time I was at the door.

"Say, man, s'cuse me again," he said, smiling, "you got a beer in there?"

"Nope."

He tried to look around me. "Sure you do, man. One beer."

"No. No beer."

He shook his head. He was still smiling, but now the expression suggested a secret: that I was afraid. "Come on, man. I just know you got a beer in there, and me and my friends could really use a beer." He took a step closer.

I examined him, wondering if it was worth the effort to get my two dollars back: yes, but I didn't deserve it. "Parole's a bitch," I said, by way of making conversation.

"What?"

"Doing time is a bitch, too, but—" I nodded toward the van "—but night patrols, that was hard. And remember how the mortars sounded coming in? "I smiled. "What *did* they sound like?"

He looked blank. Only I was smiling now. We had a secret.

He stepped back. "Hey, man, you know, just to make a few bucks."

"And a beer, whether I want to give it to you or not. You have three minutes until I'm on my CB. Grasp that?"

This breed: they're always so shocked when you raise the ante and call. Aggrieved, they look, deeply wounded. Sometimes I wonder that guys like Parker, who had an obscene number of kills as a sniper in Vietnam, don't come after trash like this.

Naturally, this piece whined. "*Fuck*, man. *Fuck*."

"Yeah. Parole is a bitch."

<hr>

I watched them leave. I do have a CB, a gift from Steve, "just in case." But I've never set it up, so I walked over to the restroom complex to call Highway Patrol. I had a pleasant conversation with a dispatcher. Aggressive panhandling is no big deal, nor is lying for pity. "But you be careful," she said. "We had a killing last week one stop down from where you are."

I sighed. "Yeah, well, I'm from Oakland. I always say my prayers."

After that I lay down in the bunk above the cab, looked out through the skylight and listened to the low rhythm of a truck running a refrigeration unit. Before my sleep image arrived, I remembered rice *paddy* spreading out to the horizon, tracts squared by low berms and speared by eight-foot termite mounds and the occasional tall tree with branches beginning way up the trunk. There often seemed to be a light green glow above the deeper green of the rice marsh, as if the life of the plants rose in mist.

Malaysia, not Vietnam. I'd been in the Peace Corps then, in another silly effort to do right, that one much more expensive than a pocketful of change. We hadn't listened to a lot of mortar fire, though I'd heard some ten years before, in the Golan Heights. Never mind that: what my blond beggar-besieger hadn't seen behind the door jamb was a gift from Parker loaded with— nice irony—Israeli percussion points. Parker had insisted I keep it for awhile, shaking his head over my own little .22.

⟶┼◆⟶○⟶◆┼⟵

I called him in the morning, and he got a kick out of the story. Nothing too much was happening yet: The "60 Minutes" crew had tried and failed to get an illegal roust on film, settled instead for a dinner of *Camarones ala Diablo* at La Fiesta Brava. Parker was feeling pretty good though.

So was I until I called my editor. We argued: I just couldn't convince him that certain parts of the story were important.

I drove away swearing, then parked and stared at the Sacramento River. The great big Sac, lower river below Redding, is a wide glide of runs and riffles that intimidates me. I know that I should fish each seam as if it were a small river or a stream, and I tried to do so for an hour with a nymph-and-indicator rig, feeling the tug of current against my waders, distracted by the sun.

It was not, I decided, a day for the long rod. Though I'd flyfished since my teens, the tactics sometimes called for a faith I did not quite feel, a confidence I couldn't find: rods like fragile wands launching line instead of more tangible weight; reading currents to sink flies that could blow out of my palm in a breeze. Fighting fish without gears or ball bearings, relying on the slip of fingers…I just figured fishing a fly rod for big fish or in big waters was like asking a ballerina to help you fell trees. She might be willing, but to expect success was optimistic. Optimism did not describe my mood.

The spinning rod with a soldier's spine felt better. Realistic, anyway. Immediately I hit a fish at a drop-off into slow water.

Big fish. It fought deep, throbbing. Every shake of its head drew down my tip-top 10 inches. Sac rainbows can get enormous, the size of the steelhead that also run here; and Chinook salmon bucks in this system may reach 50 pounds. The slack water coves trenched out at marinas hold good black bass; shad migrate up in thousands reduced from a hundred times that; and, in the deepest runs, living ever in darkness, edging along the bottom in their armor, swim sturgeon as long as a rowboat.

This was none of these, but a much-hated native, a squawfish. I'd done a story on them several years before, at the pleading of a guide. For two days we'd talked with other guides and old fishermen in trailer parks. "The damn squaws marry the hen salmon," said one of them, "follow her up on the redd. A buck will try to fight them off, but there's so many now, 30 or 40 at each nest, that he'll lose, with damned squaws on one side tearin' in when he's fightin' squaws on the other. Rip the redd to pieces, is what they do." I'd continued to drink with this man until, late, he had allowed that in his life he'd done more than a squawfish's share of damage to the salmon, while owning an orchard along the bank. "Open them gates to irrigate, suck up water and salmon smolts in the pipe. They come up in the trees and lay there like silver, like silver snow, coverin' the ground and shiny, thousand of 'em dyin'." He shook his head with self-disgust. "Now we always talk about the good days, how good they was, how bad it is. Like it's all a big, damn surprise."

I thought about some of that, with the squaw cutting smaller circles near the bank. Eight pounds or nine, easy, with triangular jaws about the size and shape I could make by putting my hands together, forefinger to forefinger and thumb to thumb. I tailed the fish, then looked around for something to use as a priest. It was mostly earth bank there, with trees smallish and wrapped around by blackberries, so I hauled the fish up to the parking lot and swung it against the asphalt. The first blow certainly killed it; I suppose the next three or four were for emphasis. When I found a blue garbage drum stenciled "Trash," it seemed very clever to hang the remains on the lip, leaving them to bleed.

It seemed clever at the moment. Twenty miles down the freeway, it struck me as small-spirited. A squawfish did what it knew to do and killing one was a chore, not a moral triumph.

There was something wrong with me.

What, exactly?

The sense of bewilderment tugged at me many times during the next two hours. I gnawed on feelings of fault and blame, getting nowhere; then stopped, napped, woke with the need to drive.

I did, down a long and rutted road above Lake Shasta, taking some satisfaction in the thump and grind of Viola's six wheels and arriving, at last, at what had once been the mouth of the McCloud River. The lake was thirty feet down after four years of drought; now the river ran an extra mile before reaching still water. Too bad; I'd hoped for a familiar place, a chance to angle water I understood. Instead, I drove around, seeing rapids where once I'd drifted at leisure in a fat red inflatable. Finally, I hiked down and took a smallmouth on a streamer. Only one though, a fluke; I drove out, pushing Viola hard with the hope of making the Williamson by early evening.

It was later than that, edging twilight, when I came close; then I could find neither my butcher's maps nor any public access. I was furious. With the sun falling I was also exhausted and desperate, so I stopped at a diesel garage built near the river.

The guy called himself Dizzy Dean and, looking me over, seemed not entirely pleased. I hadn't checked a mirror, but I guessed I looked shaggy and rather hollow. "I just want to get near the river for a few minutes. Before it's dark."

"Where'd you say you were from?"

I could see another man, also in his sixties, watching me from the shadowed garage. In the house adjacent a curtain moved. "Oakland. California."

"California."

"Right."

He nodded, weighing this. "There's an Oakland in Pennsylvania, too," he said.

"Next to Pittsburgh," I said.

"You know Pittsburgh? Hell, I worked steel there near thirty years ago. Nice town, but dirty."

"Cleaner now," I said. "Mostly just nice. About the friendliest people I've met in a city."

"Yeah, I remember....Well, hell, I suppose you might as well park your rig over there."

I offered him a fish, if he wanted one. "I wouldn't mind. The brother likes a fish, and my sister can cook 'em."

Forty-five minutes, I figured I had. Three to rig up—no time for the fly rod—and then I stood on part of a low ridge that funneled the water into a pool below. A huge fish moved below me—monstrous, certainly a carp. Another worked above a slick farther down. I took my trout just at dark, swinging the same spinner that had done for the squawfish. It was 21 inches and silver even without a moon to light it. I regretted the promise to my host while doing my duty, cutting loose offal into water that turned over and over and swept away.

>-+◆>-○-<◆+-<

Dizzy looked happy with the offering. "That'll do," he said.

Good. "You've got some big carp in there, haven't you? Really big ones."

He could look pretty mischievous for an old fellow. "There's no carp in the Williamson," he said. "Not a one."

I looked at him. He laughed. "Show you what I use," he said, and led me to a couple of rigged rods leaning against a wall. Light saltwater stuff, 20 pound mono-knotted to nine-inch, broken-back plugs."

"For trout," I said.

"For trout."

He didn't invite me for dinner, but he did suggest I sleep right where I'd parked.

"You know," I said, "I think I better drive."

He nodded. "None of my business, son, but I think you better not."

I didn't. Instead I drank Jim Beam, slowly and steadily. Because Dizzy Dean had called me son, I thought about my father, missing him more terribly than I had in years. What would he think of what I had done?

He would have been proud and sad. He would have sat quietly, smoking his pipe, his skin the golden color of cured tobacco, eyes dark beneath brows gone wiry and gray. A rager, my father, he was also a man of soft, eloquent sighs. He had excellent manners and could still say "son-of-a-bitch" with more conviction than anyone I've ever known.

He flew 50 missions in a B-17 and won medals I didn't know about until I was 20; but he had also lost battles.

"We're not going to get them, Dad," I told him aloud, and it startled me. Silently, then, "Not the big ones. Maybe we'll get some of the little ones, but the fat bastards, the architects of it all and the worst of the thieves…we're just not going to get them. And I'm tired and I feel very dirty."

I didn't imagine him speaking to me. I only imagined his silence, and drank, slowly, for a long time.

⊱┈⊰⊱┈0┈⊰⊱┈⊰

Lying on my back, beginning to doze, I had my "sleep image." I used to think everybody had one—a last picture or set of pictures in your mind before you slipped down. For some time, at least since beginning the OHA story, my own was one that should not be described in great detail. Suffice it to say that it was suffused with dread and included amputating a hand.

⊱┈⊰⊱┈0┈⊰⊱┈⊰

I woke thick. Fish were rising amidst hatches of different bugs, and I couldn't raise anything. The fly rod, an off-the-rack six-weight, felt feeble; but the spinning rod seemed too much like a killing stick, crude and sharp.

⊱┈⊰⊱┈0┈⊰⊱┈⊰

"I don't know about bugs," said Dizzy, already greased in his overalls. "But you know, there's a fly shop down the road. You could ask there."

It was Tuesday and the shop was closed. Entirely right, I thought, full of an anger far beyond reason. I needed coffee anyway, so I walked forty feet to a cafe.

It was busier than I expected. A harried waitress put a steaming cup in front of me without asking, then hurried to serve other tables. Watching her haste, the way she blew loose hair from her forehead, eased me somewhat. "You," she said at last, surely relieved that nobody had arrived after me. "Sorry for the wait. Anything else?"

"No, thanks. Just a refill when you get around to it. "

"I'm going to top you off right now."

"Thank you. I guess you get these crowds during fishing season."

"Oh, we do. Lots of folks fish."

I nodded. "Sure hope it doesn't hurt business, that suicide off the bridge."

"What?" she dropped the coffee pot down hard. "Somebody jumped off the bridge?"

It can't be a thirty-foot drop. "Not yet," I said. "But if I can't find anybody to tell me what flies those fish are eating, I don't see that I'll have any choice."

Her mouth closed. She eyed me evenly, then began a laugh that lasted a wonderfully long time. "You just wait a minute," she said between gusts.

I heard part of her phone call, repeating my story. "You sit there," she said when she returned. "Judy's still laughing; she's coming down to see what you look like." A big smile. "You know, one last look?"

⊱┄⊶┄○┄⊷┄⊰

Judy Carothers and husband Steve run what was then the "This and That" store, selling flyfishing supplies and local crafts. Judy's also a sort of patron saint of old flyfishermen around Chiloquin; she tended Polly Rosborough and Kelly—"just Kelly"—for many years. She was grinning when she sat across from me. "That's so sad," she said. "Is there anyone I should call when you're done?"

We talked caddis, at first, then the river. Indians, water wars. She had fled the same area I'd come from, where her ex-husband was a cop. I thought I was listening to her voice, a soft sound full of smiles, sometimes wistful; but four hours later—the last two in the shop she opened for us—I'd told her the whole story.

She sighed. "Brother. That's just how I remember it. Same sort of stuff."

"Same and same," I said, as if I had some perspective.

"So you came here, fishing? That was smart."

"I hope so."

"Me too. Listen, there's some great water up here, and not just the Williamson. If you can stay I'll get Steve to take you out with Kelly on the Wood. Maybe you can do a story about that. You'll love it out there."

"Wish I could," I said.

"You have someplace else to go?"

She knew I didn't.

"Or do you think somebody will find you here?"

I shook my head.

"Ah," she said. Then she told me that, when I came back this way, she would send me out on the Wood.

I appreciated the invitation, along with every minute she'd spent talking and listening. "It's a feeling," I said, trying to explain. "I need…speed."

"Maybe," she said.

I'd had the offer of rest and could not take it. I felt bad about that, driving away, but I left the truck engine running when I stopped to say a farewell to Dizzy.

"Hell, stay," he said. "Park where you were. Stay a week, if you want."

I smiled, shook my head.

"Come back, then."

I nodded. Thanked him. And began to move fast.

Many of the following days are dim. If I'd expiated anything over coffee it certainly didn't decrease the restlessness, though maybe I drank less. Often I drove until I was exhausted, never bothering with campgrounds but sleeping on dirt turnoffs and back roads. I fished the Upper Santiam, sometime in there, and the Deschutes while cutting across to the coast. From a gas station I called my friend Steve to hear that my story was out. "Yeah, it's chaotic here. Now every newspaper's got it." Likewise, the Sheriff's Department, DA's office and Public Defenders, all of whom were now scrambling to take credit for a sting operation overseen by the FBI and BHE. Only three years late: the same bunch had failed in their duty so many times, destroying an awful lot of good citizens in the process. Some good cops, too: one of these, Jonathan Allen, they'd allowed to be beaten, jailed and fired after he had repeatedly tipped off other agencies to corruption in his department. The chief of police had been in on that humiliation. "Now, people say he's bragging that they'll never get him," Steve said. "Because he worked for the FBI."

"You think it's true?"

"I don't know. Parker and Donna"—dispatcher, Parker's girlfriend, vital to my story—"are sure that the investigator the FBI assigned is a former partner of his, been a drinking buddy for years. They say the guy's calling the chief from the courthouse."

"Jesus Christ." Secret investigation, you bet.

We would just have to wait. I would do so at speed.

The Umpqua. A clerk at a convenience store said her brother caught lots of fish "Where you go left after the big turn to the right—first road, park anywhere." I did, and from a perch on a boulder, took more squawfish and a couple of tiny smallmouths with the spinning rod. Walking back to the road through trees I heard a truck rumbling. Somebody called my name. I stopped dead for an instant, then slipped deeper into shadow.

From shadows, I saw a green pickup idling alongside Viola, with a man at the wheel. A small boy scampered about on the roadside, picking up garbage. The man called my name again and the boy answered. I stepped out and walked toward them.

><+>+O+<+><

"Hey there," the man called loudly. "Catch anything?"

"A few." We were talking over the sound of the engine.

"Uh-huh. Think you'll stay here much longer?"

It was an owner's question, proprietary. "Not if you can suggest a better spot."

"Uh-huh." He turned off the engine. "What I was going to suggest is that this private property."

I looked around, then down. "I'm sorry. I didn't see any postings, or a fence."

"Yeah, that's right. Because people tear the postings down, and there's nothing to fence but these trees. You have any idea what they're worth an acre?"

"Half a million?"

He nodded. "More." He chewed this over in his head, watching me. "You see all the trash people leave? You see the fire pits?"

"Yes."

"What do you think?"

"That they also owe you an apology. I'll make mine again: I am sorry." With that I slung off my vest and pulled from the big back pocket a couple of bleached Coors cans and assorted other scraps. It's an occasional hobby of mine, to pick up junk.

The man looked impressed and disgusted. "Uh-huh. Well, not so much you, then. But that's what I hate most." He pointed to a coil of monofilament, 10 or 20 kinked yards probably stripped from a tangled spool. "That stuff is deadly. What's the matter with people?

Don't they know what that does to animals?" He shook his head. "They don't care."

>-+-<>-O-<>-+-<

His family had owned the land for three generations, had once run a mill. He noted my California plates, asked what I did, then said that if I was a fisherman and a writer, he imagined I supported the spotted owl policy. I told him I'd thinned timber and cut pulp for a while, and yes, I thought the timber companies needed limits, but that I mostly blamed the government for selling us all off too cheap while failing to enforce their own regulations. He didn't mind hearing that and, half an hour later, was pleading with me to write a piece about how one of the big cutters had ruined a remote stream he'd grown up fishing, logging right down into the water, running equipment through the bed, violating every established law and policy until, as far as he could tell, no trout lived there any more. "I'll show you the whole thing, take you out there myself. Just don't use my name. I have to live here."

"You know," I said, and I knew how weak it would sound, "that's something one of your local people should write about. Some reporter from here or near here. Not somebody from California."

He thought about that, his expression grim. "I guess that's right." We both knew no one would. "I ought to get home." He called back the boy with my name, who by this time had dumped into the truck bed several square feet of cans and cardboard, Styrofoam, plastic Sprite bottles, a bra, an assortment of colorful potato chip bags. "Brother," he snorted, and started the truck. "Stay as long as you want," he said. "Maybe you can even keep an eye on things. Like fires."

>-+-<>-O-<>-+-<

I was soon on the road.

Portland at night; they say it's a nice town. Then up into Washington. Phone calls along the way: Lisa missed me at home, my step-kids hoped I'd be careful. Parker and the other sources were ripping down threats posted on a bulletin board in the office: they'd made a pact, and made it known, that they would retaliate for actions taken against them. I didn't consider the caution idle: Parker had been a sniper in Vietnam, then a weapons trainer at Quantico.

My publisher was excited but edgy as a cat, waiting for libel suits. Steve said the legal community was buzzing. "You'll get awards for this one," he said. "Meanwhile, they say I look good on camera." Formerly an investigator for the Public Defender's Office, Steve had discovered the corruption in a HUD-run security force with guns, badges and Peace Officer Status. His superiors had forbidden him to look into it. He did anyway, on his own time, in secret, for two years, risking his life and career a hundred or two times before he quit the county to go it alone.

"What about the chief?"

A pause. "He's telling the media it's a racist plot. Compares himself to Marion Barry."

I considered: "That's about right."

▻┄◈┄○┄◈┄◅

Driving at night was best. The dread of those first days steadied into a low drone that harmonized with Viola's little engine. I fished bait, when I fished, but I slept a lot during the day. At last, in King's County Washington, outside Seattle, I parked Viola at the house of a friend's father and got a ride to the airport. I flew across the mountains to Walla Walla, where another friend, another Steve, picked me up.

I spent three restless days there with him and his family. Steve read a draft of the story I'd brought with me. "Let me get this straight...These cops would just walk up to you, tell you to pull down your pants, take your money." He was laughing.

"Probably not you," I said. "You're white: you might sue. Mostly blacks they leaned on."

"And they're black."

"Mostly. Sometimes though, a lot of times, they screwed up and got middle-class types. Those are the ones they had to make sure they arrested or cited for something, so it would be the officer's word against theirs in a courtroom."

"They did this how many times?"

"Allen, the officer the chief had arrested, guesses three to five thousand."

"I don't believe it."

That had been the problem: the scope of activity was too wide. Maybe a jury wouldn't believe it either.

"Allen's the same one who went to the DA and to the public defenders?"

"And somebody in the sheriff's department."

"So how come they didn't do anything?"

I shrugged again. "I don't know, exactly. I think because their directors are elected. Nobody wants to take on a black police chief, his black boss, a black sergeant, and mostly black cops. Not in Oakland."

"I don't blame them. How come this guy Allen did?"

"He's honest. And he's black."

Another night, Steve staring across the glow of a single malt Scotch, "You know, this whole thing is just like you."

I looked at him dubiously.

"I'm serious."

"What are you talking about? I've never done an investigative piece in my life."

"Maybe not. But how many other people get thrown out of the Peace Corps for sabotage and sedition?"

"I wasn't *thrown* out of the Peace Corps. I was thrown out of *Malaysia* by a stinking Islamic government. I was asked to stay in the Peace Corps, anywhere in the world they had an opening. The whole Peace Corps was out of Malaysia in a year. That was *nothing* like this."

Steve began to laugh. "Remember in college? When we were taking bets who would get you first? Those Black Panther wannabes, the Chicanos, or the Arabs? Remember that?"

Now Steve was giggling and spilling 30-dollar scotch from the edge of his glass. I didn't think any of it was all that funny, and I couldn't figure out whether he was making me out to be better than I am or suggesting that I was a racist and a malcontent. I reminded him that I had an Hispanic girlfriend at the time, that the step-kids I'm nuts about are Hispanic, and that I'd been working civil rights since I was 12 years old.

"That's not it," he said firmly. "The problem is," he groped a moment, "that you don't let anything rest."

I must have puffed up like a pigeon. "How could I let this rest?" I demanded, sounding so pious I winced.

"Easy," he said.

This Steve is an oncologist. Sometimes he saves people's lives. The local hospital has built a clinic around him. He also has three neat sons, a wife I love, a sprawling comfortable house with a kitchen the size of most Oakland apartments, a collie, two horses, and a pasture. He lives in a town that, in its entire 150-year history, probably hasn't seen as many murders as mine has during any 12-month period since

1980. He even has three split-cane fly rods he hasn't the faintest idea how to fish.

>‒+‒◆‒◦‒◆‒+‒<

One of which he gave me when we parked at the airport. At the time we were sitting in his Volvo with leather seats; he also has a new Suburban. It wasn't necessary for him to say aloud, "There are other ways to live."

"You know," he said, "there's something I expect of you."

"I can imagine."

"That you'll take care of my boys if anything happens to me."

I looked at him. Steve's father died when he was eleven. I was living in Steve's house twelve years later, when his mother's cancer moved into her brain.

"You can marry Mary if you want to," he continued. "But you have to raise the boys. I want you to swear to that now."

On the plane I tried to imagine what such a life would be like. It was odd to feel the relief.

>‒+‒◆‒◦‒◆‒+‒<

It didn't last beyond the landing. Fred picked me up and we went back to his father's house. I stayed three days, the trio of us taking day trips into the mountains. It was wonderful to see the two of them together. Fred is six and a half feet tall, impoverished by a life of scholarship, and very, very ill. He did manage a short hike up a trail in the Cascades, stopping often to ask his dad about trees and to discuss geologic phenomena they recognized.

Along the way I caught something, maybe a chum salmon, on a spinner in a river; then two gorgeous cutthroats from a tiny lake, keeping them for dinner. It was almost magically relaxing, sitting in Fred's father's house, urging him to explain things: he is one of the people who make the world work right, a genius engineer-without-degree who headed a development team for one of the aeronautics companies in Seattle. Looking around his house, examining things closely—from the wood stove he welded together to hinges on his fruit cellar adapted from the hood of a Volkswagen bug, and a mulcher which turns two hundred pounds under the pressure of two fingers—it's magnificently clear how each device has been thought through. Fred's dad takes Aristotle to heart.

I was almost quiet for moments. Except late at night, every night, around two or three a.m., when Fred's sister, who has her troubles, would begin to mow the lawn, quietly, the well-oiled blades whirring as they nicked a single day's growth. Once, lying in the bunk above Viola's cab, I watched her hang out white bed linens in the moonlight, moving bare-foot and silent in her white nightgown, with the sheets billowing a little as she lifted her face upward and skin glistened across an expression stern and utterly intent. I remember the rustling sounds of heavy, damp cloth.

Of course it was strange, but I also found it just a tiny bit familiar, as if our demons had nodded once in passing.

⊱—◆➤—◦—◄◆—┤◅

Steve, the investigator Steve, said in a phone call that an attorney he was working with had filed suit for 42 people illegally detained and arrested. The DA's office was now abandoning virtually every new case in which one of the rogue OHA officers was involved. The black-sap sergeant had been called to one already pending and, wearing full uni-form, had actually taken the Fifth Amendment about his name.

"What do you mean, 'about his name'?"

Steve laughed. "He took the stand, and when the Deputy DA asked him his name, he refused to give it, on the grounds that it might incrim-inate him."

"His *name*?"

"He took the Fifth again when asked if he was a sergeant in the OHA."

In another case in progress, a judge dismissed all charges against a defendant because he found the testimony of a twice-convicted drug dealer "more credible" than assertions of the arresting officer and the chief, who'd made "misstatements" about the officer's "good" record.

"What about the chief?"

"Haven't touched him. Not even suspended."

"And all the guns they found in his office?"

"Nobody's paying attention, so far."

Nor would they ever.

"They're not going to get him, are they."

Steve hesitated. "It's a little early to know that."

Lisa wanted me back home. My step-kids missed me at dinner and worried. It was time to drive again. South, home.

I traveled in fits—short stretches suspended by sudden exhaustion, moving like one of those lizards with a single-chamber heart: dash, rest, dash. Always stopping by water, sometimes I didn't even fish, as on one big coastal stream, where, hunting access, I saw a man with a spinning rod on a bridge. I parked, walked out to watch.

It was surprisingly shallow water below, a riffle really, ten to 20 inches deep. He had cast and now leaned his rod against the railing. He did not care to talk—barely nodded as greeting. But all I needed to do was follow the course of fluorescent line to understand the game.

He had a chartreuse diving plug on the end of his line. It wobbled wildly in the current, plunging a few inches, then rising. Every so often it would actually bump the nose of a five- or six-pound steelhead suspended in the clear, shallow water. When that happened the fish would turn its head slightly or back off a foot or two; then the angler would move his rod a little, to place his provoking plug back again in front of the steelie's white mouth.

I continued to watch for three or four more minutes. Wobble wobble, slip back, move the plug.

"That's it," I said at last, more to myself than to him. "That's how it's done." "It works," he said curtly.

>—+◦+—O—+◦+—<

Eight or ten miles upstream I saw a long glide above fast water. More from duty than anything else, I spent an hour hauling with the fly rod. Nothing. By then, however, I'd seen boils at the head of the pool, beneath another bridge: chinooks. I couldn't hope to sink a fly to them, so I broke out a steelhead casting outfit I often use for striper. I tied on a lead-tube and glow-bug outfit, and walked—climbed, really—upstream from the pylon, setting up below a spillway. Second cast, the drift stopped.

A buck, dark, probably 25 pounds. He fought deep, holding to strong currents, but I was armed for him and brought him to hand pretty fast. The pink bug had stuck him just at the tip of his lower jaw and came free quickly. When I looked up I saw a small cluster of children watching me from the bridge, talking together in words I could not hear for the spillway falls.

The second buck was much the same, big and dark. The fight reminded me of splitting log sections, the heavy impact of a sledge into green wood, the kind which resists the wedge, forcing you to hammer deep until fibers begin to tear, barely ripping by inches instead of cracking apart. Again the bug came free quickly.

I thought I heard a noise and looked up almost directly into the sun. By the hat, I took the man for a highway patrol officer. Silently— I think—he pointed at me, then swept his arm to a sign posted near the bridge pylon on the opposite bank. I couldn't read it, but his next gesture, swinging from my chest to the river behind him, the downstream side of the bridge, seemed clearly to indicate that I was standing off limits.

I nodded, reeled up. He nodded back and stood watching me. When he saw me appear below him on the bridge's downstream side, he walked away. I wondered if he would have been so tolerant had I killed the buck.

>-+-»-0--<-+-~

It was different water, a run not particularly promising, so I switched to a heavy spinner without any expectations. I was tired and didn't much care that I'd been moved. It occurred to me then that I'd really not felt the two fish, not exhilarated in them. This made me unhappy in a muted sort of way; then I struck suddenly and savagely in midswing, bending the stiff rod way down into the butt.

The males had been slow, weary; this hen was not. Her first run was a crazed streak, the next, downstream, an arc that began to fail as she faced the fastwater stretch where I'd earlier tried for steelhead. Perhaps I had surprised her on a nest, at some climax moment in her journey which, now, I would finish: two hooks of trebles had gashed her under the throat, ripping gills. She bled a slick on the beach when I tried to revive her, wasting herself, unable even to struggle.

I cursed and cursed, furious that I had not settled for the pair. It didn't help, and eventually, I dragged my kill up to Viola. With my hand in ripped gills and my arm extended, her tail touched the asphalt.

Once again a pickup pulled up beside Viola, this one beat to hell, also with a man and his young son. Both gaped. "Jesus Christ," said the man.

"Look, Dad!"

"Foul hooked," I said. "Do you want her?"

"Jesus Christ," the man repeated. "The season closed on salmon two days ago."

"God *dammit!*"

"Dad!" the boy cried. "Look how big it is, Dad!"

The man glanced around quickly. "Throw her in the back," he said. "I'll smoke her. Throw her in the back—right now."

I did, on top of scraps of pine bark, as the man jumped out to pull a tarp over her. He shook his head. "Thanks. We've got to go."

"Dad—"

"Jimmy, will you shut up a minute?"

⊱┉◈┉⊰

I drove hard, thinking hard. After the first flare of irritation and remorse, I settled into grim resignation. I've killed thousands of fish, I imagine, angling since childhood, working three summers of my teens at a fishing camp. Even so, snagging a hen salmon—maybe on her nest and certainly out of season—was no small thing. I'd been flat-out lucky to find somebody who looked to need her. Lucky, too, that the trooper hadn't stuck around.

Such luck isn't the best kind; it's the luck of the lousy. This would have bothered me longer if, after an hour of driving, another feeling had not reared up to disturb me, beginning as I wished again that I'd quit fishing after the bucks. Suddenly, I realized that, in truth, I didn't even care that I'd caught them.

That's bad, I thought.

The idea had legs and ran, especially when it occurred to me that, hell, I hadn't cared much about any of the fish I'd caught on this trip, though the Cascade cuts were pretty and it was pleasing to feed Fred and his Dad. With none of them had I engaged—found that sense of connection and excitement that had salved me all my life, drawing me ever to water, especially in the worst of times.

Like this one; but it wasn't working. Why?

I was unnerved and confused. In a burst of ugly self-pity, I thought, "*This is not fair.*"

It really wasn't. I had no reason to be ashamed of my role in writing this story, in living it, off and on, for two years, the last six months of which were so intense and loaded—literally, with wary sources who made a point of showing guns—that drinking myself to sleep was as forgivable as it was unwise. My pay for the effort would come to something less than a dollar an hour.

Well, nothing to be ashamed of save the one thing, which wasn't shameful—maybe, maybe—so much as galling, a compromise I'd made for good reasons:

When I'd first submitted the story, it was written as an insider's view of what happened in a scandal we assumed would be already revealed, widely reported, rampant in every media outlet around. The indictments we waited for would assure that and would also provide protection for my sources.

None of that happened, or so little it hardly mattered. Without such exposés, sources like Parker and Donna were terribly vulnerable. So I placed an embargo on publication.

Parker was exposed by the DA's office that had promised it would not do so, named as a source of information on a search warrant conducted on the force's central office. The rogue officers presumed collaboration from Donna and others. Retaliation began, official and unofficial: vacations were canceled, sick and funeral leaves denied, checks withheld; then those vehicles vandalized and sabotaged. Street contacts told Parker that a sergeant had bought a contract to kill him. The same officer assigned Parker to walk a night beat alone in one of the worst housing projects, where he was shot at. According to Parker, his reports of those incidents were not passed on to the Oakland Police... and then, the Sergeant sent him back in.

Looking it all over, Parker at last said "Now," and the others agreed.

I went to the weekly that held the story. "They want it out and to hell with the indictments."

For months both the publisher and his editor had been hounding me to say just this, even threatening once to write their own story if I refused. Suddenly, the editor seemed to balk.

"I'm not sure about, well, exactly the way this will play," was the sort of thing he said, along with other vague directives that prompted me to desperate rewrites.

Finally, over the phone, I put it directly: "What do you want?"

The silence that followed couldn't have lasted five seconds, but it was dark at my end. Then he reminded me that I had early on asked for his help with the story before going it alone. He'd done some important work, he insisted. He wanted to put it in.

"You want your name on it," I said.

His answer was to the effect of "Listen, it's not like it's a Pulitzer-winning story, you know. If you hadn't been involved, it would have been mine anyway. It's been a lot of work just going through your stuff. And I have things to add."

It was an easy decision, thinking about Parker under the chief's thumb. It was also like swallowing a slug of somebody else's spit: do it fast. "Do it," I said.

Steve and Parker were particularly angry. "Take it somewhere else," they insisted, "screw 'em." I dismissed their objections. Bluntly stated, it took great courage to run the story as I'd written it; this paper had that, was willing to take huge chances. And now, with the timing so critical …all other considerations were mere vanity.

>−+◆>−O−◁◆+◁

Wasn't that right?.

I just needed to go fishing, to feel better.

Now I couldn't feel the fish.

Which was entirely unfair; and it was time to go home.

>−+◆>−O−◁◆+◁

I slept somewhere, drove, ended up in Bend that afternoon, a Sunday. From another pay phone, I called around until I found a shop open, to ask for suggestions about where to fish the evening. A kid—I think his name was Joe—suggested either the Rogue River or Crane Prairie Reservoir. I chose the lake because I'd been hauling my fat float tube around with me, living around it, eating with it sitting across from me at the table, for nearly three weeks now, and had only fished from it once, in the early days in some quiet bass pond. I would drift into the evening and dusk. I might as well throw a fly.

Near the boat launch I met an officer from Oregon Fish and Game who was checking in catches. We chatted. He didn't flyfish but had heard that those who did here favored brown flies, "kind of a cinnamon color." He also mentioned that the lodge nearby sold live "bugs" as bait, which

I figured might be either damsel or dragonfly nymphs. Before I left, he asked that I keep any big fish I caught, if I did, for tissue samples: it was a mystery to Fish & Game that larger trout were seldom caught.

>−+◦>−O−<◦+−<

I pushed off about five-thirty. A modest number of fish were rising. I took one, a little rainbow, while kicking out toward a drowned forest. It ate a brown A.P. nymph.

I kept kicking out, casting. I landed another fish, bigger, almost a foot, which was kind of fun. I kept kicking: two hundred feet away stood a flyfisher in an elegant, lacquered wood pram. He wore a flats hat and was throwing a split-cane rod. I figured he likely knew something I should. When he noticed me, I gave a small wave. He looked at me a few more seconds and then, very deliberately, turned away.

The world's full of 'em; or, to be fair, he wanted no distractions and lots of space. The lake certainly had that: more amused than rancorous, I began moving away.

I missed a strike, then fished for five minutes before I deigned to check my fly—broken off. I tested every knot after that, on a leader which at this point looked like some kind of industry experiment, four or five colors of mono stepping down. I thought to tie on fresh tippet I'd bought from Judy Carothers, 6X, and was pleased that I did so, if only because in the time that took I noticed a damsel nymph swimming up. The fly I chose represented it pretty well. It was a cinnamon color.

>−+◦>−O−<◦+−<

I made what for me was a long cast from a tube, maybe 60 feet, let it sink, then turned to see what was ahead; so I struck on instinct. I looked back to see the boil, and a tenth of a second later, this salmon leaped clear of the water—enormous, silver and red. In my excitement I wanted to shout at the distant pram man, "Are there salmon in here?" Only after the second leap did I—suddenly, with disbelief—connect the jumper to the fish on my line.

The fish leaped again and three more times within ten or twenty seconds, humping like a porpoise on a bow wave. Maybe 400 feet beyond the last splash, a couple at anchor in a white boat turned to watch.

I had no drag on the reel, a twenty-year-old Korean knock-off of a thirty-year-old Medalist, so when the run began I simply held on, slipping the last thirty feet of fly line through my fingers. Then came 100 yards of Dacron backing; that seemed to take 45 seconds; after that I was gripping 10-pound mono, of which I hoped to have another hundred yards. By that time my mouth was making an O shape, but I had nothing to say, not even when cork rings in the 6-weight started to separate beneath my thumb.

The fish stopped, although I certainly hadn't turned it. When it began again it headed at a right angle to the first flight, in the direction of the pram man. It jumped behind him; he looked too late to see. I watched the yellow fly line making a belly a hundred feet away, waiting for drag to snap the 6X, but the fish doubled back.

It swam directly at me. I reeled and reeled, then stripped. Only the weight of circling line kept tension between us.

The fish turned back out, moving again in a vast sweep. Slowly, inexorably, it picked up all the slack until once again the little reel was whirring, loosing mono in coils set two or three years before. This time I might have managed some sound with the O mouth.

Then I shouted. The fish was headed for the white boat. "Pull anchor! Pull your anchors!"

It's a stupid-feeling phrase to say, I remember thinking, along with "they can't in time."

They did, each of them on a rope, as fast as I'd have hoped to manage if I'd been there myself. Then the two of them watched the fly line slide beneath them. When it passed, the man yelled words I could not understand and gave me an "OK" with his thumb and forefinger, which made me laugh.

All that took little time. Then it got fun—it got to be so much fun. The fish made run after run, often heading toward the drowned forest, but always turning in time. The tube would jerk whenever he began one of these, rocking; then rocking more wildly when the fish changed direction and I reeled. The couple in the white boat neither anchored nor cast again, and eventually I realized that even the pram man had stopped to watch.

I laughed and laughed, excited, feeling nuts. "Six X and holding!" I remember gloating, and maybe I shouted it, though of course the miracle couldn't last long. Not with all the drowned timber and so much line out, with such a fish and a fool like me on the other end.

So much fun—I was happy even knowing how it would end. The excited words that came to my mind were from boyhood, some from my kids. "Cool, bitchin': a lark, a gas, hecka-bad." The fight was no less a thrill for the futility. I still laughed even as the lactic acid built up in my forearm and the tiny rod whipped over like a riding crop, ridiculous against the odds. When the couple in the boat called out, enough times that I finally understood, "Do you need a net?" I just shook my head and laughed some more. A net would never end this battle.

Twenty minutes or thirty, I enjoyed the game. Gradually—with the adrenaline fading, I suppose, with my blood sugar falling—the pleasure began to fade. The runs were slowing a little, less streaks than slugging rushes, heavy and hard to hold. Long moments went by when the fish swam within a small area still distant from me. I would lose and retrieve the same piece of line over and over again; finally I turned and kicked toward the fish, until I had a few stripes of backing on the reel; the mono pained me to hold. From the effort, I found myself inhaling deeply, sighing out.

The move had brought me closer to the white boat. Perhaps sensing my weariness, the couple in it began to call encouragement more often: their names were Bob and Apryl. I was then in the state of mind to think, "Apryl is certainly a pretty name; I've always liked it."

"Hell of a show," Bob shouted.

April tried to remember that famous story about the old man who fought a fish for days.

"You sure you don't need a net?" Bob asked.

I told him that the tippet was 6X and would break at between three and four pounds test.

"Christmas," he said. "Then you are going to need a net. How about I do this: I tie one of ours to this cushion, drift in and toss it to you, then get away quick?"

Sure, why not. He did as he'd suggested, and after kicking over to where he'd left it, I found myself staring at this tiny little trout tool with a mouth about ten inches across.

I told him I didn't think so.

"You want a bigger one?"

"Not now," I said.

Not for a long time, and it wasn't a good time any more. I started to shiver as the sun went down. My shirt was light cotton, wet on the sleeves; and, though I was in neoprene waders, the cold had invaded. Twice I cramped up in the calves. The ambient air temperature had dropped, no lower than 60 or 65 degrees. But I felt the change.

Far more uncomfortable than this, however, was a feeling I might have recognized by now: I was going to lose. From the instant of hook-up this fight was doomed. There was no way in hell I was going to land this great fish on such light line. With the fun part over now, the waiting began to tire me.

Not once did I associate this with a story of police corruption. Still, it was a familiar weariness I felt.

It didn't help my mood when another boat joined us, this one with a guide and a woman, his party, who drifted near where the pram man had taken up station. Their conversation crossed the water.

"How long's he been at this?"

"Hell, I don't know, about an hour."

I thought I heard the the guide snort, say something about beating a fish fast.

"How big do you think that one is?" asked the woman.

"Six or seven pounds."

>⊶⊷⊙⊷⊶⊰

What annoyed me was knowing that, when the fish broke off, I'd never get to put it to him.

Bob announced that it was eight o'clock and had been an hour since the fish swept under his boat. After the first jumps I'd never even seen it. The fight was reduced now to surges, waves which ebbed and flowed, shakes of a head. With alarm I realized we were now much closer to the trees, and it was nearly dark. Bob set out his running lights.

"I'm going in," said the pram man.

"Please stay," the woman said to her guide. "I really want to watch this."

"For a while," he answered reluctantly.

>⊶⊷⊙⊷⊶⊰

I changed again. At about an hour, I think, in no particular moment that I remember, in a process as unconscious as getting cold and dispirited. But this was a great turning over—like an epiphany with neither insight nor trumpets. It was almost as if I awoke from a fugue, a disassociation of unknown duration. Big change, with no connection to the ache in my arm or the stiffening of my legs. Nobody, certainly not me, said an inspiring word.

And yet, suddenly, I was going to catch this fish.

No quotes around this. None of the sort of self-conscious boldface with which I've framed other determinations in my life. I really had no instant image of what it might look like or feel like to do so; no grand assertion like "I'm no loser" or "Victory is at hand." Since I'd had no first wind of hope, this wasn't the second. It just *was*, an absolute sense of what I would do, without question, without doubt.

This is my fish. Something like that, that's all. And it was this conviction I held into the second hour, those last thirty minutes.

Which were not without event. The fish came in to circle me in the tube, round and around. With assistance from the fins, I spun like a clumsy top. Then a sudden short run bumped me against something solid. "What was that?" I demanded. "How deep am I? How deep is it here?"

"Plenty deep," said the guide, with the kind of condescension in his voice that can get you punched even in a nice bar. "You just worry about the fish."

The woman, his passenger, said softly, "The depth finder says four feet."

"Just fight the fish," said her guide.

"You're going to win," said Apryl, and I almost smiled, seeing her now in the half-light huddled in a coat.

This time Bob floated out an aluminum salmon net with a 20-inch handle. I pushed it away when I realized I could never get the angle. Besides, my left hand had cramped into a claw from pinching line.

In the last light I saw a tail. *My* fish's tail….was nearly a foot deep. The *tail*.

It was almost time to try.

The fish slammed into my legs—I mean *slammed me*. I shouted.

It slammed me again, striking just above one knee. In a life of fishing I had never experienced such a thing.

It hit me a third time, a ramming stroke with the side of its head. I felt it sliding hard against my thigh, pressing into me.

"A tree," I hissed at Bob, amazed and certain. "It thinks I'm a *tree. It's trying to grind the fly off on my leg.*"

Bob didn't know what to say, I suppose. I did. "Let's do this now."

When I saw the line cutting back toward me, I kicked at it. The fish rushed away 20 feet.

"I'll net him," said the guide. "I've got the right net. Bring him over here."

He'd pulled his boat up a dozen feet behind me. Bob and Apryl's was about that distance in front.

I said, "Bob? You got your net back?"

"Got it."

"Are you ready for this?"

"No way," he said. "Not me."

The guide said loudly, "I'll do it." I bet he already saw himself in the photo, his name on the caption.

I laughed. "Get ready, Bob."

"No. No, seriously, I'd never forgive myself if I screwed up."

"But I would," I said.

I felt fantastic.

➤┤◆〜○〜◆├◄

First try, Bob got him. From a dozen feet away from me, locating the fish—somehow, incredibly—in the water beneath his running lights, stabbing deep and lifting this great silver slab of fish, shining silver, so impossibly large that three or fours gasps just made one. I was laughing and shouting and shivering, thrashing about, rising up in the tube to kick over, so Bob could lay in my lap...such a weight. And I was laughing still when the woman with the guide, Sally Merlin, shot a photo. She shot another of Bob landing me, dragging me over the gunwale like a cod; and I was still laughing, because in all my life I'd never seen a three-foot long trout, a wild rainbow, and now I had.

➤┤◆〜○〜◆├◄

Changes. But first: Apryl, Bob and I got drunk that night, after they fed me dinner, the three of us talking until four. Apryl took care of kids; Bob was a guard at a model prison. But all that came after we weighed the fish on the scale on the lodge porch: 17 pounds, four ounces. One of the people who pounded out of the campground said he thought it might be the world record on four-pound test line. In fact, it was a couple pounds shy.

The pram fisher came, and that was wonderful. He stormed up, demanding—"I *demand*—" he actually said—to know what fly I'd used. "It's in the fish," I told him, still attached to a piece of 6X tippet. When he, sneering, really said "What the hell do you call *that*?" I told him it was the one that was half-off at Payless Drugs and he should make sure to go get some.

The cords stood out in his neck. I'm not kidding.

Sally Merlin gave me her card and promised me copies of her photos. She delivered. One of these is pinned to the trophy board in Judy Carothers' new shop. Another hangs in the office of my friend Steve, the oncologist. Across that one I wrote "And I owe it all to Steve Iacoboni." The same shot appeared in a *Western Outdoors* story I wrote to thank Apryl and Bob. When the rod maker of my little six-weight made me a "VIP," I bought them a pair. Some time later—nine months to the day, I like to imagine—they sent me a birth announcement of their baby.

Both the local lodge and Oregon Fish and Game wanted the fish. I gave the guts to F & G, the rest to the lodge for a mount.

>-+-+)-+0-+(+-I-<

Four of the officers I'd investigated went to federal prison. The entire force was placed under permanent supervision by a lieutenant from the Oakland Police Department. I hear they're better now.

Steve was right: I did win awards—the Harrah and Golden Medallion, along with a Pulitzer nomination. The prize money from the pair almost paid for the transportation and parking it cost me to pick them up, but Lisa was proud.

In his turn, Steve also won: he was the first nonattorney in California history to receive the Skip Glenn award for service in criminal justice.

Parker, one of the real heroes, suffered enormously, his police career apparently ended when he resigned. We kept track for years. Last I talked to him he was working as a security guard, raising cockatoos, selling special bird feed. He still had a suit pending against the force.

Donna Smith, also a vital source, also paid dearly. Eventually she settled her own suit, for too little, given the toll.

Jonathan Allen, the officer jailed and fired, did better. He now runs a security company in Las Vegas with three times as many officers as the force he tried to bring down.

The Chief's secretary, Elizabeth Natalie, who also testified for the Grand Jury, lost a suit, because, I was told, her attorney failed to prepare. Probably he thought the defendants would settle at the last moment.

He had some reason for his presumption, though not one that would excuse any incompetence: the 42 litigants represented by the attorney Steve worked with, Daniel Horowitz, settled with the city of Oakland for a great deal of money, an amount still kept secret. Millions, let us say.

And the Chief of Police, as he'd boasted, stuck around. A third of his force indicted, perhaps half the remaining officers willing to testify against him—on "'60 Minutes," Parker referred to "criminals with badges"—he was instead assigned another job and is due to retire soon with a sizable pension. It's some kind of testament that in the same time frame, the misconduct of four or five officers out of thousands (the Rodney King case) would bring down William Gates in LA.

"60 Minutes" was so horrified by the faint response that they did the story again. Maybe it created a stir in other places.

>—+—◆>—○—‹◆—+—‹

And I don't do investigative reporting any more. Unless you count a battle Steve and I fought for five years with a scab of three realtors and a pest control company operating under many names. After we won five judgments of fraud and five more of negligence, gross and regular, we publicized that a little. But no more investigations, not for me, save some conservation pieces for flyfishing magazines.

That was the other thing: I stopped spin fishing after Crane Prairie. Like the mental turnaround I had experienced in my tube, it wasn't so much a deliberate "Let's put this away" as the natural result of a visceral conviction that "This is possible, this can be done." Eventually, I began writing also for flyfishing publications and found, to my vast delight, that editors and publishers in that market were a great pleasure to work with, primarily because they assume they have smart subscribers who don't need help with ideas or big words. Some actually believe readers will even wade through a piece like this one.

The new focus has let me write the kind of things I always wanted to. To a small extent—it still feels fragile—I'm also able live the way I'd like to. Even my sleep image changed, for what it's worth. Now, every single night, my last conscious image is of a bow flexing, the limbs looking much like a fly rod loading to cast. When the arrow flies, so do I, which I think only means that there are options sometimes, and more than one way to win.

A Most Practical Companion

Breen is back from Africa again, this time with 200 McClellan saddles he traded for a multi-megabyte computer. At least this visit he wasn't charged with felonies. His last stay ended with him fleeing police troops. His *own* troops, as it happens, since he was still some province's Chief Prosecuting Attorney. "A practical problem," as he describes it. "Because they're so short, we didn't see eye-to-eye." All I'm sure of is that I ended up tying streamers from Greater Kudo hair, adding this to my stock of wild boar and nutria, courtesy of my high school fishing companion, who didn't fish, but lived to hunt and to eat fish—

>−+◆>−O−◆+−◄

I met Terry Breen in high school, freshman Spanish class. Not counting Terry, I was the least attentive pupil. In fact, I was drawing trout when I noticed Terry sketching what looked like an anorexic pike.

"Well, buddy," he drawled in East Texan. "It so happens that this is my new ship for the Navy."

"That?"

"Four miles long and four feet wide."

"What?"

He leaned his long frame forward. "You betcha," he whispered. "We sail it straight at the enemy, and he never sees us coming."

Yes sir, he had the dimensions written right there on the page. "What if you get turned sideways?" I demanded.

"Now aren't you clever? That's the genius: during an enemy assault we split into 27 pieces, each one a ship its ownself…Now we got a convoy."

I went back to adding fins to my trout. No doubt this Breen was somebody to watch. From a distance, if possible.

>-+-+>-O-<+-+-<

"Care for a Coke?"

Midsummer it was now, and the sun scoured color from the mountains around us. I'd bumped into Terry at a store on the edge of town. Coke in hand, he was soon confessing his 4-by-4 ship's fate. "You'd think that with all those narrow minds in the Pentagon a skinny ship would suit them just fine. But, no. *Heavens* no. Say, how 'bout we drift down to my house, saddle up Major and the pony, go for a ride? It's just a couple of nautical miles."

>-+-+>-O-<+-+-<

Remarkably few distances in the desert are measured that way, but by the time Terry and I finished floating downstream in the canal, that's about what we traveled. As we mounted up, Terry pointed out his summer project, a patch of disturbed earth at the side of the corral. "You know how those bone-heads at school love their bleached jeans? Ruin perfectly good Levis in the washer? Well I buried five pairs in the corral where these horses do business. Gonna sell 'em to dilettantes as 'Genuine Piss-Cured pants.' Make me a mint."

What?

Terry smiled. "You got to understand, buddy. I'm a very practical guy."

>-+-+>-O-<+-+-<

Soon thereafter Breen and I partnered to serve our obsessions: his to hunt, mine to fish. Mountain meadow to desert canyon, we rattled along in "Blue," his English Rover, sometimes accompanied by "Brown," his lion hound. Terry taught me to use a 12 gauge. I gave him extensive, utterly fruitless lessons with spinning and fly rods. If fishing was poor I would hunt; if no game showed, Terry dredged worms.

Inevitably we'd argue. Loudly, about "practical" matters.

"You did *what* with that bass?'
"Threw her back. It's spring, Terry. She's full of eggs."
Pause, frown. "You can't eat the eggs?"

⋗┅⋗┅○┅⋖┅⋖

At the golf course pond where we sneaked in nights to fish—
"C'mon, buddy! Who's gonna miss a couple white ducks? So fat, so
trusting… We'll deep six those babies in my mom's Coke sauce!"

⋗┅⋗┅○┅⋖┅⋖

Of the sixty-odd topics about which we disagreed, cattle ranked high
on the list. Terry had punched a herd one summer, on horseback, while
indentured to a rancher. I'd spent my fishing career fleeing the beasts on
foot. Consequently, insisted Terry, "You are wildly prejudiced against
them. More ignorance you've got to get over."
And he'd help.
We'd seen the bull relaxing in a cottonwood grove on our hike in along
the river. He wasn't there when we force-marched out—Terry *needed* a
Coke—so when we entered a narrow, grassy swath bordered by cliffs on
one side and rapids on the other, I told Breen to ready his shotgun.
"Now *there's* an absurd idea," he announced, expounding on this for
the five minutes it took to trap ourselves in the canyon. Then the bull
plunged out from willows 30 feet ahead.
"Breen, he's going to charge!"
Terry had looked alarmed, but my warning calmed him completely.
"Ridiculous. You are so *paranoid*."
The bull pawed the ground, tearing up chunks of riverside sod.
"Shoot, Terry!"
"Shoot? *Shoot?* Why, do you know what that animal's worth? In
United States dollars?"
"Shoot to scare him!"
"Oh yeah? And who pays for the shell?"
"Breen. He's going to—"

⋗┅⋗┅○┅⋖┅⋖

I honestly don't remember the next several seconds. I draw blanks
until I see horns shaking beneath our heels as we clung to the cliff's
coleche wall, then the swing of bull tail as he sauntered away.

I berated Breen for something more than an hour, taking advantage of an uncharacteristic silence. "*I'm* prejudiced, *I'm* ignorant, *I'm* absurd—"

At last, Terry said sternly, "That is all affirmative."

"*What?*"

"I figured it out; it's a practical problem. You see, cattle are deeply sensitive animals. You upset that poor bull—"

"*What?*"

"—with unkind remarks. Frightened and hurt—"

"*He charged!*"

"—in desperate flight....He simply ran the wrong way."

It's lucky I suppose, that Breen held fast to his shotgun, given the high price of shells. And as Terry pointed out last week over Cokes at the airport, "If you'd killed me then, think of the trouble you'd have getting Kudu for flies. Not to mention a good McClellan saddle."

"For the horse I don't own?"

"In San Francisco, no horse? Listen buddy, let me explain the practical advantage..."

Nay, I think not.

Reflections in
Moving Water

An airport porter saw me standing with rod tube at the curb and knew just where I should go for fat catfish up to three pounds that eat liver and worms. He would be there himself as soon as he could; but for the time being he'd be glad to imagine me sitting on the shore of a lake thirty miles south, taking one whiskered fish after another. Surely, I would do well.

I went north and did well with brookies instead, then east for rainbows and browns. He would have savored every one of them, I think. He sure did look pleased when he wheeled his cart away.

⋙⟶⟡⟶⋘

Resonance. Empathy. Identification.

⋙⟶⟡⟶⋘

I met myself moving away on the Truckee River one late afternoon, seeing me slight and gray, wrinkled as a tortoise but slower still as I edged through long grasses down to a riffle where, bent with scoliosis, I cast for two hours over a caddis hatch. I didn't have many such days left. Believe me, I made the most of that one.

⋙⟶⟡⟶⋘

I met myself long gone in a discount store, dragging my mother along on the leash of an eight year old's absolute will, picking out a saltwater surf rod to match a crummy little spinning reel I held in my hand. My mother was bewildered but I knew I "Need a big one" for the great beasts of water and imagination that I would soon battle.

Met me again, 12 or 14 years old now, dangling a nightcrawler under a bank on the Owens, squatting like a Bombay beggar as I turned pages of a hard cover edition of *The Red Pony*, no kidding…About 1968, page 84 of *Native Son*, I hooked a five pound carp on the Salt River outside Phoenix, believing it was a bass for five exciting minutes, soiling the book with carp slime when I returned to it the next cast.

>─┤♦>─●─<♦─┤─<

As a 20-year-old I talked to me, grizzled and smiling and twice that old, outside the Cow Palace in San Francisco. With an awkward pride I told of how I'd dashed across the Trinity River in a float tube to release a steelhead from a steel stringer snap. Almost two decades before, I'd insisted that a Clear Lake park employee examine 15 crappies and bluegill I'd kept because of their open tumors, eyes sealed over with opaque film, grossly humped bodies. He'd refused because "You're not a biologist," and because "water testers are coming in October"; so on that June afternoon I slung the fish across the floor of his air-conditioned office, then gave him the finger when he swore he'd call the cops.

>─┤♦>─●─<♦─┤─<

"As a conservative Republican," wrote a man in yesterday's Letters to the Editor, by way of placing himself and his ideas within a context of people, philosophy, history. "As an obsessed fisher," I suppose I should try by way of doing something similar. And I would have a constituency: of boys hurling out bobbers with bolo casts, bass anglers covering rocky points stone by stone, midge fishers staring along glistening tippets in the morning's half light.

>─┤♦>─●─<♦─┤─<

Not so absurd, these pursuits, even from the perspective—now—of a flyfisher. Why, several years ago I was an incorrect guest at parties of a certain profession, and there discovered, in the kitchen beside the jug wines, a rock codder, yes, and he had human speech. He fished a Boston Whaler off the Bolinas reefs, Duxbury, calculating currents and weights, the spawning seasons of great gray ling cod. We argued not about tactics, but whether it was better to fish solo or with a fast friend. "Male bonding," said the other guests, speaking through professional half-smiles just as if they understood something; but we were too busy, too pleased to have each other to bother with them. We had the common ground of water; and though he was altogether wrong about absolutely everything, his heart was in the right place.

>–⊷–○–⊶–⤙

Resonance. It's a fine thing to fish alone, even for a lifetime. It's fine also to turn a page and find "for other anglers whose eyes are going with age, and who are still trying to tie #20 hairwing flies, I'd like to share this tool which you can buy at any drugstore." It's fine to lean on a counter and hear about a brown trout somebody fished over for three hours, and caught, or didn't; a happy thing to see somebody else absorbed completely in a pursuit you share, feeling the tension in their arms as they poise for a strike you can feel and even celebrate as the line tightens…I've sworn aloud when a stranger missed a fish I wanted him to have.

Because, of course, he, or she, wasn't such a stranger after all

Religions do it. Communities, other sports—all Mudville groaned together when Casey struck out. Fishers are a fair-sized tribe, or collection of same, even if consisting of many solitary players. We have our differences, naturally. We split into factions for good reasons and petty. We have serious problems, at times, sharing resources; yet it's reassuring to see a light I recognize in someone else's eyes, to shake my head in appreciation of how a ling cod attacks a bullhead in shallows, imagine that maw snapping shut. "Bleak" is the name of a tiny fish which excites anglers on the Temes. For weeks I stalked jungle streams for an *Ikan Klee*, finding my only satisfaction in the grins of Malay farmers who hoped I caught one, and who would have applauded if ever I did. I've shared thrill and frustration with a Bora-Boran friend named Ke-ke, as we tried to troll up a marlin bigger than our boat.

Fishers need share no spoken language to understand each other. The pursuit itself casts a shadow on the wall which others so inclined will see. Often enough our prophets or gods fish for souls; but we mortals put our faith in waters, aspiring to a catch worthy of our station.

Of Grace and
a Caddis Case

The clerk at the general store leaned back on a stool, steadying himself with one hand on the register. He had the sort of sly, share-a-secret smirk on his face that I associate with dime store thieves, which may say more about me than him and maybe not. "Gin Creek," he said slowly. "Yeah."

I added a mustard bottle to bread and bologna I'd set next to my map on the counter. "Right. How to get there."

"Doin' some fishin'?"

"Right."

"Huh."

I waited.

"Carson Road will get you close. You ought to take worms. I got some nightcrawlers in the 'frig."

"Carson is this one here?"

He didn't look. "Only one nearby. Mind if I ask you who told you about it?"

Yeah, I did. "It's on the map."

He counted me change. "House up there, you'll see."

"Private property?"

He shook his head. "Not to high-water." Then he grinned. "Don't need to be. Crazy boy out there you should look for. About the size of a grizzly bear, but more raggedy ass. Talks to trees."

It's good to get away from the raw rub of the city, if only to frame rustic daydreams with the wormy lumber of locals like the clerk.

And of course, to remind myself how I feel on little creeks like Gin, a pretty meander tumbling through mixed forests of oak and pine, deep pools set apart by quick riffles and dark runs, just as I'd heard. It takes a while, perhaps an hour or two of stalk-and-cast, before a sense of right-ness comes to me—longer if I'm well out of sorts. But it will happen, speeded this time by two tiny rainbows and a brown which rose to my hopper dapped in behind stones. The silence helped too, or the sound of woods and stream, early autumn leaves turning against each other, which goes beyond silence.

It happened, kept happening while I waded my way up, moving slower as I eased into the rhythm of the place. Though the hopper was working fine I took time to examine the life beneath rocks: in a clear eddy I found caddis who'd made their houses of black iron and flakes of fool's gold. Jewels.

On the walk back to my truck I was surprised by how short a stretch I'd covered, not even a mile. What was above? After racking my tackle I drove farther up Carson Road so I could start on new water in the morning; then I set myself a cold cut dinner warmed by a measured glass of bourbon. Gin would have been appropriate, perhaps, but when the air cools I prefer brown drinks. Besides, gin is the only liquor which makes me mean. "Or meaner," as my oldest son once said, laughing with his head thrown back and his eyes full of play. "You're not so bad."

I'm always glad he thinks so, him and his sister. Both married now, they were conspiring to make me a 41-year-old grandfather twice over. "See if you can find a grandma," each advised me in our traditional parting phone calls—a conspiracy, I'm sure.

And an unlikely prospect. As their-mother-my-ex said once "You're a fine father and no one should have you for a husband, nobody." I'd agreed at the time; still, one could always hope.

After another half shot of bourbon I took out the manila folder labeled "Retire Soon" and tried to figure out, just in case, how I could *ever* retire on a stream like Gin Creek. Difficult; yet I was certain that one more year of what I was doing would break my heart in a way I could only begin to define, break something fundamental in me that had worn thin like a piece of good steel grinding against an unyielding edge. Or an edge which when broken showed another, was replaced endlessly with a new one even sharper, like a row of shark's teeth shifting forward to fill gaps.

><+>+O+<+><

The next morning I discovered more of the stream which made me happy right through lunch and into the afternoon when I realized that the clerk was right: the boy was big as a bear, ragged, though not especially dirty; and he looked to be talking to a tree. A stump, to be specific, surrounded by a tangle of wood split to kindling.

"Mom said not to," he was repeating while shifting from foot to foot. "Mom said not to."

There was no way around him, not without back-tracking or making a noisy detour he'd notice anyway. Besides, after fifteen years of study I could read him well enough, the flat gaze, the monotone mantra, what we used to call the "Stelazine Shuffle": schizophrenia does not scare me. The heartbreaking job I had to leave was on a locked ward.

I waited. He turned at last to include me in his stare. Big, yes, but not as old as his size would suggest—17, just getting fuzzy on the chin. "Mom said not to," he said now to me, and spread his arms slightly. He had a hatchet in one hand. The other was so bloody it looked like a glove.

"Mom said," he began again, but then seemed to realize I might need more explanation, "Mom said not to *cry*."

That did it: he'd been trying so hard, but the combination of audience and speaking "cry" aloud collapsed his resolve. Tears welled up and his voice caught. "I hurt myself."

"You did," I answered softly, and set down my rod. "What's your name?"

It's important to get a name. To how may interns and trainees have I said that? With his disease a name is magic, a critical reference when the membrane between *self* and *other* leaks; a name, so you can remind him who he is when he loses track.

"Jimmy," he said.

"Jimmy. My name is Will, Jimmy. May I look at your hand?"

He raised it, flinched at the sight of his blood, looked back at me full of woe. "Will you, please?" Then, as if repeating a lesson well-learned. "I won't hurt you."

"I know," I said.

The cut was clean and deep to the bone on the top of his thumb—not all that bad, but he'd let it bleed so long it looked worse. "Okay, Jimmy," I said. "You need to put pressure on a wound. Keep it closed together, hold it above your heart."

I'd bent his elbow up while I spoke, so brought his face close to mine. There was an exotic smell about him, not unpleasant—sweat and smoke and something else. His hand was relaxed, and the blank expression had surrendered to incredulity. "Me, touch it?" he whispered. "I can't."

"Sure you can. Hold it like this." I gripped the thumb in my palm.

"No, I *can't*," he hissed.

"Yes, you *can*," I hissed back.

He shook his head. Then, with complete and utter sincerity, "I'll do it next time, Will, when it's your blood."

I laughed—I just had to. I've seen rather a lot of blood, my own and other people's; and the earnestness in his face was the stuff of bathos. His eyes opened a little wider, but he smiled.

"Look, Jimmy. I can't hold your thumb and drive you to the hospital at the same time. My truck's a stick shift."

Now there was fear in him, a great fear that would have caused him to jerk his hand free if I hadn't held tight. "*No* hospital. *Never* again. Take me home. *Please*."

My gaffe was right there, obvious as his injury. Of course, no hospital. "All right. All right Jimmy, I'll take you home."

What a pair we must have looked. Because of the rough terrain and his shuffle, I had to put my backside to the front of him, clasp his elbow beneath my own and hold his injured hand up beside my cheek while I put him in tow. I'm just less than six feet—Jimmy had eight or nine inches on me, maybe 60 pounds—so this arrangement forced him to stoop over low, forehead to my back as he lurched along like a drunken hunchback. All we were missing was a horse's head at my end and tail pinned to his hiney.

"How far?" I demanded after 100 yards of this.

"A long way," he panted back. And so it was—or a quarter mile, anyway, the last bit of which was simply hell because, at the sight of his house, Jimmy gasped "There" and collapsed forward like a felled ox.

"Jimmy! Dammit!"

"Sorry, Will."

My back, which hasn't been the same since a restraint in 1986, will never be the same as it's been since then.

>⊷•—○—•⊶<

The door was open. Through a veil of sweat I spotted a picnic table, the heavy redwood kind, in the middle of a large, confusing room; there I lay Jimmy on his back. He whimpered a little, mostly from relief. "Hang on."

The bathroom was right off the front door, spare and surprisingly clean, with an old pull-chain toilet. In a wooden medicine cabinet I found an abundance of medications, many of which I recognized from the hospital: Haldol and Mellaril, for psychosis; Artane to minimize the side-effects of those two; two half empty bottles of minor tranquilizers and a new antidepressant that had only been on the market six months. Behind all these stood the hydrogen peroxide I needed, along with a neat little box of bandaging materials.

By the time I'd taped over a tight row of butterfly stitches, Jimmy was feeling much better, probably because he could no longer see the injury. "Hi, Will," he said hopefully. I grunted a reply.

"Will? Did you know your flyfishing vest is all bloody? And can I call you Willie?"

"Yes, then no," I answered "But you can tell me who it is that takes care of you, and where the hell they are right now."

He looked around carefully, as if I was missing someone who might be close by. Which wasn't such a peculiar idea: a closer study of Jimmy's home revealed an elegant riot—less a cabin than a small, plank-walled meeting hall converted to home-cum-forest full of decorative figs, local willows and immature oak trees in wine barrels, planter boxes full of herbs and spices and God knows what else. The plants reached out toward dusk light streaming through banks of big windows and, set crudely into the sloping roof, three skylights. Below, sets of Japanese folding screens created sections; the one Jimmy and I now shared had, in addition to the table, an iron bust of Rodin's, a map of the world circa 1700, a bookcase full of vials, a vase of ferns and another of mixed ostrich, peacock and pheasant feathers—

—none of which spoke "Jimmy" to me.

"Lilly," Jimmy said. "She's my sister."

"Lilly," I agreed. "Where is she?"

"At the store?"

"Jimmy…are you asking *me*?"

He considered this question. "Yes," he said finally.

I sighed a little, and worried. I'd left my rod back where this adventure began; it was now close enough to dark that already I hadn't much chance to find it. To stay longer would make returning to the truck a stumbling trek all by itself. Still, I couldn't leave Jimmy on his own.

Jimmy, who was now staring at me, was silently mouthing words. He stopped when I returned his gaze.

"Hi," he said again.

I relaxed a little; this too would pass. There was probably a driveway I could hike out to Carson Road; I'd find the rod by morning light. So be it. "Hey, Jimmy. How are you feeling?"

"My hand aches and I hear voices," he answered.

"Yeah."

"Is that okay?"

"Sure."

"Okay, Will. Will? How come you're not afraid of me?"

"That," said a low female voice, "is a wonderful question."

>-+◆>-0-<◆+-<

"Lilly!" Jimmy said happily.

She stepped out from behind one of the screens, barefoot, draped in a sheet she'd gathered about her. Dark-skinned, or so she looked by contrast with the linen, tall, with black hair disheveled in a way which suited the weathered prettiness of her face. Mid-thirties—34. In the midst of annoyance, I could guess that we'd caught her napping. Still, she might have made her presence known.

"I'm sorry," she continued evenly. "But I wasn't expecting you. Then, you were so involved in what you were doing for Jimmy…" She glanced to her brother. "He did as good as a doctor, Jimmy."

"Are you a doctor?" Jimmy demanded.

It was to him that I spoke. "I'm a nurse, Jimmy. And now I've got to go."

"You do?"

"Wait a minute, please," she said.

I was already standing and turning toward the door. "Excuse me, but it's getting dark."

"We need to pay you."

"No, you don't. Nice to meet you, Jimmy. Keep that hand up."

"Okay," he answered, throwing a salute.

"Please," said his sister.

"No," I replied.

"Jimmy—get the caddis."

What?

"Which ones, Lilly? the black ones?"

"Yes."

I turned in time to see her moving, the sheet falling from its drape to reveal her. She saw me see her; I jerked back around feeling heat in my face.

"Here," said Jimmy. "Look at these, Will!"

> ɪ ◊ · O· ◊ ɪ <

It certainly was irritating how quickly *he'd* recovered. Now Jimmy was pushing one of the little vials at me.

Black-cased caddis, in a clear solution. The little jewels I'd found between stones, built of fool's gold and iron.

"That's the real ones," said Jimmy. "Now look what Lilly did."

I hesitated a moment. "You can look," she said.

I turned into the glow of the hurricane lamp she'd lit; by that light I thought I saw a blush. Maybe, but she was holding her head high and, in an outstretched hand, a small plastic fly box.

I took it. Nestled there were three dozen nymphs, black and gold, some ingenious combination of dark fur and wire. I picked one from the foam. She—or someone—had mixed flakes of pyrite into the dubbing.

"You flyfish?" I said stupidly.

She crossed her arms on her chest and shook her head. "No. I never have. Our father did; he taught me to tie. So now I do for a store in Castle Rock." She stopped, then said quickly "Not this pattern, of course. They say these are too unusual. I tie hoppers, Adams—all kinds of dry flies. Streamers. Anything you like, really. You can have those or something else."

I wouldn't accept anything, of course, but the box was still in my hand as I stepped over to the vial shelf. Samples, dozens of samples: more caddis, larvae and adults; mayflies of a half dozen species; stone-flies from little goldens to pteranarcys like baby dragons. On the cap of most bottles was glued a shaving of wine cork; to these she'd pinned her matching ties.

"Some of those I've never taken to the store. I mean, I don't really know if they would actually fish very well. Maybe you could say. Or even try some tomorrow..."

I looked at her.

"...and would you *please* stay for dinner?"

⊱―◈―○―◈―⊰

Jimmy conked out, not before devouring two plates of rice and beans flavored with cilantro. Cilantro—"We grow it!" Jimmy bragged—was the odd scent I'd smelled on him during our horse-walk.

There was wine also, and my own brand of bourbon after Jimmy went down in some distant part of the house beyond screens. About then the butterflies began to dance in my stomach; so I poured more bourbon to soothe them.

Didn't help. It only got a great deal worse when by lantern light Lilly stood too close to me while laying out her flies, describing in detail how she'd tied each, what she hoped for—even the influences of tiers about whom she'd read. I've tied for a decade and haven't one tenth the background. Such questions: "Like with mayflies, the nymphs—Sawyer says they swim with their legs tucked up, but André Puyans puts legs on his. Then there's those soft hackled flies...What's right?"

So close, she was standing. She'd dressed, now wore loose jeans and a looser sweater, neither of which could dismiss another image from my mind. I did my best with answers, barely breathing.

She must have noticed; she sat back, smiled, shrugged during a silence. Then, "So that's what I do, now, for money; we have that and Jimmy's Social Security. Oh, and I read a lot."

I nodded.

She smiled again, then laughed softly. "I was thinking...that if I was you, meeting Jimmy—if you didn't know him...like from *Of Mice and Men*?

I laughed too, a little ruefully. "If I didn't know him? '*Androcles and the Lion.*'"

She enjoyed that with more laughter. "Yes—but a *bear*! In town, they call him a bear."

I shrugged.

"It's all right, really it is. Actually it's good. For me, I mean. Sometimes you have to rely on people's fear to stay safe." She looked around her, what we could see of the room. What began as an idle gaze changed; suddenly she studied it all, perhaps seeing it new for my intrusion. After a few moments she smiled.

It had been my chance to study her; so it was that I thought I knew something she might like to know..

"Flyfishing," I said, speaking as carefully as I could, "is a little like you in this room."

She looked delighted, but uncertain. "'Why do you say that?"

"Because…there is a passion to it, an inward passion which connects every instant to this bit of the world you've chosen to see. It's…artifice, but all about your life and other lives. Trout, caddis." I shifted uncomfortably, wishing I'd kept my mouth shut. "It wraps you."

"Wraps me," she said then paused. "Wraps you."

"Yes. I mean—"

"I understand. You choose what to live with, when you can. What to see or build around you." She laughed. "A caddis case?"

We shared a silence, then she asked me about my work. I told her the long story about the hospital; how in the beginning it was difficult to get distance from people suffering illnesses that stole their minds for a while or a lifetime, how poignant and painful it was to see them struggle inside schizophrenia, until you reached a point where you became professional about it, because you had to do that or leave. But then, after many years—so many that you've spent more time around the mentally ill than the sane—the professional distance can start to fade away. When that happens you might look around like I did and discover again the people within the diseases, especially the brave ones who you've known so long, from so many trips to the hospital, and you wonder how it is that they can still work so hard at keeping their spirit, hold to hopes, try to salvage dignity from ruins of lives. Try even to hold on to love. "And suddenly, while you're admiring them, you realize that for a long time they've been your tribe, that their triumphs and failures are more important to you than mortgages and politics. And then there's a day you look around the ward and suddenly understand that its in here that you've found your heroes. Your villains too, maybe, but certainly your heroes."

It was a long speech and she just sat there quietly, listening. At last, she said "Your heroes…sometimes they're well for a while?"

I nodded.

"But sometimes they're very sick a long time."

"Yes."

"I guess that sometimes they die."

I didn't want to talk about that. Instead I said, "For me, the hardest part is watching the ones who are mothers or fathers. The ones who got sick later, after having kids. A lot of times they gave them up, because they had to, or because that was best for a child or children at the time. Other times they hang on so tightly, getting well, if they can, so they can have their family again. They tell you these dreams they have for their kids, these fears…"

"You're a father."

I nodded. "That's a lot of it, I suppose. But there's more." She looked at me. I think I smiled. "My ex-wife used to tell me, not too nicely…That I was somehow looking for my own redemption in theirs. In clients. And that since they could have none, neither could I."

After a while, Lilly stood, began to clear away her flies—"Don't get up"—putting them carefully on a shelf below the vials. Jimmy's sleeping presence slipped back into my awareness. And Lilly's, "Do you think," she said softly, "that it's hopeless? Schizophrenia?"

I shook my head.

"When is it not?"

"For some people, the medications work. Pretty well. Some people, they get sick once and never again. Then there's people who have so much inside them, so much…grace…that even with the disease, they win their lives."

"Win?"

"They fill them with…wonder. Love, even. They make their hopes real."

"Grace," she said.

"Yes."

When Lilly returned to the table she leaned against the edge just before me and took my face between her palms. Her skin was warm and rough and her touch very gentle. "Grace," she whispered. "As in 'There but for the Grace of God.'"

I said nothing.

"As in 'Saving Grace.'"

"Yes."

"Yes…will you please stand?

I felt fear and what should have been shame and not enough of either to stop me from standing. And when she kissed me I was trembling,

trembling terribly, until she enclosed me and I whispered into her hair in a rush "Lilly, I know all about you, about Jimmy and this place. Your mother told me, Lilly, over so many years, almost since Jimmy was born. About Gin Creek and the trout there and her daughter, she was so proud of her daughter, Lilly, who ties flies and takes care of Jimmy. I have to tell you, I should have told you before that I know so much about you, even that those medications in the cabinet, Lilly, some are yours—"

"Yes," she whispered.

"—but that you struggle the way she did, your mother, only you might even have won, already beaten the disease, but that no matter what you *will* win as she did, because of grace—"

She was crying now, against me. She didn't seem shocked or betrayed, only sad.

"—and your mother, before she died, made me promise to come once to see, and I have because Lilly, Lilly, your mother was a hero of mine."

She was still crying, but when she kissed me I kissed her also. And she made me feel then, and ever since then, many wonderful things, beginning with what she whispered as she drew me down whispering in a rush "And you came Will, you did...and that makes you a hero of *hers*."

A long time later, hours, Jimmy called from some far corner of the house. "Lilly? Lilly, will Will teach us to flyfish?"

Lilly laughed against my chest. "Hush, Jimmy. Ask him tomorrow."

There was a disappointed silence, then a loud grumble from Jimmy's quarter. Part complaint, mostly plea—

"Well, *Mom said* he would.'

Getting Away

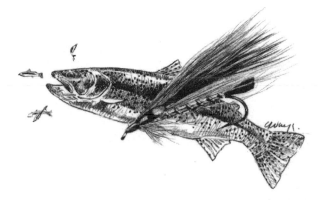

It was a fast run spilling from a pool, narrow, perhaps three feet deep. At the top a broken tree branch trembled in the current, but I was working 12 or 15 feet down from that when the fish took my point fly, a nymph intended to mimic the smallest of rock worms.

I struck and the fish turned; I thought I'd never seen such a crimson color, sweeping through the green. I still see that vivid side these years later; still feel the triumph rushing through me even as the fish headed upstream until it reached the drowned branch and stopped.

Bit of a fluke: the dropper fly had caught and pulled its partner free. I've got a good guess as to the size of the fish so released and I have several times lost larger. But this was one of those fish—maybe it's the day, the place you are in your own passage—that left me feeling hollow. Made me step out of the stream and into a shadow, sit down.

Losing things. Losing things of value. Grief surely overstates a case like this one; one does not properly mourn, of course. Usually I find a wry appreciation for such a brief battle, an ironic sense of variables and risk, "better to venture"—that sort of thing. But that day I didn't, and I still remember that I didn't; so today, sitting on the back stairs looking over the bay, I started wondering why.

If anybody else has managed to bitmap their brain, I'd like to hear about it. I haven't, so I can't quite tell you why Kenny came up. I did know him about that time, I think; and he could well be living out in the city over which I stared. Maybe it's something like that, but it's more likely the prompt was of another sort. That there's a file in there, keeping close unrelated items in a safe of Regret.

⊰•◆•○•◆•⊱

He was 19 years old when I met him, a very big kid with broad shoulders humped by muscle and eyes always wide with astonishment and fear. Those expressions mitigated against the professional contemplation I was tuned to those days, which ran to assessing how effective a flesh hold would have on a body that size: this was C-Wing, the door was locked and the fleece-lined leather restraints near to hand.

It's too long a story, but Kenny was one of those important people who give you a sense of hope doing a job where hope wears pretty thin some years. He'd had a schizophrenic break in his mid-teens and might have gotten into trouble—the records were unclear, and his mother a poor historian. What we did know was that she had locked him in the house then, and kept him there for more than three years—that his apprehension was about this chaos of people and stimulation he found in a hospital of a hundred patients, the maze of well-lighted hallways hung with murals and photographs, a public address system calling codes, nurses checking him off on clipboards or leading him to the station for medications and juice...

Kenny spent the first week pinned against a wall. He spoke so few words we weren't sure how many he knew. When he drew a picture during one of the low-functioning groups to which he was coaxed, a self portrait on a sheet of paper 17 by 21 inches, his face filled only three of those inches, faintly sketched in pale yellow crayon.

"This is you, Kenny?"

He nodded.

Kenny was no less than six feet four inches tall, the color of mahogany. I had never actually figured out how I would contain those arms.

"This is you?"

Only a nod.

⊰•◆•○•◆•⊱

The medications worked for Kenny, but that was not the cure. People were the cure, good people among the clients and staff, who really liked him. It generally started with the kind of relief folks feel when they find a gentle soul in somebody who looks like he could tear your arms off; that gave them the time and presence of mind to notice his shy kindness, then to savor a smile we saw some months into his stay. The fondness went beyond that when, holy holy, we saw that Kenny was getting well, coming out so far beyond what was early visible—and *hey*, did I have a part in helping here? Because if so, I'm really glad I came.

Kenny left after about nine months, as I remember. By then he was working in a sheltered county workshop program where he'd been "Worker of the Month" three times during the transition to that placement. He still hunched over a little, but now his wide eyes were always looking for a reason to smile. The last self portrait he did for us filled that big piece of paper with a rich brown face, grinning from ear to ear.

Three months later there was a fight on the assembly line. Another client threatened Kenny, who rushed away and didn't come back. The staff at the workshop made no effort to find him, and baffled me when I tried.

Kenny just disappeared, leaving us that last portrait. Over the years my sense of loss about that has remained constant. I mean, you just don't cure that many people in the mental health system...so where the hell did Kenny go?

Losing a man is so different from losing a fish that it seems an insult to compare the two. I'm not. Or if I am, it's the way the gunshot victims compare taking a slug to getting punched: perhaps nerves of mind, like those of the body, are only able to register a degree of impact. After that it takes some sorting out, a careful spreading of edges or probing of tissue to determine the depth of the wound.

And perhaps we also need, at times, to study the nature of the balm we apply. For certainly balm is required, and distraction.

Fishing may serve as these, and well. Last week I stumbled across a photograph of myself holding a big bass, and for once it's not the fish which fascinates me—usually after one of those "I really look that bad?"

double-takes—because I really do look bad, as bruised and distorted as a half dozen fractured bones in the face can make one look, with the arches around an eye collapsed, my mouth twisted by the broken piece of cheekbone driven into the jaw joint. The surgeons wanted to wait three days for the swelling to go down before reconstructing—

—so of course I went fishing. It was obvious, at the time, that I should go fishing.

>–·‹›·•·O·•·‹›·‒·◁

It's not always so, nor should we ever require such reasons to search the currents; and I truly, truly cannot remember ever thinking of Kenny while sitting beside a river. I would certainly not welcome such thoughts—I hope never to find my fishing intruded upon by such cares. While I do credit a trout for once exorcising my spirit, the rescue probably had more to do with finding something in myself and other strangers.

Fishing may or may not ever be metaphor—though a metaphor is whatever we make it—or symbol, or echo. It may be an activity entirely contained, a tiny galaxy with its own physics and biology, chemistry and codes, triumphs and tragedies. When we choose to enter here we suspend disbelief—that this is only a fish, fishing for it a trivial exercise undertaken in idle time. We believe in fishing's value with the same conviction we confer upon pieces of paper printed with president's pictures; so it's as silly to suggest that fish on my point fly was only a fish as it was for the staff at the workshop to dismiss Kenny as just another client, one in a pool of many thousands.

Silly and worse.

>–·‹›·•·O·•·‹›·‒·◁

Sitting on the back stairs I found in my mind both regrets. One does not put the other in perspective any more than love of a river is diminished by knowledge of the sea. Kenny and a trout link together in a dumb bond of "Lost and Wondered About." There's a difference, of course: I can still hope the trout lived well its life, rightly fitted to the world.

The Ugly Angler

"You're casting sucks," observed a recent fishing companion. Note that I use "recent," not *late*, though the idea had appeal; but no, for I am truly an ugly angler.

"I know that," replied I. "I've been down to the casting ponds ever Saturday for a month. Instructor there says it will take years to set me straight. By the way, have I mentioned that you're losing your hair?"

⊱━━━⊙━━━⊰

It's not that I'm amateur, you see: if casting's an art form my "mature" work should hang on a refrigerator door. Worse yet, casting's my strong suit: cats who chase moths see my flies and flee; my home-carved plugs strongly resemble Studebakers with eyes. In a sport of details I keep a tackle box which might be mistaken for an aerial photo of "Hurricane Andrew Hits Bob's Sporting Goods." Bob could still be in there; or, in a vest resewn with any fiber I found handy, wearing waders gooped from waist to sole, *I* could be Bob just dug out. Sometimes I'm tempted to stand near streams wearing a sign "Will Wade for Food."

All that's left is to offer up my life as a moral tale to frighten children: "Here's what will happen, Little Petey, if you continue to live your life like a grub."

Grubbing well describes my childhood pastimes. Born in the desert, I was forever foraging in dirt for lizards and other small life forms. Dad blamed my habits on Mom. Not that Mom grubbed much, you understand, but it was her idea to leave my babysitting to a collie named Cam. "Lord, the boy's caught another gopher," Dad would observe. Then, "What I don't understand is why the dog can't teach him to lick his clothes clean." Cam didn't, and so established my primitive dress code.

At five or six I discovered water—in irrigation ditches and canals—and immediately immersed myself. "It does keep him cleaner," said Mom, and Dad, encouraged by this improved hygiene, began a daily game of catch. By the age of 12, I was a Little League All-Star and firmly set in one of the most improbable casting strokes you'll see on a stream.

You will notice, I hope, a similarity between throwing a baseball and casting a spinning rod: both intend to accurately move a small object some distance. Unfortunately, my baseball career began as a pitcher, with a kick like Bob Feller's and a follow-through which launched me so far toward home plate that I could catch my own curve ball. Translated to casting, this meant I was often in position to net a fish before the lure actually reached him. I was also in constant danger of drowning. Luckily, Cam was a strong swimmer.

"Was it a cast? Or a try at suicide?" Dad would wonder as the dog towed me ashore. After numerous such episodes I believe he rooted for the latter—a suspicion compounded when Dad locked Cam in the car while shouting, "There's a big one in the deep hole above the rapids, son. See if you can cast to him off the cliff."

Perhaps it was Dad's despair that led him to give me a fly outfit for Christmas. Certainly he knew nothing about that end of the sport; so I spent a week struggling to get the fat line through a hook-eye. By the summer I went to work in a fishing camp, however, I'd learned to enjoy the whip-snap, single-haul style I named "Sandy Koufax With Stick."

Which turned out badly: first try on our lake, I KOed a bat with a false cast. I carried my victim back to the lodge for convalescence. "That's what you caught?" asked my boss.

"It's only my first time."

The boss considered. "So what's next? A duck? Hey folks, the kid's wingshooting with a fly rod!"

>─┤◆─○─◆┤─<

I wish I could say it got better. Unhappily, the corruptions of youth stayed with me, partly because—despite habits disdained by peers—I do catch fish. I've even developed an attitude about this. As evidenced last year:

While flyfishing a reservoir from a float tube, I slowly finned my way toward an angler casting tight loops from a gorgeous wood pram. Even at a distance I could see that everything about him was perfectly in place, from flats-billed hat to fitted vest and gleaming varnish on his split-cane rod. His dry flies, I'm certain, nested prettily in a walnut box, lined up by size and alphabetized. Why, the man was probably playing with an abacus while Cam and I picked ticks from each other's ears.

I hoped for a little advice or just the chance to watch, but he must have seen me casting or may have spotted the multicolored stitching of my seams; perhaps he noticed the hatch of flies impaled to various parts of my tube and hat. In any case he turned away from my greeting with exaggerated deliberation. After silently suggesting he go procreate himself with a power tool, I shrugged, which helped set my hook into a rainbow trout which missed three feet by one-eighth of an inch.

The haughty pram-man caught up with me at the dock. His face was flushed and furious. He looked me up and down, taking in all my ugliness. "What the hell were *you* using?" he demanded.

I returned his glare but he remained intent. *"I want to know what fly you were using."*

It was easy to smile then, and to hold to the light one of my battered creations.

"What...is...that *thing?*"

I smiled wider, showing canines, then carefully explained how to tie, cast and fish "Cam's Ugly Grub."

One of those moments to treasure forever: I thought veins were going to pop in his neck. It wasn't even necessary to follow-up with the observation that he, poor chap, was losing some hair.

The Merciful Rod

Max took the rod from me, swung it up and down, let it settle, then waggled it horizontally while mindful of his bedroom walls. He smiled at me—an even smile, now that his braces were off. "It's not like a really good one, is it? Really expensive?"

I shook my head. "It's a very good, very cheap rod," I explained, "with a slow action which will forgive some mistakes."

"So if I accidentally break it?"

"You don't owe me anything, but I flog you with the pieces."

He laughed. Head and shoulders thrown back, rod flexing with the movement. An easy, strong laugh, full of familiar relief: it struck me that he'd needed to know that the rules hadn't changed—that just because we were heading together into another domain, the game was still the same, no different in principle than the one we'd begun when I moved in with him and his mother and the girls.

That was four years before this day—important years, often wonderful—a span of time in which you can get a good education, even learn new sets of rules by which to live. For Max, that also meant understanding differences in the natures of adults around him: his mother was a passionate woman who played life with an emotional repertoire that ranged from elegant symphonies to sudden bursts of dangerous noise. With her, it was important he watch closely, take certain care.

Not with me. He knew that, shaking the rod he worried to break. But it was important to keep the idea visible, even now—especially now, as the game ended; I would not be living in the house he left.

"Three days we're going, right?"

"Yep. Starting now. Let's hit the truck, buck."

"Violet," he said. "Oh God."

"Silence, wretched child."

><+>-O-<+><

There're things you give up, merging your life into a family already four. In my case a work schedule, which let me fish most of a week, along with the studio apartment cluttered as a curio store and fitting me nicely. Habits, too; but my truck, Violet—a mini-motorhome, four cylinders dragging 4500 pounds—was something I'd kept hold of and kept in the condition of chaos natural to me. Max's mother hated it, of course—"It's so you can leave us whenever you want," meaning leave *her*—but to the kids it was a kind of wacky castle, a lair full of insects and amphibians in vials, bird wings, furs on the walls. Bunks piled with blankets made forts and nests; the photos of friends in far away places offered clues to the mysterious life I lived before I shared theirs. Even so, Violet had a wildness which frightened them in an exciting way—so messy and unlike the environment their mother maintained. "Crazy Violet," they called her, and refused rides even to the grocery store. "Who *knows* what'll happen. Violet *squeaks*."

And rattles—once in a while things fall down or off when I drive. So after clearing a loose fly or two, a screwdriver left out after some fix-it, Max sat the shotgun seat with an exaggerated roll of his eyes. I put my hands on the wheel and looked over at him. "What?" he said. "What?"

"Just seeing if Violet likes you there. You know how she can be when she's pissed."

"What? How?"

"You don't want to know."

He laughed. We rambled over the drawbridge, through the wicked town beyond, out into the central valley. By dusk we could see the mountains where we headed, feel the cool air off their flanks drafting

Violet's various cracks between gusts of the heater. We ate on the road while continuing to move into night, talking about Max's life in school and on the quarter-mile track where he runs. We remembered stories about us and the family—all the kids love to do this, ascribing mythic status to events from only a week or two old, committing these to a history they love to retell. Then, late, we lapsed into a comfortable quiet. I was entering the state of grace I find going fishing. I thought Max was near to sleep when he said softly, "I've always wanted to do this.."

"Really? No. You think flyfishing is nuts."

Another laugh, softer. "Well…I guess I don't mean the flyfishing part. Or I don't know if I do; I don't get that yet, even after all you've told us. Maybe I'll understand it afterward."

"What, then? You wanted to see the places."

I could feel him shake his head, see him barely in the penumbra of light from the dashboard. "I just wanted to see who you are out here. When you're free."

The last word surprised me a little; I had to consider what that meant. Some time during that process Max did fall to sleep; and off a dirt road where I could hear the stream, I pulled out the table bed, put him down and stretched out in the bunk above the cab. I pondered whether I should have forced Max's mother to let us take this trip earlier, years before; then remembered why I hadn't.

⊷⊶⊙⊶⊷

Max was a stranger to the world he woke into. He'd been camping before, with the Boy's Club and scouts; but there's a significant difference to the feel of outdoors when you're on your own, even in as civilized a fashion as Violet provided.

Over breakfast: "This isn't really a campground, is it?"

"Nah. I avoid them. I see enough of crowds on the island. So, tell me everything you know about flyfishing."

It was a lot, at least in theory, from using the weight of the line to cast, to the hierarchy of who eats whom in the water.

"Did I teach you all that?" I asked him.

"Yup. And 'A natural order beautiful and savage and mysterious beyond knowing.' Whatever *that* means."

"I forgot. Sounds good though, doesn't it?"

"Oh yeah. But I think you said the same thing about women and sex. Remember? After the part about—"

"Silence. Rig your rod."

>─┼─◆>─◦─<◆─┼─<

We did some casting. Max is an athlete anyway, and we'd had a few sessions with a stick and yarn outfit; soon he could lay out 20 feet of line without causing serious injury. About the time he mastered that, we saw a fish splash. "Can I try? Can I try for that one?"

"Sure," I said slowly, then noted there was not yet a hatch. What fly would he chose?

From the box he took a stray steelhead number, big, pink and chrome. "How about this?"

"Not a prayer."

"How about this one?"

"A lot of fishers would try with that. Why would you?"

"Because...it looks cool?" He glanced at me. "Okay. How do I know?"

From my vest pocket I unfurled a collapsible insect seine. He grimaced. "The bug thing."

"Follow," I said. Then, as we waded the riffle, "I'm going to hold this like so, while you kick up the bottom upstream from me... *Up*stream, I said."

I did, he did; the seine came up with three golden stone nymphs and two small caddis pupae. "Gross! You're not going to make me touch those?" I kept the stones, then seined up a second batch.

>─┼─◆>─◦─<◆─┼─<

The trout's lie was in a trough below a riffle—clear water, but with enough turbulence to hide the fish. We left the rods behind to make an approach on our knees.

"Isn't he gone by now?"

"Not unless we scared him. You remember where he came up? Watch."

It was almost a straightforward drift down from where I flicked the hapless stonefly nymph; we could see its yellow belly tumble. It hesitated in a current cushion, slipped on, disappeared in a flash of silver and red.

"Whoa! *Cool!* Do that again!"

I did, with identical results. Max remained impressed. "You have some more?"

"For you," I said.

"Come on—no way! You *know* I hate bugs."

"Come on yourself. It's not a bug; this is Nancy the Nymph and she won't bite."

It took less coaxing, since Max was eager to see the fish move again. But he wasn't comfortable with the nymph's feel, so his "Yechh" throw missed the lane. I held a second nymph out to him. "Try."

"Come on!"

Again, too far off line.

"I've got one left. Make this a strike."

He did, but at the last moment the nymph caught the cushion and slid left of the lie. "Shit!" Max muttered, then "Sorry!" just as the rainbow dropped back, tracked its prey and, with a grand lunge, took the stone from beneath the surface.

"Did you see that? Did you see that?"

I grinned. "*Now* what fly would you use?"

>—+›—O—‹+—<

Max lined the first fish—sort of crashed him, actually—then the second we found. Before the third I fixed him an indicator. "If I blow it this time," he groused, "maybe I should just put one of those things on live."

I stared at him. "You…would do that?"

He laughed.

"To Nymph Nancy's sister?"

"I know, all right, I know. But wouldn't that be lots easier?"

I crossed myself in mock horror.

"All right, already."

The next time I had him cast well ahead of the fish, counting on the loop of slack he tended to throw to serve the drift. It did. From instinct, Max struck as soon as the indicator dove—fish on.

A good one, it turned out, a holdover stocker big enough to give Max a struggle complete with shouts and slips and enough splashing to spook the dead. I landed the fish gently, then made Max hold it in current, knowing that as he did so he more than half-wanted to keep it, if only to show the girls. I told him he could, but Max parroted my maxim: "Don't eat the ball if you want to play the game tomorrow."

"It's true." I said, then slipped a pocket camera from my vest. "Smile."

As I framed Max in the viewer it struck me suddenly that this might be one of the last pictures I ever took of him.

"What?" he said suddenly. "What's wrong?"

"Nothing," I said. "But we'll take another, to be sure."

━┼◆━○━◆┼━

The rest of the day continued as idyll. Max caught two more fish and started insisting that I fish also. A caddis hatch came off in the late afternoon and, after missing a half dozen strikes to his own fly, Max had the fine experience of hearing me swear a streak when I'd done the same. As he gloated over that, I advised him that "flogging" was within reach. He only smiled wider. "I'm not so sure you can do that," he said.

I looked him over ruefully; he's taller than I am, if not so heavy. "Neither am I. And how I wish I had, more often, when I still had the chance."

He started laughing, then stopped abruptly. I wondered what thought had struck him and found out over dinner.

━┼◆━○━◆┼━

I'd poured myself some bourbon to follow the beans. Max was watching me intensely. "You want an inch?" I asked him.

He shook his head. "But you'd give it to me, wouldn't you?"

"Yes."

"Why?"

I thought he knew the answer to that, but he'd asked the question with some serious intent. I put the bottle down. "Because you're just about a man now. Because most of the time you handle yourself like one. You've watched me drink for years, seen how much I do and don't; I'm not worried you got it wrong. I have...significant faith in who you've turned out to be."

A long silence, then "I don't think my father would agree."

We knew I had no need to address that. While the subject of the kid's father wasn't forbidden, over years we'd developed protocol: they could talk about him but I would not. A religious zealot who made good money scamming stock investors, he was now $30,000 behind in child support. Early on, I'd treated him with elaborate deference on his irregular visits, even when he played Santa Claus while keeping from his children their due. Then he went too far for my tolerance. After that, the visits came rarely; he occasionally called.

Max was watching me again. "I know," he said. "You don't care what he thinks."

I shrugged. "About you? Forgive me if I trust my own judgment." I toyed with my glass. "And I might as well say, that if it comes down to you deciding what to think of yourself...for what it's worth, I hope you will consider my opinion."

I couldn't see Max's eyes in the light. But his voice was low when he spoke.

"I have to tell you something."

I nodded.

"I always wanted to. But I didn't know how."

"That bad?"

He nodded, sighed, spoke slowly, then in a rush: "Look...I was in the garage that night."

I wanted to say *What?* then *all of it?* but didn't. I pulled bourbon instead, so I'd have some moisture in my mouth.

"I didn't mean to be," Max raced on. "But it got so crazy in the house. Mom screaming, and the girls..."I couldn't...*do* anything. I tried, before you came, but I was so scared."

"Not your fault. Max, you were 12 years old."

"I know—I do know...I try to. Then, when you came in I ran out, so when you both came out to the garage I was hiding there and...I saw everything."

There are things you do in life, that I've done, to which there's shame attached; but even in hindsight you can't see another way it could have happened. The alternatives you think of years later, however reasonable they might sound—to your conscience, to a jury, to God—they're not real. Not solutions. What you did had an awful logic to it and you'd do it, that way, again.

I'd warned Max's father—I'd warned him—that if ever he beat his ex-wife or children again I would hurt him; so it wasn't like he didn't know. Of course he had his own rationalization—"that marriage was made in heaven, divorce only in court." I reminded him he'd married three times now, but he didn't see that it made a difference: in God's eyes he had rights and responsibilities I could not deny him. If he thought it necessary, he would not "spare the rod."

I was supposed to believe we had different perspectives, merely that. But even in the poor light that night, I could see malice in his eyes, an assertion that he would do as he liked not only in spite of me, but in order to spite me. I understood then that to him this was mostly an issue of dominion and possession. If I intended to interfere, he told me, now was the time; he didn't believe I would or could. What frightened me wasn't how big or dangerous he imagined himself to look, so full of Faith's fire, but how little his children meant to him in that moment.

So in cold fear I beat him. And when he was on the concrete, swearing he'd return, I pulled a small lock-blade knife from my pocket and put the blade in his mouth. With my face next to his I explained to him that he had better hope for God's mercy because the next time he hurt one of mine he'd have none from me, and as he tasted the clean steel we both knew this would never happen again, because we saw each other clearly.

Max had seen it all.

I didn't know what to say, except "I'm sorry. I'm so sorry. I wasn't try-ing to drive him away. I swear."

Max shook his head. "You would have cut him. I think you would have killed him."

There was no denying that. There was so much more to it, but we couldn't speak it just then.

⊱–⊰⊙⊱–⊰

In the morning Max smiled at me weakly; by that sign I knew we would not take the conversation farther. We fished instead, finding safety on the stream, in the learning and teaching of knots, in the immersion in water and the rhythm of casts. Once again, I had him study life in the seine, this time chromatids and mayflies from a still-water pool. I wor-ried that now this all seemed trivial to him, inconsequential; perhaps for that reason I grew pedantic, lecturing him on the ties of one thing to the next, the intricate necessities of dependence. He laughed once that I remember, when I told him how some insect species live years as imma-ture forms, crawling about under water until they fly as adults for only hours or days: "Then they find sex, which kills them…didn't I tell you it could happen that way?" He caught a half dozen fish, including a medium size brown with gorgeous color that he landed with a look of quiet satisfaction and revived with great care. "So," he said slowly, "in a way, fish are where they have to be, aren't they? Like the bugs—where they can eat and hide and breathe."

"Right. Though sometimes it's much harder to figure out where that is, or why."

He looked up at me. "But we're different. People—we can choose. I mean, if we wanted to, we could fish with the real bugs or worms. Or not fish at all."

"Right. Mostly."

"What do you mean, mostly?"

I looked around at the woods. "Some things you can choose. Sometimes, though…it's a trick to know if you're choosing even when you believe that you are. We think more than fish, but I'm not certain that I understand the reasons I do one thing or another when I do them. I try to. Sometimes afterwards, I figure it out. Maybe not. I do try."

"Right. I try, too."

"Right."

"Some people don't, though."

I looked at him, but he was looking at the stream. "Trout don't," he said firmly.

"No; it's not in their contract."

He didn't laugh. "You feel really good out here, don't you?"

I hesitated. "Yeah, I do. Water, woods—they draw me out. Flyfishing, for me—helps me live to the edge of my skin."

"That's how I feel about running."

"I know. I know you do. I can see it in your face when you race." I grinned at him. "I love seeing it there."

He blushed a little and things felt easier after that. We watched a hawk for a while, and in the late afternoon saw three does on the ridge waiting for us to leave. Max picked a baetis dun off the water and we compared it to ties in my box; then he practiced loading the soft rod, sensing the moment when flex reached the butt, began to spring. I taught him the roll cast, which he liked immediately. He put a fish down with one, but knew that he had. "Still," he said, "you'd think it would appreciate how hard I'm trying."

I enjoyed that: "Now there's a distinction for you: takes a mammal to appreciate intent….*I* appreciate the effort."

"You usually do."

><+>+O+<+><

Fine time; we brought two good moods back to Violet for dinner, to the table where we'd spoken the night before. Naturally, I'd left out the bourbon. "It's still light," I said quickly. "You want to eat outside?" We did, sitting on logs opposite, talking softly into gathering darkness. At last he said, "We leave tomorrow. So can I have that inch of bourbon? Or half an inch?"

I laughed. "Okay. But I don't want you saying 'yecch' to Jim Beam."

"Yecch" is what he said by way of making us laugh. Then we settled into silence. I finally geared myself to say what I'd been planning all day. "Look, Max. About that time with your father...I don't know what it's meant to you, how it's felt to hold on to that so long. I just want to tell you—"

"I know," he said. "I guess I've known a long time."

My face must have asked him *What?*

He sighed. "I think what I wanted to say last night, even if I didn't really know it, was 'thank you.'"

I looked at him.

"Just...thank you." He shrugged. "The thing was, you know, that I felt bad about feeling that way—I thought I should *blame* you. I thought I should be angry, when really I was glad about it. Or glad at least that you made him stop what he was doing to us—like he was God, or something. I guess the real thing is, that I was blaming myself for letting him do it, that I couldn't stop him. If I could blame you for something instead..."

"You can, if you want to."

He shook his head. "No. I can't. I mean, I don't like my dad much. I love him, because I have to. But, as a dad...He did what he did to us because of who he is. Not because of anything we ever did. It's just who he is."

"Yes. Yes."

"And you, you did what you did to him because...for us. Maybe you chose us, I think you must have; and when you did, part of what that meant was that you would hurt him if he hurt us. Because that's who you are...so...there's really nothing to be mad about."

He looked me steadily in the face, then smiled. "Remember, when the girls came in and said, 'We adopt you.'"

I laughed. "I remember."

"Well, we did." He nodded, then looked down. "But we also know, we've known for a long time, that you don't love our Mom. We know— I mean, she yells it at you—that maybe the reason you're still around...is because of the girls and me. That's why I wanted to see you out here, where you want to be. Because we feel bad, that you stay because of us."

"Max. Listen."

"I know. I know what you're going to say. But we feel bad. We feel bad, because we don't want you to leave. The girls, you know, they're not little any more; they understand. And when you asked me to come out here I *knew*, I knew that you're going, because you can't stand Mom and all the stuff that she does."

"Max—"

"No. Listen, please."

He was trying not to cry.

"We don't want you to leave, but we don't want you to stay. That would be like…I don't know what it would be like—like making that brown trout live in dirt. Right? So I just want to tell you, from us…that you can go."

What I had to say was so important that I stood, walked over to him and kneeled. His head was still down when I got there. "Max." I shook him. "Max, listen. I am supposed to be with you. I'm sorry I don't love your Mom any more; that's not about you. But there are some things you do choose, that you make the way you want because you know deep inside you that it's got to be this way…I've got to be part of your life and the girls no matter what, no matter what; and if that's the way *you* want it to be, it will be. I promise. If it's what you want as well."

He was trying to steady himself, take this in.

"Yes," I continued in a whisper. "I'm going to leave your mom. But I swear—and she knows this; she won't try to stop it—that if it's what you want I will always be there, always. That I will see you every single chance I get, and whenever you want. I will be there."

"I want," he said simply. "The girls want."

"Then Max, that's *how it is*."

⊱┈◈┈◦┈◈┈⊰

And that is how it is, a decade later. Once in a while the kids come fishing with me; more often I see them where they work, or for dinner, with years behind us now of school plays and PTA meetings, races won and lost. I call on my way out of town. They tell me to be careful, call back later to leave messages on my machine for my return. I think of them when I am in the mountains, on a stream alone, consider them when I start to wade too deep or climb higher than I should. Sometimes I know where the fish must be, and why; but it is always that I have a sense of these children in me, for there are requisites of man as compelling, and natural, as any that keep a fish in a stream and stoneflies in a riffle. To the heart we cast in our way, and some takes are forever.

Legends: of Madame X and Cats

I met Maurice Kelly by threatening suicide. A fisherman, you know, must do whatever it takes.

━━━━◦━━━━

The Williamson River is a shorter trip to a finer water than most California anglers understand. All morning fish rose around me. They dimpled and slurped and three of the greatest rainbows I'd ever seen gouged troughs through a slick downstream. Two thousand casts with twenty-seven flies annoyed them not at all.

I considered switching religions. A local suggested I try a fly shop near Chiloquin instead, just a mile down 97. But "This 'n That" was closed—now don't the Hindus have a river god?

Next door at the coffee shop I found a friendly waitress. "Nice place," I observed. And didn't they see lots of fisherfolk, this time of year? Sure they did, so it would really be a pity when word got around about such a horrible death—

"Somebody *died*?"

"Not yet," I admitted. "But if I can't find someone to tell me what those fish are rising for, mam, I'm taking a trip to your little bridge. Not much of a fall, you're thinking—but head first, on those rocks? Awful messy. What a shame."

I like laughter, and that's what I heard when the waitress passed me the telephone after dialing Judy Carothers. Then, in a voice still smiling, "Stay where you are, drink some coffee. I'll be over in a bit."

Fours hours later I'd heard lots about the town, the rivers around it, Polly Rosborough, and the origins of the fly shop Judy runs with husband Steve. Judy speaks softly and well, and listens with a kindly expression that encourages people to speak. Me, anyway; by the end of the conversation I'd confessed that I was a writer on the run from retaliation for a crime story she'd soon see on "60 Minutes."

"Usually when I'm fishing, I meander," I told her. "This time I need a little speed. Some distance." What I needed, I felt, was to move on.

Too bad, said Judy, but if I came back this way she thought she could show me something special. "There's an old fellow here who knows the Woods River really well. You could write about that."

⋗┼⋖⊶⊙⊶⋗┼⋖

Two weeks later indictments came out and I did return, arriving late, hung over and relieved. I packed camera and tape recorder to meet Steve Carothers and Kelly at the shop. For the record: "Kelly first name, or Kelly last?"

He grinned. "Just Kelly." Mid-seventies, I guessed him, lean and erect and quiet without seeming taciturn. Long, elegant fingers in which he always held a Salem. Despite the pleasant presence, I couldn't get much sense of the man.

While off-loading the boat at a remote ramp on the Woods we suffered an unlikely delay: a pair of kittens, unchaperoned, too fat and friendly to be feral, played around us, mewling as they rubbed our ankles and tangled our steps. You could mark us as three animal saps by the way we passed the cats back and forth, agreeing "They shouldn't be way out here, that's for sure."

⋗┼⋖⊶⊙⊶⋗┼⋖

Launched at last. Compare the Woods to Fall River—you can't do that with too many waters—a broad stream wandering meadows as it settles toward Klamath Lake. We motored upstream watching clouds stack up on volcanoes. Below us weeds streamed in current, sheltering trout in channels, Kelly said.

Other than these interchanges, we were quiet, three men in a boat, one a stranger.

Steve handed me a Madame X. Kelly checked his knot on the same sort of fly. "I'll watch a while," I said.

Kelly nodded and flicked out some line. He false-cast a couple of times, loaded his rod, released. The Madame passed my ear with a hiss so pronounced it sounded like a raptor stooping to kill. For a moment I didn't even realize the sound was his cast.

Seventy feet away, six inches from an undercut bank, Kelly's fly settled down. I turned and stared at him. I couldn't have been more startled if he'd stood on point in a tutu.

I didn't know then that Kelly had traveled and fished these rivers for five decades, that he was legend already, along with "Pregnant Whale," the fat raft he strapped to his truck. He was beloved for his quiet kindness, for his championship of conservation; as author and letter writer, Kelly was so scathing in his attacks on "bloated politicians that a local paper banned him. (Kelly simply had others submit for him, under their names. "Such a clever and pointed man, with such a gentle way," as Judy Carothers would say.) I had no idea that he was a founder of the fly-tying exposition in Eugene, or an award winning tyer himself...

>—•>—()—‹•—‹

No clue; never mind. Ignorant, I could only wonder at how many years it took to put together a movement of such power and grace, a coordination of hand and rod and eye and wrist. Later, I remembered other people in my life who defined themselves by physical gesture—a shy girl who could burst your brain cells with a kiss; a psychopath listless as a toad until he attacked—but at that moment I realized Kelly revealed with one cast aspects of himself I had not suspected, demonstrating a mastery I don't imagine I'll achieve.

>—•>—O—‹•—‹

For hours he cast so well, oblivious to my awe; he had drifts to look after. We drifted also, searching for rainbows which never rose, waiting for the trucks to frighten grasshoppers from fields of alfalfa, creating thereby a terrestrial "hatch" for which the Woods is well-known. Over Carothers' objections I took my turn at the oars; later I switched to nymphs, which prompted Kelly to speak, if only a little, about his dedication to dry flies. My hosts worried that we caught no fish. I did hope for one to illustrate a story. More silence, more searching.

Encounters of brief duration often offer gloss—reflections of super-
ficials, shiny enough, meaning a little. In some small, special way, Kelly's
casts changed that. Then we came back to the cats.

>─┼─◆>─○─<◆─┼─<

They romped around us as we winched up the boat, still unattended,
obviously hungry. During a vague, monosyllabic discussion, the three of
us allowed as how we really must take them back to town. So we did.
Then the conversation went something like this:

Carothers: I thought you were going to keep them.
Me: Me? Well, no. I mean, I'm traveling in a truck.
Kelly: Yeah. But I thought you were taking them, too.
Me: Me? Listen, I've got two male cats at home. Mean males,
    territorial, still with balls—
Kelly: Four, my wife's got. Can't walk around the kitchen
    as it is—
Carothers: Three, we have, and two dogs. That's one of my dogs
    over there. See the way he's watching those kittens.? Look at
    that, will you?
Me: Wait a minute...I'm in a *truck,* with two males at home—
Kelly, in a whisper: Polly Rosborough.

Carothers and I turned. To me the name meant fuzzy nymphs, but
Steve replied "Polly? No chance. When that cat of his disappeared he
swore he'd never get another one."
    "I know," answered Kelly, and there was light in his eyes.
    "I mean, that he won't take them."
    "I know."
    "*Besides*—he's out of town. Won't be home 'til late tonight—"
    "I know."
Carothers and I watched the grin spread on Kelly's face.
    "And I've got the key to his trailer," he said.

>─┼─◆>─○─<◆─┼─<

The next morning I woke beside the Upper Sacramento, just months
before the spill. I tried to make my casts fly like Kelly's, let them fall so
lightly so far away. I failed, caught fish anyway. Over breakfast of

Grapenuts and summer blackberries I smiled, remembering Kelly's face as we skulked through the trailer park in a late August evening carrying two tiny mewlers and a key.

Is it still a giggle when you're 35 years old? 40? When you're 70-something? Exactly what do you call the sound Kelly made when he popped those kittens through Polly's front door?

Steve made that sound, too, or something like it, and so did I; then the three of us slipped off in the dusk. For a minute there we were no longer two men and a stranger—just a bunch of *boys*, yeah.

⊱──⊰◦⊱──⊰

Only two years later I returned to This 'n That, a bigger store now, bright and friendly, with an AKA of "Williamson River Anglers." I brought the Carothers a photo I'd dug from a pile: Steve and Kelly perched in the boat prow, gazing out over the Woods' gentle current with clouds and volcanoes rising above. Judy looked a little moist and Steve's voice dropped, I think, when they remembered Kelly. Their last shot shows him bent by the cancer that ate him so fast, with so little mercy.

Kelly fished until the end, of course, sneaking Salems whenever he could. "And you know," said Judy, shaking a smile onto her face, "He really loved telling the story about that night, about Polly's trailer and the cats....He was so proud of that prank."

⊱──⊰◦⊱──⊰

Imagine. A man that accomplished taking such pleasure in such a small escapade. Perhaps that's a measure of Kelly, and a lesson of its own.

Abstaining from Trout

There's nothing wrong with failing to fish for an extended period of time. After two weeks I'm a little restless, sure, cranky and distracted. At three I start to question existence; end of a month and I'm convinced that my soul has shrunk to the size of a raisin. "Other than that, First Lady Lincoln, how did you like the play?"

But one can't always go fishing; one must cope. Divert energy. Consider aerobic exercises for that thumb which convulses for want of resisting cork. Personally, I try not to false-cast during staff meetings, or disguise the motion if I do. "Yes, Madame Director, I only raised my hand to say…that if I may compare this situation to raising a brown trout from beneath an undercut bank, late evening on the Owens River, then I'd drift a paradun, size 18, in olive or black. I hope that clarifies things, and I thank you for your attention."

⊳⊶⊷⊙⊶⊷⊲

Part of the problem is that the cats are tired of me. Like Hat Creek rainbows, they used to thrive on a catch-and-release program, the one I conducted in the side yard. Oh yes, I remember the days when I could take a nine-pound, six-ounce Siamese on every cast. Lay out a Matchstick Muddler between my lemon tree and the gas meter, twitch once and get set for his run to the live oak—

No more. I think his tabby half-brother convinced him this was some sort of *dog's* game, the idiot occupation of a spaniel. Now the Siamese just sits there, watching me with one or another of his crossed blue eyes. It's all I can do to make him hold still for a dubbing raid disguised by "Nice kitty, let's comb-out the fleas."

><+>•O•<+><

Then my tying goes wild. I've confessed that my flies resemble road-kills—"Stoner's Bass Bug" evolving into "Dead Buck On I-5."; so now I'll admit that I've also tied the "Brown Buick" that caused the collision. And on a 6X shank, a "Wooly Greyhound" that followed; then a hot-pink "Ferrari Steelhead" that swerved in the other lane—

No kidding. Be sure to write for my marabou series, "Mammals of Africa."

><+>•O•<+><

Symptoms, sure. I'm supposed to grope for a cause, come to grips with underlying illness, practice my speech for the Angler's Anonymous meeting. "I'm an addict," I'll sob, waving about pieces of my five-weight, "and it's ruining my life. My neighbor, Terry, hasn't talked to me since I congratulated her on spawning, then said baby McKenna was 'pretty as a brook trout…' "

But they say you have to want to be cured for that sort of thing. I don't. Not even when The Woman Around Here advises once again that "There's more to life than fishing, you know."

"And just what is that, dear damsel, my little nymph?" I inquire politely. Then I get to sleep in my camper.

><+>•O•<+><

It's not so bad, really. I'll sniff the scents of Viola's last trip, dust from some Lassen dirt road mixed with lingering odors of line-dressing and hash. I'll find an old *Trout, Steelhead and Salmon* beneath a mattress, pant a little as I point the flashlight; then lie on my back, close my eyes and pretend that traffic sounds are rushing water, that the barking of Betty's brain-dead Doberman is a distant coyote. The wisteria I smell through the skylight climbs a stream-side willow, somewhere; and maybe in the morning I *will* try a cricket pattern, for once, given the pleasing racket they're making tonight. Well now wait—I'd better hold off till the sun warms the air, start instead with a streamer in the dawn, tuck it back into that slick beside the riffle, stack slack to let it sink...

I'll sink. If I'm lucky—I'm often lucky this way—I'll dream of a rainbow slipping through current, clean and bright, utterly intent. In silence I will watch, poised in my neurons for a pursuit of beauty and strength and speed—do I breathe?—until I feel my fingers load a wisp of rod, stretch back and, still in silence, cast.

In my dreams I catch fish. Carl Jung speaks to that, I'm sure. But I hardly have enough time to read Lyons and Brooks, McGuane and Kyte and Chatham.

>─┼─◆>─○─<◆─┼─<

No, in life I have no time for a cure, or even the search for reasonable explanation. And I suspect that situation will only get worse, when at last I get that spaniel for the side yard.

Knight and Day
of Merced

Consider the protocol: it's seven a.m. and you're stringing a Sage five-weight, slipping 18 feet of fresh leader through the guides, about to knot on a grey nymph before you clamber 100 feet down to a river below...when some shaggy guy in baggy blue and pink shorts his kids gave him for Father's Day shuffles up to your car, saying "So if I'd like to fly-fish a little, maybe this is the place?"

Think—-then he launches this unlikely explanation of how he's fled jet-boats on the local reservoir and has forgotten his shoes—his shoes, for Christ's sake—but does have these flip-flops, also blue and pink, along with his off-the-rack rod and, by the way, "Are there trout down there?"

You say—

" 'Trout,' hmm—that's some kind of fish?"

or

"Sure are. Go for scorpion and rattlesnake patterns, because there's so many hiding in poison oak along the bank you're going to hike down half-naked—"

or

"I don't know, but let me show you some fly patterns I've invented, then we'll try here for half an hour. After that I'll lend you some shoes and spend twelve hours guiding you on a terrific smallmouth stream while sharing thirty-five years of fishing experience before I take you to a secret bass pond on private land I have permission to fish—"

Maybe the answer depends on your mood. On your level of tolerance. How you were raised.

>─+─◦─◦─◦─+─<

The angling end of Gary Azevedo's biography: he bought his first flyrod in 1956 with money he made selling peanuts during ball games at Louisiana State University. Flyfishing was not quite the rage around Baton Rouge that spring; nor had it caught on in the Central Valley town to which his family moved soon after.

" 'Eccentric.' Boy, I sure got tired of being called that because of my flyrod," Azevedo confesses with a short laugh. By "brim" fishermen with bobbers and bamboo poles, by catfish hunters with broomsticks and braided Dacron cable, by bass anglers with level-winds and by striper-folk throwing plugs the size of two dollar cigars.

But flyfish he did, joining thereby one of those lesser known limbs of the family tree. You've got Pennsylvania people, the Upstate Brigade, Montana legends and the Key West/Cuba Tarpon tribe—everybody milking ancestral "memories" of English chalk streams... Then you have guys who grew up alone in their sport outside of towns like Turlock. Men, and women I'm sure, who thumbed backwards and forwards through a Joe Brooks book and learned to cast by watching their shadows. Maybe they did like Al Martin of San Leandro, who made his whole family line up in the back yard to tell him if his loops looked anything like the ones he saw in Jim Freeman illustrations...

Mokelumne, Tuolumne, Merced. Stanislaus and Owens and Rush—even Wildhorse in the heyday of that Nevada water. Azevedo remembers stretches of streams where thirty fish days were the rule—"now empty, just empty..." He began his own program of catch-and-release in *1964*.

I learn some of this during the hour I delay him on the road, while carefully perusing the fly boxes he opens. Save for a few terrestrials and two Brown Grizzly Bear Black nymphs, he carries no trout flies bigger than 16.

Why's that? I ask 1100 questions and get as many answers. Then, by accident we share one of those awful, vest-kept secrets which can destroy a fisher's reputation these days; we're both fond of Fenwicks. That's right, we stood there and said it, *mano a mano*, and the heft of my old Eagle in his hand brought back memories of the nine-footer he lost in a fall. "All the fish that rod took me... All the grief I got for using it" from the *now* generation of tackle elitists."

I learn more as I waddle after Azevedo in my flip-flops, navigating the trail with an occasional scream. After the Fenwick confessions other intimacies come easy: both our careers turned for a time toward criminal justice, Gary's into the strange and frightening world of domestic espionage, mine into investigative journalism, and as adjunct to a program of criminal justice pseudo-psychology.

Talk, talk. In the meantime the dam opens above us—this is a tailrace—apparently shutting the mouths of all trout about. After half an hour or so we climbed back to our cars to suck Cokes and carry on.

"Any interest in smallmouths?" Azevedo asked. Oh yes. "Well, I grew up on the Merced near here. Don't have the right tackle with me, but if you've got poppers in your box..."

I did, which left us both staring at my already battered flip-flop feet. "Doubt it," he murmured, "but maybe my spare wading shoes would stretch to fit you."

You bet. That is to say that they were a size and a half small and worn through on the inside to expose a hard plastic honeycomb that lamed me after three steps: "Sure, these are *great*."

How to describe the day after that: 105 degrees or so—that magic temperature at which I expect Heaven's Hand to descend and baste me with a brush...We waded half a mile of a river thin from drought, mostly clear, mostly fast. Cattle moved on the shore and crashed trees near the water as the best bunch of frogs I've found in years *chirr*-erupted from hiding. Azevedo and I continued to talk.

About fish, a lot. It's one thing to share time with an expert, something else to learn from a local. When somebody is both, it goes like this:

"Believe you'll find bluegill holding just outside that current—usually are. Now that pretty popper you have in black—"

Jeff Yamagata's, actually, from his A-1 shop in Oakland.

"—would work wonders here at dusk. For sun like today I tie a white one with black legs. But I think if you cast that big humpy you like out beyond the cut—"

Bang, bluegill.

"Smallmouth under the little tree there—see him? Lay it out, dead-drift it by him, oh, three times. Last cast, give a little twitch—"

Three drifts and a twitch—bang, smallmouth. *Wait just a minute...*

"Now we'll hike a hundred yards up from that riffle. Show you some channel cats and smallmouth in a run where we can watch them. Couple black bass, too. That little grasshopper you tie? I do think it would raise one."

Smallmouth. Bluegill, bluegill, largemouth, smallmouth. Azevedo took a big squawfish on an elk-hair caddis. "Now if you'd just move ahead of me here—oh no, thanks, really, I can do this any time—we'll have bass from the current line all the way over to shore."

We talked of things not fishing—about family, about fathers for a long time. Stopped in current, we marveled at how very different men lead us to such similar conclusions. Azevedo gently thanked me for an act I committed to protect a step-child; then he told me why it meant something to him.

Smallmouth breaking up into sun. Bluegill kissing the fly, then turning broadside to current. The bright threads of fish knit into our conversation, each prompting admiration. Wherever it wandered, the conversation came back to fish, to water, to memories and dreams.

In twelve hours there's time for ideas to circle, themes to surface with a swirl that's soon familiar. Azevedo had several. One was always tinged with regret.

He would begin with a recollection of some great piece of water and the wonderful fish in it. Qualifiers shadowed what would follow: "before" they put in New Melones dam; "until" the drought drew down too much water; "back then" when a stream was unplundered, wild, running through gravel instead of silt left by erosion from clear-cut hills... Oddly enough, Azevedo never conveyed a sense of "You should have been there"; instead, his voice sounded of bewilderment, of disbelief that such treasure could be so utterly wasted. "If people only knew," he said softly but often, "the fish that stream could support...how much that river once offered...what good management could do, if we gave it a chance..."

The earlier of Azevedo's stories had a solitary sound, I noticed, the meanderings of a boy who fished alone, escaping through "eccentric" pursuit from a sometimes brutal reality. Later came Marty and other partners who shared the days. Yet when Azevedo brought forth the full picture, fleshed out this theme, I could sense the impact of those solo years.

We were neck deep at the time, shed of our vests to cool in current and to drink through our pores. "How can I say this?" he wondered. "but it was Marty who got me to taking photos, you see, then videos of the trophy fish we caught—wild trout of over three pounds. We've got maybe, oh"—he mentioned a number I believed because of the day, then looked at me to check my reaction.

"Anyway, we've taken just a whole bunch of 'fish of a lifetime.' Sometimes Marty or me, we talk about writing a book, doing a film, or something. Then—

"How can I say this? If everybody really put pressure on fish—I mean, a size 14 nymph is just a show tie, most of the time—if everyone fished trophy fish the way trophy fish eat, and *killed* them...And if I played a little part in telling them how...

"I don't need the money that bad. Maybe if half the great waters of California were catch-and-release... Maybe, if I believed that all these new flyfishermen really understood, knew *from their own lives* how good it once was and could be again...I'd do it. Write, film, I don't know. Am I selfish? I feel selfish. Of course, I'd feel foolish acting like I knew something special anyway. Even with Marty's pictures... you know what I mean."

I tried to reassure him, a little, about the integrity of flyfishermen as a tribe. He believed me, a little, I think. Then, as I sniffed the scent of my own hypocrisy—do I share the best waters I know? Sometimes. Do I ever reveal a secret trusted to me by another fisher? Nope. Azevedo hammered again at his theme. "You see, if they realized when they took a fish of five pounds and wanted to mount it, that once such a trout wasn't rare in that place, that the water could again produce them in numbers... If I really believed they believed in *what was and could be*...

>—•>—O—<•—<

A great day dimmed to evening as we waded the bass pond, putting poppers up against reeds, in pockets of weed, under overhanging branches. Talking...

As we trudged back to our cars, I bit back groans from my battered sole; then we stood another two hours telling stories. We shook hands, twice, laughed about what a good time we'd had, made arrangements to meet in October—

End of story, not reflection: I do believe that Azevedo's tactics are unusual and deadly. I'm also convinced that in his hands they don't deplete our stocks—that to Azevedo the process of fishing utterly dwarfs any "product" of fish. I honor the idea that he would not contribute to more effective depredation. From that I wonder—

Perhaps the catch and release ethic does not rise very high. Perhaps it's only as pragmatic a practice as I once explained to four meat-hunting kids: "If you eat your baseball, tomorrow you have no game. You won't catch your dead fish again."

Perhaps there's more to it than that. But even if an odd chivalry does apply, maybe that's also self serving: those of us with grim vision—show me a law enforcement type whose eye is still clear—need a sport in which honor and reverence persevere, if only to maintain our faith in those virtues.

Worst case, I suppose, flyfishers might be merely the elitist dilettantes we're often made out to be.

Still, imagine streams with stewards of Azeved's bent. Imagine rivers tended that way—for the last thirty years, say. Paint a picture of what was and title it "Ten Years From Now."

Imagine all that, and perhaps your five-weight will feel like a sword, your odd ideals as worthy as King Arthur's or Azevedo's.

The Rhythm
of a Woman and Line

I listen closely to stories about how a flyfisher came to the craft. I read with special care those daring writers who mate flyfishing to romance or to sex, but it's never quite what I'm waiting for. What I truly want is already settled in memory; so I visit.

At 18 years old I began to understand that I had little understanding of my heart or anybody else's. Specifically—and to my great dismay—I hadn't the faintest idea of how a heart beats in the breast of *Woman*, though much of my interest did not penetrate near so deep. Never mind that—*Woman* was for me an abstraction with less definition than fast water in sunlight. Besides *Her*, I was obsessed with fishing for trout. At least the latter were accessible to a young man working the summer in a fishing camp.

Sixty-five hours a week was about all my boss could use of me, for room and board and $40 a month. His schedule left me two hours at dawn and dusk, a full one-sixth of each day, to wade the lake shallows or quietly slip a canoe through the mists, usually alone on the lake save for osprey, early-rising or late-homecoming raccoons, and irritable coots. During these winsome times of day, I was so utterly intent that I felt at ease in the tension of my age, the reign of confusion that is half hormonal and half wonder. Which is only to say that I had brief respite from the thoughts and fantasies that drove me the rest of the day and raided my nights.

Until *Woman* became Eliza.

><-+>-•-O-•-<-+->-<

I didn't know her name or sex that first morning when she simply appeared, standing brown and green and waist deep along my favorite shoreline. I'd been paddling parallel to the low sunlight while flicking a Mepps spinner into shallows: for an instant I actually thought she was an animal, maybe a bear—until she seemed to lift a 40-foot ribbon of water from in front of her, slung it up over her head, then waved it toward the water again.

Flyfishing. An exotic angler had moved into my time on my turf from God only knew where. The surge of resentment that invasion prompted promptly evaporated when she pushed a felt Stetson back from her face to loose a long fall of hair.

"Hello," she called softly.

I didn't return the hail, only sat silently, drifting with my rod poised and spinner twisting on the line. Understand that our lake was something of a blue-collar destination, a remote put-and-take with a fair share of secrets and no blue ribbon reputation whatsoever. Beyond the rarity of her technique, I'd never once seen there a woman fishing alone; so I certainly wasn't prepared.

"Hello?" she said again, as my canoe continued to slide toward her. I believe I'd actually hoped that she would magically stop seeing me.

"Yes," I said, suddenly, and with this bit of repartee, drove my paddle down in a familiar motion now desperate, turning back the way I'd come, hoping that it wasn't a low laugh I heard at my back.

><-+>-•-O-•-<-+->-<

My first chores in the morning were to stock the store icebox with a day's soda and beer, then slice a Velveeta loaf into the slabs we sold for bait. Because of the dawn's mishap, I got an early start, much to the surprise of Noel, my boss. A small, strong man, Noel was clever in ways I wasn't, especially about people. Around the time I finished the cheese, I noticed him grinning at me from a perch near the counter. "Well, well," he said.

"Morning."

"And a pretty good one for you."

I eyed him warily. Noel had a wicked sense of humor that made me careful. "Why's that?"

"Well now, when's the last time you had a chance to earn twenty bucks in one day?"

"There's a fire?" It was my great hope to get on one of the emergency crews.

He shook his head. "No, no fire. But I had a young lady come in to cabin five last night. Says she wants a *guide*."

"A guide?" We really were *not* that kind of camp.

"Right. I told her we had none. She said she'd be satisfied with somebody who knows the lake pretty good and can handle a boat."

I scowled.

"Right. So then I said we didn't have anybody like that either, but that you'd caught a fish in—when was that? May? A—and could sometimes row halfway cross the bay without sinking..." He laughed. "Virginia packed you a lunch."

I had an awful suspicion. "Wait a second—what does she look like?"

Noel laughed some more. "You'll see."

I did: Out of her waders she didn't appear bearish at all—more like a deer, or like one of the antelope I liked to watch out at Sunflower Flat. I stared at her as she walked down the dock: she had a steady, easy stride, without much side-to-side movement, and wore clothes that hung comfortably along her body. Her face showed little emotion at all, not even amusement about the earlier encounter. In one hand she held a rigged fly rod, in the other a khaki-colored vest.

I was already stationed in the boat I'd chosen, a 14-foot wooden job stable enough to dance in; so I was looking up at her when she stopped.

"It is you," she said evenly, in that low voice I'd heard laugh. "I thought it would be...Hello again." She stepped down into the bow, barely rocking the boat, then sat to face me. She neither smiled nor frowned.

"Good morning, ma'am," I said softly.

She probably wasn't even 25 years old, but she *was* paying 20 dollars. "Ma'am," she said. "I'm Eliza. Noel tells me you're Will, that you know the fish here, and that you can row."

I nodded.

"He also said that you are, and I quote, 'Not badly brain damaged, just shy around women.'"

I froze, wondering instantly if it were possible to stalk and kill Noel in his sleep.

"That's all right. If it will help make you comfortable, you can pretend I'm your sister."

I pulled a stroke or two, just to free us from the dock. "Yes'm."

She looked at me steadily. "You don't have a sister."

I shook my head.

"All right. I'm not keen on this, you understand. But I would like you to be more or less at ease. So, Will, you may pretend I am your mother." She smiled faintly. You *do* have a mother, Will?"

I dug in the oars. "No. Where would you like to fish, ma'am?"

That was part of my job, of course. Oddly enough, the awkward bent I'd put in our conversation made it a little easier for me to direct the conversation to the task. "I don't know too much about flyfishing except what I've read in magazines. You want me to try to find fish on top?"

Yes, though she could, she explained, put on a line that sank. She'd prefer not to: did I know of any place where the trout would be hunting closer to the surface? And had I ever seen an insect that looked like any of those in her box?

I checked. "This one, not quite so brown. They start to move around in the weed beds about now, creep up on the tulle stalks in the cove east of the dam."

"I see," she said thoughtfully. "This is a nymph, a damsel fly nymph. Your cove sounds like a good place to start."

Yes, but a long row. As I got to it she set up her rod, freeing a fly—I recognized it as a streamer—from the hook keeper, then adding to that a length of monofilament and another fly, smaller and dark. After that she stripped out a couple dozen feet of the fat fly line and, with several waves of the rod, laid it out at an angle from the wake.

I couldn't help but watch, seated the way we were; so it was a relief when she turned sideways to troll, her face and body in profile. Sort of a relief: the position pulled her clothing taut; and from the new angle I was at liberty to examine various curves and the way her light brown hair drew back behind one small, surprisingly flared ear. I looked away, of course, when I felt the fascination; and because I feared she would discover my study. But it *was* a long row, and she was intent on her fly.

Yes, I was 18, not a child. But Dad's last job was in Saudi—that was after Alaska, where I learned to fish—and we'd been too far out in the desert for any of the foreign staff compounds; so from 15 to just a couple months before, I'd schooled at home with my father, which I liked; and played, when I did, with Saudi boys from town—soccer, mostly. The situation had worried my father so much he'd brought me a *Playboy Magazine* he'd found—contraband, in an Islamic nation—May of 1963. "Strictly for the purposes of anatomic study and cultural indoctrination... And so you won't eventually confuse species or suffer some sort of mammal deprivation."

I didn't. Get confused, anyway. Still, I'd had remarkably few opportunities for interaction with girls or women, save for the occasional visit from the wives of my father's colleagues, in whom Dad observed, "You do provoke the most awesome maternal drive. Half of them are ready to nurse you before we've reached dessert."

An interesting image, but not one I could fix to Eliza that morning, as she stared down her rod while I stared at her, the two of us lost to our separate consideration. It was possible that she was more aware of me than I cared to think.

"Osprey," she said suddenly. I paused in my rowing to follow her point. I watched the bird wheel; I'd even found where they nested.

"Hunting over the cove," I said. "He does that, about this time."

She nodded. "That's a good sign."

Her rod twitched. "Yes," we both said at once...

⤁┄◆┄○┄◆┄⤃

It was a small fish and it planed more than fought—a keeper, but I could tell she was disappointed. It was a fish, though, and I felt a tiny relief that at least we wouldn't be skunked. As she drew it near I pulled the metal stringer out from under my seat.

"We won't need that," she said.

"They get bigger," I agreed.

"We won't need it at all. I don't keep fish."

I held still from surprise. Around the lake, I was the only one I knew who didn't kill a catch.

She misinterpreted my hesitation. "It's not required, you know."

I nodded. "No. It's a waste."

By now the fish was by the boat. I slipped a hand under the little belly, slipped the hook free.

"Thank you," she said. Then, "You don't keep fish either?"

I shook my head. "I think it's like eating your baseball after a hit. But it drives Noel crazy; he wants them to feed me." I laughed.

Sometimes I close my eyes a little, when I laugh. When I opened them she was studying me closely. Her eyebrows, I noticed suddenly, were almost as brushy as mine.

"It's easier to release them on a fly," she said. "They don't take the hook so deep."

I nodded, unsettled by her gaze.

"It's interesting that you think that. As you seem to look carefully at water…I wonder if you wouldn't like flyfishing."

It didn't seem like a question. "I did try, once."

"You have a rod?"

I nodded. "My Dad gave it to me. As a joke, sort of. We were living in Saudi at the time. Saudi Arabia."

"I've heard of it." Sometime soon she was going to have to let go of my eyes. "What happened when you tried?"

That pulled me free. "Well…" I shook my head hard. "I whacked a bat."

><+>-O-<+><

She laughed. I remember the way she laughed, showing such a different side of herself; but I was still puzzled about the gaze she'd fixed on me before, hard and careful—not maternal at all. What was she thinking? Maybe, I thought, she was getting even for the long watch I'd settled on her. Maybe, by suggesting that fish were of value I also had earned some small value in her mind. But even as she laughed, head back to expose her throat and the line coursing from there down to the V of her collar, I had a sense that her earlier appraisal was of consequence, of significant meaning; that it suggested something about me I had not yet grasped. Years later I would understand better, if not well: But *what was she thinking*, I wondered then, before the humor broke her away?

"A bat," I repeated, happy that I'd made her laugh, wishing that she was still looking at me with that incalculable expression and grateful that she wasn't.

"It happens."

"Does it? Noel said I was wingshooting without a license. I felt pretty bad."

"I can imagine… Well, it doesn't happen *often*. Maybe you'll see something today that suggests you can *also* catch trout."

>─┼─◆─○─◆─┼─<

We were both more relaxed after that, moving into the cove. She rerigged with the nymph I'd picked from her box, telling me about damselflies as we approached the weeds. When a good fish boiled, however, we both focused on the task that presented itself, joined in intensity.

>─┼─◆─○─◆─┼─<

Tough fishing it was, too. The sun was high enough that visibility was good through the half-dozen feet down to the tops of weed beds; and the fish were spooky for it. There were indeed damsel shucks on the tulle stalks and bright blue adults in the air, zipping along in those quick bursts that always remind me of electricity. But aside from that first riser, no fish came to see, or none that stopped the fly Eliza dragged slowly along. She was tensed for one anyway, half an hour later, when I noticed a fish working well out from shore.

"There," I said, and she squinted.

"Yes, but that's not about damsels…*baetis! Callibaetis.* You see the little sails?"

The bugs' wings, she meant; she was already biting off the nymph to tie on more monofilament, then another fly she greased from a bottle.

"Can you row us closer? *Very* gently?"

I did, careful not to bang the locks.

"That's far enough. I'm going to stand."

She did, putting me in her shadow and making me crane my head to watch the action of her cast. *Now* she was casting, extending to reach a greater distance than she had while fishing blind.

From my angle I could see the rapid swing of rod, the sudden snap forward of the tip when her hand stopped. Coils of line snaked through her fingers with a speed that should have hissed. After a while I could see the way the muscle movements of her upper body tied to those of her hip, even the slight shift of her foot as her calf tensed.

I could also see the results of this rhythm, line flying out from the unloading rod in a motion reminding me at once of both an arrow and the bowstring from which it sprang. The fly, I saw, settled more slowly, for the resistance of air.

Nothing. Another fish rose, or the same one farther out.

"Stay here," she whispered, then began the process again, as did I, seeing now a tiny spot of perspiration below her arm, and smaller movements of her wrist as she halted the line at the end of the backcast. This time she let out a tiny "umph" as she released, a funny noise that made me smile.

Two more casts; then a third to another fish rising closer by. The excess line curled around one oarlock until I flipped it free— "Thanks"—so I wasn't watching as she rocked the big boat a little, crying "Yes!" then "No!" as she lost her balance, touched my shoulder for an instant, then cast again so quickly I still hadn't time to raise my head. This time her "Yes!" met with the rod buckling above and the loose line slipping quickly out through the guides.

"Yes, yes! Did you see that? Did you see him?"

"No. I was—"

"*Just right.* You were doing just right. Look."

It was a much better fish than the first, also a rainbow, as were the next couple, bigger than average—fish likely stocked that spring. I did see the other ones rise, each with a bright little lunge, each accompanied by her "yes!" and a dance with the rod. On the next strike she lost her balance again, missing, falling back just enough so that I felt again the touch of her fingers on my back, a little longer. More than that, I had again the strange experience of actually smelling her scent, not perfume, which was to my amazement both like that of my own body and different in a queerly familiar way. A scent both moist and dry, touched with sweat and something like the wind I remembered coming across sand from sea.

I liked it. I liked also a little habit she had: whenever I landed a fish, she made me pause for just a moment, so she could look at it closely. Once or twice she remarked on a feature, a color or the shape of a fin. Mostly she just stared intently for a second or two. "Okay," she'd say.

I do exactly the same thing.

"Wonderful," she said at last. "Wonderful. God, I'm hungry. What's for lunch?"

She *was* hungry. Sitting in the shade of pines and an oak, on a downed log that thirty feet farther ran into the water, she ate half of a bologna sandwich before I could pass her a Coke to go with it. "Wonderful," she said again; then she was done with the sandwich and moving on to an apple.

She ate the second sandwich—Virginia had packed three because I always eat two—and after I insisted; she finished the Coke, then another apple. "Catching trout makes me famished," she said by way of apology, "So do mountains. I'll be sorry, though, if it gets any hotter."

It would. And since I'd never fished the lake so late in the day I was fine with just sitting back a few minutes. I only wished I could strip down for a swim.

"So, Will," she said, with the sound of somebody full; then she stretched out along the log with her eyes closed. I was too far away, but for half a second I thought I caught her scent again. "So."

I looked away. It really was confusing: one moment she was, well a person, hungry, then happy and full. A fisher, making sense when she talked, with what she did. Then all of a sudden she was something else altogether. Or I was, getting a sense of her that wasn't merely physical, but something ethereal as well. Then she was a fisher again, which made me laugh.

"What?" she said. "What?"

I tried to explain. "It's just, you know, the way you go about it. The focus or something. The..." I knew the word but had a hard time saying it. "You know—the way your eyes search for fish, your hands tense up, so ready. I just liked it, that's all. It reminds of me of me."

"Does it? And you find that strange."

What did she mean by that?

"It is interesting to watch. Flyfishing."

She smiled, then nodded to herself. "And to do. How many fish did you count?"

"I didn't."

"You don't count?"

"No. With fish...for me, there's the first, the last, and the next. Most of all the next."

"First, last, next," she said. Then after a silence so long I thought she was asleep, "I don't know about that. It sounds rather...superficial. Some things have a lot more consequence than that. They last. Or they're supposed to."

I figured she was talking about memory and probably not about fish. But she'd lost me, and her pleasant mood as well; there was something raw in the sound of her voice.

"I'll tell you another thing, Will. It's a lot harder to fish with you watching."

It was?

"Believe me." She rolled her head over, cocked one eye open at me. "No doubt because you've never seen someone cast a fly before."

I nodded.

"Or is it, maybe, that between Saudi Arabia and no mother, you've had the training of a monk, without a monk's motivation?"

I could feel heat in my face.

"I'm not trying to embarrass you, Will. But if you'd stared any harder today I think I'd have put on a trench coat. I mean it."

I couldn't think of a thing to say. Caught, wide-eyed—betrayed, some-how—I could only stare at the pine needles at my feet, feeling humiliated.

"Feral," I managed to say at last.

"What?"

"My father says he's afraid I've gone feral. Like a dog, you know, that—"

"I know what it means...Now wait—I really didn't mean to upset you. And I am sorry that...well. The truth is, that it's a little disconcert-ing, is all. Some women like it. Sometimes. Even expect it. Just not so...*intense*, that's all."

I couldn't look up.

"But you're not *feral*. You're really quite sweet. Polite. Gentle. You remind me of my husband, or what I used to think my husband was, before he evolved into a jerk."

I still couldn't look up, but a weight shifted. "I'm sorry."

"I'm not. I'm pretty sure now that I saw only what I wanted to see."

"Oh."

"It happens. Besides, now that he's gone, I can go flyfishing when-ever I want, as much as I want."

"That's good."

"Yes, it is. Will? You can look at me, you know."

She was wrong about that.

"Okay, you can't. I only meant to say that...it's *interesting*, to be looked at like that. Impersonal, maybe, but flattering in a way it proba-bly shouldn't be. I could have made you stop before."

I made another sorry sound.

She laughed. "Boy, for somebody with such a tan, you certainly can turn colors. Let's go find some fish, shall we?"

⊱──◦──⊰

We didn't. It was hot, the water white and glassy, the fish down too deep for even her sinking line. We gave it a quiet hour anyway. She talked about her job teaching. I recovered enough to tell her that I hoped to go to college in the fall, but that I'd never technically finished high school—had taken both the GED and SAT in the first week we got stateside. She asked about my scores and when I told her, raised her bushy eyebrows. "My, my. Why don't you skip college and just become a professor?"

"That's what my Dad says. The skip college part."

"Your Dad. It sounds like it's always been just the two of you."

"Yeah." I'd been rowing, slowly, one oar at a time, to give her fly some action. I wasn't quite sure why I went on. "My mother left, then got sick," I told her. "I don't know her."

She was quiet a long time.

"Your father never remarried."

I shook my head. "They never divorced. She still needs his insurance."

"I see."

"Yeah. I like him to have a girlfriend, at least, and once or twice he has. But the way we move around, the places we've been…"

I shrugged into the oars. Eliza turned around to watch her line streaming back. I made a wide turn, to make her fly rise, like I do while trolling spinners. When nothing happened I suggested that nothing would until after the 3:30 thunderstorm cooled the water, then cleared.

"If we quit now," she said, "will Noel let you go in the evening?"

"Sure. If I do what he needs done before then."

"For the same $20?"

"I think so."

"Heck of a deal. Consider yourself a bought man."

I didn't get it, but she found that amusing enough to keep her smiling all the way back to the dock.

⊱──◦──⊰

I loved the lake that evening. The light, the reflections muted and long, the sound of frogs along the shore, the smells of mud and reeds rising into cooler air. My last and favorite chore of the day was to swab out the boats, hauling out the aluminum ones onto the floating dock, rinsing them, flipping them over and back, sliding them home to their berths. At the same time I could check on the lake birds or watch for deer picking their way down the meadow's east side, even listen to conversations in the campground across the bay, amazed at the way the lake amplified sound. The paddle boats were a pain to bail, but I could soak the sponge with one hand and, while it filled, dip my other for the fathead minnows to nibble. Best yet, when I was done with the paddlers I was *done*, free to slip into the water after a look-around for the ranger, who went home early, and didn't care much anyway.

From the dock it was 100 yards out to a buoy, set there for no reason anybody seemed to know, dead-away toward the center of the lake. I usually swam with my jeans on, to wash them as well as me, and they got heavy fast—a challenge to kick hard enough to keep them higher than the chill water that lay just beneath the lake's warm skin. I'd frog it, but sweep my arms in a crawl, the way the Arab kids swim in the Red Sea. Sometimes I timed myself with the Timex I left on the dock.

Not this evening though. I just did a couple of dashes, thrilling to the cold and thinking about Eliza; then I shook off like a dog and did another dash back to my cabin to change. By the time I came down again she was waiting and the first fish were rising off the point. I noticed with satisfaction that she'd brought a windbreaker. I'd already put a flashlight beneath my seat.

"That looked like fun," she said. "The swimming."

"Yeah. We have no showers anyway."

"I noticed. You could bring that rod of yours, if you want."

"Thanks, but I'll watch."

"As you like. So what do you suggest?"

>─┤◆〉─O─〈◆├─<

At this point in the evening we hardly needed the boat, the trout were in so close. But it was special to be out on the water, moving silently on the lake, watching for fish. Insects she called caddis were coming up, fluttering like moths; but I told her a secret: that the big fish, holdovers from last year and even the year before, were likely working the shore for fathead minnows and mosquito fish."

"Small fish on dries or bigger ones on streamers—that's a hard choice," she said. "I hate that kind of decision."

I grinned. "There's another secret."

"What's that?"

"Can't tell you yet, but maybe you'll let me see your boxes."

I saw what she'd need in the first one, but asked to see two more anyway. "Yep."

" 'Yep' *what?*"

"Can't tell you. But you might as well fish the top."

She glared. "Have I paid you your $20 yet? Because for a shy boy, you're getting pretty...*spunky.*"

And she, I noticed, was looking young. Or younger than when she had come down the dock that morning. I'd finally decided she wasn't much more than five years my senior, however much wiser she was about the world; and in the failing light, sitting in the stern with her rod at ready, she seemed more present, more real. Perhaps it was only because she was just more aware of me, feral or not, in a friendlier way.

"I'm waiting," she said.

"The fish aren't," I answered. And for the next hour we had fishing much like the morning, but prettier, and faster, with rainbows of the same size and smaller. The camp owl came out, coursing toward his hunting ground off the horse pasture behind the cabins. Twice we saw water snakes slicing sine waves through the tulles. I continued to row us down the shoreline, back toward the bank where I'd seen her at dawn as it began to darken.

"Wonderful," she said at last.

I waited, listening.

"And...frankly, I just don't see how your secret could be such a big deal compared to this. Besides, I'm going to get cold soon."

"You brought a windbreaker."

"Oh, did I? What else did you happen to notice?"

That shook me. However rhetorical the question, there were a couple of things.

"You smell nice," I said firmly.

She put down her rod and held to both gunwales. "You know, Will. I think I preferred it when you were scared of me."

I could never have answered that; so it was with great relief that I heard it. Or we did—a slurping sound sixty or seventy feet away, accompanied by a boil of water broad enough to see at that distance.

It blew everything else out of her mind. "What?" she whispered, "was *that?*"

I passed her the flashlight. "The black fly box."

She stared at me an instant, her eyes catching light. Then she dug for the box.

I had her hold the light as I found the fly I'd seen. "I told you about the holdover rainbows. Did Noel mention browns?"

"Not a word. Is that what that was?"

I laughed. "Well, if a camper asks, we tell him it's a beaver. Sometimes it is."

"You're saying it's a brown trout?"

"Sometimes."

The next boil—like a big bubble bursting—couldn't have been 20 feet away.

"God damn it," she said, then bent over to scan the water as low as she could. "What are they after...*sails*. Will, I see sails."

"Like the ones this morning, except—"

"*Hexagenia...this is a* hex *hatch...*"

Like I said, the lake had its secrets; now I had a name for this one. I'd actually fished it several times, using a spinning rod and a float. I'd broken off twice and told her so as I held the light for her to tie on. Her hands were shaking.

"Why didn't you tell me before."

"I didn't know you before."

"I mean—Jesus! How big are they?"

I thought. "Imagine a German shepherd with fins instead of legs."

She'd been ready to cast. That stopped her cold. "You," she began, then a fish boiled not twenty-five feet off the stern. She cast. "You little—" and the fish rose again, this time to her fly.

><+<>+<O>+<>+<

I have witnessed many battles since that evening, or night as it soon turned. None are more memorable. The brown Eliza hooked was a relic, as Noel told the story, of a small stocking many years before. He thought the browns owed their survival to nocturnal habits, immunity to baits like our Velveeta—and to the fact that few people knew about them. They were rarely vulnerable save during hatches like this one anyway.

In the next half an hour it seemed to me that I learned a lot about Eliza. That she was tough, I had suspected; but I met more of an excited kid in her than I would have guessed, even with the way I'd seen her laugh. I also saw her anxious—for good reason: the fish moved us into shallows where even in the dark we could see the shapes of snags. "Oh, Will Will Will," she went on once. "If this is a brown—"

"It is."

"—then it's the biggest I've ever hooked. God, it's the biggest I've ever heard of, I'm sure, bigger than the ones my father used to brag about."

"Is he the one who taught you to flyfish?"

"Yes, and don't ask me questions, please not now—is he heading for that branch? That's not a branch is it?"

"No, but yes—"

"What's my tippet now—four x? three x?"

"You broke it off before you tied on—"

"*Quiet please*...three x, then. Maybe four...Is that another branch? *Say it isn't,* Will. Will Will *Will*—"

"It isn't."

"*You're just saying that.*"

And on that way, which sounded a lot like the way my own mind races when I'm hooked to such a fish.

She was winning, she really was, with the fish moving slower and in shorter runs, when it did find a snag. A deep one without any branch above to warn us; but I could feel the give and take of the line when I rowed over to it, along with the heavy throb of big wood.

"Will?"

"He's still on, I think. Give him slack."

Nothing. The slack stayed that way.

"Oh no. Oh no."

I pulled again. I was almost certain I could feel a twist of fish pull back, both of us straining against the limb.

"Oh no."

"Hang on. Hang on a minute."

I stood up and stripped off my shirt.

"What are you doing? What...Will, don't even *think* about it."

I already had my boots off.

"Will. I said no. *Did you hear me?*"

We were both standing in the big boat then, almost eye to eye. Hers were not flinching, I noticed.

"I heard, Eliza. But you and I know what a fish that is, and if there's one thing I've figured out today, it's that you're like me about fish, so we're not going to lose it. There's nothing down there that scares me, and you don't either right now, so please be ready because I'm going in before that big brown gets rested and busts off."

I heard "*Will!*" in the air and again thorough the baffle of water, when I was overboard, feeling my way down the line, holding it gently and kicking while resisting the urge to pull myself along—it wasn't more than eight or ten feet anyway. I did brush against a branch or two—spooky—then against something slicker than that, and alive. The brown only threw his tail once; then I had him free.

I came up to find Eliza fighting him, swearing. By the time I had my shirt back on he was near enough to the side that I could make a sling of my hands and raise him up.

"Oh, my God...*Will*..."

They didn't get bigger than this one where we were. Not exactly a finny German shepherd, but at least a fair-sized dachshund, or even a basset.

"Will, I've got a camera. And a flash. If you hold him."

"I have to wake him up anyway."

So she took the picture, with the fish cradled by me, then leaned over to look at him as close as she could. When she put her hand to his side her hair fell into my face, adding the scent of vanilla to hers. "Such a fish," she said, and I opened my arms.

━┼◆➤─O─◄◆┼◄

We were quiet a long time after that. She asked for a "drink drink," but of course, all I'd brought along were Cokes. She took one of those, then leaned back as I began to row. Half a moon was rising at my back. Enough to show her eyes beneath the brows. Watching me, then watching me some more.

"This is important, Will. I'd like you to tell me why you did that."

I hadn't really thought about it.

"Let's say...that you weren't just working for a tip. Shall we say that?"

Nobody had told me about a tip.

"So why?"

I laughed. I shouldn't have; it made her angry.

"It's not funny to *me*, Will. So do you want me to tell you what I think?"

"Sure."

"I think you did because...you decided that I'm *like* you. Is that right? When it comes to fish."

I had said something like that, before I jumped in.

"Given who *you* are, that means what?"

"I don't know."

"Then just...how does it make you *feel*?"

There was a challenge in her voice, a tone that seemed defensive. I didn't understand it; all I could do was answer her honestly. "It makes me grateful," I said.

⊢—⊶—O—⊷—⊣

She didn't say anything after that. Neither did I, just rowed her to the dock. She stepped out quickly, turned and looked down at me. I couldn't see her face well, but I guessed it wore the same neutral expression as when she'd stepped in that morning. "You did a very good job, Will," she said. "And whatever else I think, I want to thank you for that fish."

I just couldn't understand. But I, too, was angry now. "Sure," I said.

"I'll tell Noel and pay him in the morning, if that's all right."

"Fine."

"Good night."

≻—I—⊶—O—⊷—I—≺

I sat a long time in the boat after that. It didn't help. I tried to put myself in her position, me with a fish on the line, her jumping in. The turn-around taught me nothing so what had made her so mad? Exactly what?

I started to think that I'd ended the day knowing no more than when I started, except maybe about flyfishing. That was important. It wasn't enough.

I'd ask my father. In the meantime, I had to get clean.

≻—I—⊶—O—⊷—I—≺

I stripped on the dock, shirt and wet pants, safe in the darkness and the hour. The lake swallowed me as I dove down to feel the chill; the night sky opened as I rose. By moonlight I could see the buoy. I headed toward it, porpoising to feel and slip that clutch of the deep. I turned once at a splash, wondering about browns and beaver, feeling more naked than before, which was all right.

Then it wasn't when, resting with arms linked to the buoy base, I saw the V moving toward me in the water. A big animal—very big, and moving fast.

"Will," she said.

So many years and the truth is that when a piece of time becomes history, my history, it may be fixed in a fashion that remains true and immediate, so absolute that I will look for it in the stories others tell, which are in the end their truth, important and different.

Mine is that Eliza came to the buoy to explain to me. Rocking in the water, in the moonlight. About how it was she had lost something, someone who she had counted as her first and last; that she had let go of "next" in thinking only about that, feeling her way around a loop of anger and hurt. She said that just as I had seen something of myself in her and the way she pursued the fish, so she had seen something of herself in me, something open that had closed; and seeing an old part of herself made her want to hurt me a little, tear at a quality she recognized, and maybe mourned. "But I wouldn't take it from you," she whispered, "not for anything." She spoke so quickly and with so much feeling that I couldn't grasp it all; and besides I was chilled and heated at the same time, until I forgot that a moment when she said, "So I was mad when you did something for me that someone would do for someone else they valued in a way I'm not sure I've known for a long time. And you did it when I didn't want you to, in a way that I couldn't stop, because you are, already, a man in your own way, and not just a boy I could shame for staring. So. So…"

I told her I didn't quite understand, but that I would think about it, and try very hard.

"And will you promise me something?"

"If I can."

"Promise, because this might be something your father can't teach you. Or that I can, but…promise that you will always remember what you said. About the first, the last, and the next."

She was shivering. I was too. I said, "Yes, I will."

"Promise me."

"I promise."

"Thank you," she said, then we were both quiet. I said her name for no reason I could have explained, turning it over in my mind, wondering at the way her eyes held light and held dark, at the stillness surrounding us and within me—at an instant held in place by the angle of her throat and a certainty that might be described as that pause that begins a long fall which has not yet picked up speed. And though I never looked away she had, before I was aware, moved around the buoy to me, placing her hands on my shoulders where the skin still remembered her touch from the morning; but it was surely her eyes holding her beside me with tiny currents of her movement swirling about my chest and thighs—her eyes on mine as she said, "It's all right. Really, Will, it is." Then I caught the scent of water all around us, striking suddenly, exactly as if it swept in off the desert.

The rest was only a magic I had never imagined, never mind Miss May.

><del>—▸—◦—◂—</del>◃

That night Eliza was my first. I remember that she asked me to keep my eyes open, so that I would see her, remember that she was Eliza, who was also a fisher like me. I did watch, and remembered as much as I could, astonished at what I found in her, at what must have seemed to her the simplest of things which she still made tender and fine.

><del>—▸—◦—◂—</del>◃

She was gone by the next morning, of course. Noel handed me the twenty she'd left, and a tip, then saw the look on my face. "Oh, Christ," he said. "Ah, Christ…why don't you stock the icebox and take the day off."

That was a first, too. But I didn't fish. No: I waited until the box of flies arrived four days later. It came with no return address and a note—"You promised"—so that evening I dug out my Saudi Christmas fly rod and fished for a brown. I didn't get one then; but I did the next night. More than that, I discovered the nature of yearning, not for an abstraction, but for a woman who laughed with her head thrown back and said, "So."

I tried to keep my promise and succeeded in the autumn with a girl who loved canoes and firelight. I've tried ever since, sometimes because I promised, and sometimes because I am left convinced that love and fish have in common that yearning. Because there is forever knit into my memory the rhythm of a rod loading with line, and a heart with knowing and hope.

Pilgrim's Pike:
An *Esox* Fable

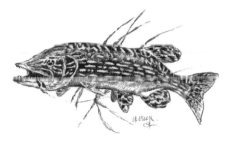

*For years I treasured a small article, gleaned from the local
newspaper, about a Russian fisherman whose dog tried
to swim a river to where his master was standing. A pike
swallowed the dog whole. The fisherman immediately cast his
net, caught the pike and cut it open. Out popped his dog
"…which proceeded to bark furiously at the pike for some time."*

For the return flight from Lake Richard, outward bound after a
week, I board the same plane that flew me in, a handsome red Air
Sanguenay Otter with an orchestra of metal-to-metal rattles. The same
pilot sits at the controls, a drop-dead look-alike for J. Edgar Hoover in
a poor-to-middling mood; he points us into a sky broken by familiar
islands of four-tone grey clouds. In the end I will even connect with
the same airline which, having briefly lost my rods on the way in, will
misplace the whole flight on the way back, plane and passengers evap-
orating from the computer without a trace.

Never mind all that. The important thing is that heading home I am
changed altogether. This time, peering down at the carpet of blue on
green, the myriad little lakes strung together by streams draining to the
vastness of Reservoir Pipmaucan, Domaine Pipmaucan, I know what
I know…

About malice, predatory malice—I do not anthropomorphize—
about green and gold beasts with binocular vision—"the better to

ambush you with, my Dear—" who accelerate to eight gs and seem utterly absent of fear. Dog eaters, a danger to pedestrians, fish that cut me bloody deep with their gills. My luggage is lighter for the flies they stole.

Denis and I took between 30 and 40 the last day, from a tea-colored bay where the fish lay up amidst drowned timber and beaver mounds, in shallows no deeper than two hands; and from the confluence of two rivers, beneath foam lines, drifting rocky bluffs and a bouldery drop-off. We fought pike until my forearm swelled like a gooseneck engorged for pate.

Now, flying out, all I wanted was *down* from that Otter, *back* onto Pipmaucan to do it again.

><+>+O+<+>+<

It began with ignorance, hope and high expectations, roughly 34 years before, right about the time I'd learned enough to read captions on *Field & Stream* photographs.

Still a tad weak in geography, I marched into my father's workshop with that magazine opened to a piece about pike fishing in Canada, announcing "We've got to go *here*, Dad, *this* Saturday."

My father looked up from the pages of his *Arizona Republic.* "A rather long drive," he observed. "Let's try the pond at Papago Park instead, save the Arctic for another weekend."

><+>+O+<+>+<

June of a year some 1700 weekends later, I was at last to fish pike in Canada. It seemed appropriate that I would spend some of my time as ghillie to a seven-year-old boy, Brendan, son of Sy, the high school friend who had invited me along. The three of us had fished together the previous summer on a California trip. This time out we will keep company with an old pal of Sy's father, a retired banker; the banker's son, a doctor of body parts rarely discussed in public; and Sy's kid cousin.

><+>+O+<+>+<

On the 13-hour voyage from San Francisco to Quebec, I have time to review pike articles, along with materials sent me by John LeBel, Outfitter, about my destination. LeBel has provided an account from the July 8, 1990 *Burlington* (VT) *Free Press*, which boldly asserts that "the Domaine *Pipmaucan* is the greatest reservoir of 'mouchetee' in the world." For these brook trout, the lodge literature suggests, "Bring plenty of wets, dries, nymphs and streamers, since it's impossible to tell what insect will be coming off." Both *Free Press* and brochure report that the nearby fishery of Lake Pipmaucan (Pip-maw-kan) contains many small pike, but neither discusses fishing these with flies. In a letter, however, LeBel writes that he imagines they'll take anything that looks like a fish.

I have flies like that. Thanks to the largesse of friendly fly designers, my boxes resemble the displays of an itinerant streamer salesman, purveyor of popper fantasies. Mike Mercer, of epoxy-back nymph fame, has mailed me a pair of sliders apparently lifted from *Jurassic Park*, each has a double-sewn, contrast-color bunny tail—crimson and black, black and chartreuse—foam cone heads and Betty Boop eyes. The Howes, Bill and Kate, contributed a shiny school of their Anchovy Looking Flys (ALFs), including several tied Katy's Tube-style, along with enough wire leader to restring the Golden Gate Bridge. "Swear to God that you'll fish these," was Bill's *caveat*. "Not like last time, hanging them all over your office wall. Swear to God that you'll fish these, and I promise to tie you some more."

So I will, along with a bunch of Tom Hnizdor's B-17 patterns, epoxy-coated, cork-bodied floaters, some with diving lips; and the plastic-and-hackle concoctions sold by Salinas Company as "Frisky Flies," lures with the action of the great Lazy Ike…

If only I had any idea what I was doing, I'd call myself well prepared. No doubt the Lake Richard hosts will prep me, yes? Pike are only a fish, no? "And the world," I'm reminded by the sigh of a Hungarian engineer in the window seat on the plane, "She is all over round, eh?"

>+∢>+O+‹+⊢≺

So is the banker's son, I discover when we meet in Quebec airport. Or more accurately, oval on a larger scale than am I yet; I'll call him Proctor, for reasons mostly legal. Sy's cousin is a big, friendly kid; Dad by marriage is jovial, and Brendan's bigger than last year, with a broader smile. Together we crowd the four-by-four Proctor has driven up from New Jersey, racing north toward a hotel in the town of Chicoutimi. Next morning is that first float-plane ride, a hundred-mile otter flight during which the level expanse of Domaine Pipmaucan appears to me—accustomed to contours of Sierra Nevada and Trinity Alps—an oddly naked, baffling landscape.

A little less so, after landing on the cushion of Lake Richard. We taxi across a bay toward the lodge's cluster of rust-red buildings constructed of half logs from the forest near by. Clean-rustic, I'd call the style: you're quite comfortably aware that you're at a fishing lodge.

At least until brunch, when co-owners Denis Normandin and Dominic Paquin serve us an unusually good meal. As one might expect: winters, the partners are chefs at chi-chi restaurants in Montreal. Between courses they hedge our bets, however, suggesting that so far, it's been an unsettled spring, with fishing not yet at its zenith.

By late afternoon I'm still fortified by the eats and convinced that D &D are better cooks than prognosticators. Or perhaps it's just that what is modest sport by their standards is bonanza by mine.

Our protocol for the next several days: on foot or in the lodge's fleet of power boats, we explore Lake Richard and its environs—nearby *lacs* and ponds, the streams connecting these. My companions mostly troll "Toronto Wobblers," brass spoons trailing leaders tipped with the night-crawlers Proctor imported from New Jersey. I score on streamers in the lakes, on nymphs in the streams; and, at Lake Richard's outlet in the evening, with big brown parachute mayflys I tie up by lamplight at night. My hand seine reveals a plethora of life forms on which the fish feed: the big may's nymphs, three kinds of caddis, sucker eggs from a recent spawn; and then a surprise—from a fast riffle comes a three-inch salamander. Denis gets a kick out of the latter specimen, asserting that it's on these that bigger brookies often key.

Such brookies. Denis, who proves genuinely a paragon of diplomacy and grace, struggles to describe them, saying at last—so softly I must lean to hear it—"I think, maybe, you find them the most beautiful in the world, eh?" "Exquisite" is a clumsy word to describe them: Val Atkinson might capture the detail of scales and skins so finely textured, the translucence of tangerine spots.

We take between 10 and 40 per angler each day, but it's Brendan who masters a novel tactic for catching the biggest: sitting in the bow of an anchored boat, he will rear back to cast, release five feet of line 90 degrees too early, and promptly drop his Toronto contraption right behind him. Never mind *that*, he continues with a vigorous forward throw and, undeterred by the misdirection, yanks his rod about for emphasis, thereby hooking a brookie from ten ounces to three pounds.

He does this over and over again. At one point, having taken eight fish in an hour to his father's and my zero, he turns to Sy with a thoughtful gaze. "Don't you worry, Dad," he says gently. "You'll catch one *eventually*. And isn't it just *great* to be out here?"

Sy, a good father, let's Brendan live.

>–•◦–○–◦•–‹

And I, good guest to the party, do the same for Proctor, despite a serious difference of style. Proctor's is to rush onto a remote pond where I am quietly wading, jump a boat and gun the outboard to troll at wahoo-speed, shouting, "I'll be out of here soon!" while his wake breaks against my chest. After three days of listening to his voice at meals, waxing-without-waning, expert enough that actual conversation is unnecessary, I've fantasized a four-weight flogging. Most of the time, however, there's room enough in this Domaine to find one's own space, sortie off solo—

Until the pike expedition.

>–•◦–○–◦•–‹

Lake Richard maintains two camps: the Main Lodge, prettily placed in the heart of *mouchete* waters; and Outpost Camp, a self-serve operation set on the shore of Lake Pipmaucan. Fishers may fly in to either, or travel from one to the other by a short, slightly complicated route. The latter involves first crossing an arm of Lake Richard by boat to the outlet where I fish mayfly dries in the evening, hiking several hundred yards up the feeder stream where I work nymphs, then crossing a smaller lake, again by boat. The hike from there up to the second stream is about a half a mile—excellent water, home of salamanders. After that comes a third lake—big ponds, really—a boat-crossing, then a last, longer walk along a lovely stream with tumbling runs, big pools and falls...to Lake Pipmaucan

The traverse is not necessarily as difficult as it seems. Paths are level and clear, the black flies abundant enough in places to provide protein when you inhale. But for our large party, with D and D attending, three ferry laps per each lake are required, making for delays...

Proctor has chosen to lead the way, guided by Dominic. For those of us in the rear, the wait for each ferry gets longer; and Brendan, bringing up the tail, suffers most for it. At three feet something tall, the trail is tougher for him—shrubs that brush my belly can slap his face. When Sy opts to carry him, with Denis and I splitting their gear, poor Brendan's head is alternately banging into branches or lost to view in a cloud of black flies....Halfway through the third portage, it becomes of serious importance to him to return and fish Lake Richard. Sy will carry him back, with Denis assisting..

Which ultimately leaves Proctor, Dad, Dominic, Cousin and I standing on a long cove at Lake Pipmaucan, looking over a trio of sturdy boats. Then comes the matter of boat crews: Dominic tries to make a suggestion, but the new partner in Lake Richard's operation—a fair-haired, well-mannered young man who doesn't quite trust his good English—is no match for Proctor. *The doctor* will captain one boat with father and cuz. Dominic and I can do what we like.

Dominic hesitates "All right. But...maybe you follow me, eh? So I can show you where the pike?"

"We'll find you later," Proctor assures him. Off he roars.

Dominic looks worried, I notice through a grin which has reduced my eyes to slits. "*C'est la vie*, Captain Dominic! You will fish also, please? " He hesitates again. "But I insist. I *need* your help to test these flies."

This early in the season, only three weeks after ice out, a low Lake Pipmaucan has sloping banks cluttered with long bones of drowned trees. Hundreds of rivers and stream arms enter the arms of the main body, forming shallows like those in the cove to which Dominic steers us. He cuts the engine while pointing to edge water which can't be a foot deep.

I am somewhat incredulous. "Here?"

"Yes. Here."

Aqua, they call that color. Aqua, with a tannic-amber tint—I could read headlines off a newspaper on the bottom. There aren't any fish—zero, zip, none. "Here, then."

I hand Dominic a small, yellow B-17 slider for his seven weight, then tie Mercer's green-bodied, chartreuse and black bunny tailed number on my eight while wishing for a nine. I am meantime sneaking glances at the darker, deeper, more promising water behind us.

Dominic, new to flyfishing this year, tests the heft of his lure, waits. "Go ahead," I insist.

"You, please."

"Both of us then."

Unused to the weight, Dominic slaps a cast 15 or 20 feet out, shakes his head. I throw out near the shoreline, let the rabbit tails soak. I'm in no hurry; I don't believe in the spot. Dominic plops his slider down 20 feet to the left of mine.

I've never understood why Hnizdor named his flies after the bomber my father flew in WW II, though Dominic's is about the diameter of a .50 mm machine gun bullet. Until he cast, however, I did not realize the SOB was loaded—

I mean, it *erupted* on impact—-imagine a small depth charge triggered in ten inches of water. In a second explosion we see jaws scissor the air; then another lunge, head on to us, the fish flying forward toward the boat until it dives into a cut-away right—

I'm gape-mouthed. It's Dominic's turn to smile. "Pike," he says simply. No frog kidding.

"My first one on the fly."

A "small one," it turns out, 18 or 20 inches, only a quarter of which appears to be teeth. After two more shorter runs, it planes in, hangs beside the boat. It is *glaring*.

"Net?" I suggest.

"No no," murmurs Dominic. Gingerly, he reaches down behind the head, clamps tight. The pike goes rigid in his hand; Dominic frees the fly. Nodding once again to the shallows I'd disdained, he says "Pike" again, then lets this one go.

I still haven't the faintest idea where the fish came from; yet my next cast is made with conviction, and I couldn't watch that bunny tail more intently if I intended to eat it myself. Nevertheless, I am not rightly prepared when the water bulges beside it, then breaks open in a frothy gash.

That misses. Incredibly, the fish misses; but I am too surprised to panic, so twitch again, once more, faster—

I get it. When the flat lake surface turns suddenly to rapids…*set the hook.*

Then hang on. Like the first, this fish begins the fight up in air, spearing through arcs, twisting in flight. The runs are short compared to those a trout of this size might make, which proves merciful, since we take four more fish from the cove in the next half hour, working both edges from depths of six inches to six feet. By then I've twice spotted attacks before they reach the fly, which is to say I saw streaks in the water for some part of a second.

When we move at last to another cove—better light—I have the chance to watch one in the making:

It's a bigger fish that I spot laying parallel to a downed log, head toward us at an angle of 30 or 40 degrees. He seems to watch me as I

cast; but when the fly falls three feet to his left it distracts him. Then he
turns back to *look at me.*

"*What* is he doing?"

"Pull it," Dominic whispers urgently.

I do. The pike swings slowly to watch. His pectoral fins flare; otherwise, he's still.

"Pull quick!"

I strip. The pike disappears; then fish and fly converge in an acute
angle—a semi-broadside assault that I strike while the pike's head is still
above water—I see it jerk—and the bunny tail swings wildly from one
side of its mouth.

Dog eater indeed. There's something else familiar about him: "Mean-
mugging," we call this pike attitude in Oakland, so during the battle I
describe to Dominic a scene from a city I know well. "What these fish
need, see, are telephone pagers, black 'Raiders' caps, and a nine millimeter holstered behind the gills…"

Dominic nods pleasantly, saying the equivalent of "My." I would go
on, even after the release, but the sound of a gunned outboard engine
rumbles toward us.

Proctor *et al* zoom around the bend. "Caught any?" he shouts.

I look at Dominic. "Did we?"

"Seven," he calls back. "You have caught pike?"

A long pause. Dad finally acknowledges that they busted one off.
Another pause, then Proctor says loudly to his crew. "Of course, *he* had
the guide."

><—◆—O—◆—><

Once again, Dominic suggests that they follow him, so he may show
them better places. This time they do.

It ain't pretty. Perhaps because of his trolling roots, Proctor decides
that wherever Dominic stops, the fish are *right under* us—he anchors so
close we've little room for backcasts, then throws right at our boat. A
better effort with a spoon whistles near enough that Dominic flings an
arm across his eyes. Humiliated, furious, I divide my time between apol-
ogizing to him and telling Proctor to back off. When at last Proctor
does, Dominic unclenches his teeth, appraises me. "I *understand*," he says
softly. "Now I understand: *you do not know this man*, I am right? You
never meet him before you come here."

We hear a hail from the shore. Denis, after returning Sy and Brendan to Lake Richard, has force-marched back to find us. He and Dominic exchange French at 78 rpm, then he suggests we head to the Outpost for lunch.

The site is occupied. A fire crew of perhaps 50 men sprawl in various stages of leisure around the buildings. Denis explains to me that they have been drafted from Quebec's welfare role, that they will lose their benefits if they refuse to come. Come seems to be about all that they've done; though almost all are smoking, none looks sooty. We wade through them a trifle uneasily, as they have the same smiling habits as our Otter pilot. Of course, if I paid as much for cigarettes as do Canadians, my world view might also dim.

Lunch, though excellent, is seasoned for my companions by memories of the morning trek and by their later lack of sport. Denis takes over for the tried-and-tired Dominic, assuring everyone that the afternoon will be better. Proctor announces that he has decided to fish flies with me, in a boat guided by Denis. Out of pity for Dominic, I concur. Proctor promptly produces a 12 weight tarpon rod; we're off.

If possible, it's a worse experience than the morning's. Suffice it to say that Proctor's casting demonstration teaches me how it feels to sit a small craft attacked by a hippo. For full flavor, consider this remark from the *second* time Proctor impaled Denis on a 3-ought: "Come on, it's not *that* deep. Besides, this must happen to you all the time. And at least I'm a doctor—I could sew you up, if I had to."

As to the rest…we endured.

>─┼◆➤─O─◄◆┼─◄

I go easy describing the day to Sy before dinner. He and Brendan had had a wonderful time; no sense interfering with their mood. Later that evening, however, when delivering a couple of flies to Dominic, including his trophy B-17, Denis asks me to sit down. With infinite discretion he suggests that he and Dominic found some of the day's behaviors "a small bit difficult" to understand.

I explain New Jersey, how the Mafia owns the state, we send outcasts and prisoners there. I mention that New Brunswick was the model for Dante's fifth circle of *The Inferno*: then suggest that part of the reason for my trip is to ensure that Americans can count on Quebecois assistance, should we need to remove Jersey from our union. "Or at least, to help fight anybody who tries to stop her, if she wants to leave on her own." I praise at length Dominic's poise under stress.

"Yes," Denis said thoughtfully. "He does say, you see, that he thought to sink the man."

"I completely understand. Did he say how deep?"

Denis shakes his head "There is something else, though. Pipmaucan is so big a lake, so many wonderful things. Today, because of—" he shrugs "because of *wind*…you do not see very much. I am sorry for this, eh?"

"Ah, well."

"But, you know, if it was just two men in one boat, tomorrow…I think it would be very fine ."

"Ah …hah."

"Only, if other people want to go…may be a problem, eh? Let me show you—"

With that he slips out a map, to trace there the traverse to the reservoir. "Here" he says, pointing to the stream connecting lakes two and three. "If, perhaps, you were to go tomorrow to fish this, I could take a path nobody knows, meet you *here*. Then, to Pipmaucan, just two."

"And you will fish, yes?"

"You insist?"

It's almost painful, to smile that way.

><+♦>-O-<♦+-<

Our first stop fascinates me: rapids of two rivers converge at the end of a long loch, not 200 hundred feet apart. A cliff face separates the turbulent inlet pools, looming above darker depths carved by a history of higher waters. Clouds of foam drift the current edges; another foam line forms behind a submerged boulder the size of a locomotive. Denis drops anchor in slack water behind this. "Along the rocks," he says, pointing with his tip-top. Then, sweeping his rod in a giant arc all around us—"Everywhere."

Denis throws a small streamer toward the cliff, waits. A fish takes on the sink. "Deep," he says. The pike goes pike-wild, then sounds. In the end, it proves a bigger fish than we'd seen the day before—25 inches. By the time Denis lands it, I've tied on an ALF. Per my host's suggestion, I use no wire. "We give them a chance, eh?"

Too good a chance: as designed, and as tied by the Howes, with synthetic hairs applied in a layered in side-to-side style, ALF sinks in the horizontal attitude of a suspended whitefish or cisco. At least it does for the four or five feet I can see it at the end of a cast. It's not for lack of light that the fly disappears though: the head that takes it—that seems simply to swim through it, maw open—must be more than a foot long.

A gentle tug, and I am ALF-less.

I glare at Denis. "What…was that?"

He shrugs, smiles. "Sometimes, you know, the big ones do that to the line. But with wire, we would catch them all, eh? And there are so many more…You will see."

⊱┥╍┿┝╍╟╍╢╍┝╍┷

I'm trembling as I tie on the next fly. Denis is working in from against the cliff again, so I throw into the foam line beside the locomotive boulder—very deep. I decide to count eight. At six the rod doubles. "Denis," I crow, but he's busy with a hook-up of his own..

My fish goes down, takes to the current and sweeps toward the stern. Denis' races 50 feet to the side as if intending to meet mine. He does catch my line, then cuts under the boat to grind us both against an anchor rope. I'm hissing like a cobra; then Denis' fish cuts off. I don't know what those French words mean, but I'm free to fight my pike in open water.

There's another problem boatside. By now I'm somewhat accustomed to the hand-landing technique Dominic showed me, but my paw won't span this pike's back. "Net?" I ask hopefully. Denis shakes his head, begins to put down his rod.

"No, I'll do it," I insist, because I am bold, or because of that head injury in 1981…Tucking my own rod in my right armpit, I reach with my left hand for the top of the pike as I slide my right under its belly. Incredibly, the pike accepts this embrace with equanimity. I lift him.

It's a trick…*he's in the boat and VERY annoyed.*

Berserk. In the three-fall match that follows—two of them mine—I let a thumb slip up the gill slits past the rakers. From there nerves relay a question "Did the recipe say *diced*?"

Maybe Denis doesn't know what those English words mean; and soon enough I plug my mouth with the wounded thumb. This is, it turns out, only my first experience with yet another "Pike Thing," this one a Trojan tactic tried by about one of three fish. A pike coming to the boat has not necessarily given up. Instead, he may be looking for the source of pressure—it's a particularly poisonous look—*just hoping to fight at closer quarters.*

"They are like that," Denis agrees. Then, casually, "I think today, we catch…50."

It isn't every cast. Not even after I notice an interesting phenomenon: the more fish we hook and play, the more excited others become, rising in the water column to take flies at lesser depths. Finally, they begin assaulting lures just as they splashed down.

By this time I've sacrificed half a dozen ALFS and resorted to wire by way of keeping the remainder. Denis, meanwhile, develops an abiding passion for one of the "Frisky Flies," a 2/0 black-bodied number with grizzly hackle and shimmy to kill for. "This," he says twice, "is a pike fly."

Some flies are not. When I switch back to surface lures, Mercer's slider produces, but a gold colored popper is avoided cast after cast. A slim solid silver streamer fares little better, giving me time to wolf a sandwich as I retie an ALF. Back into a fish I tell Denis "I could do this all day."

"Yes," he says thoughtfully. "But then, we miss the good fishing."
Pardon?
"So we finish lunch, then move."

>—+—+>—O—<+—+—<

Our second spot could not be more different from the first. After making a run down the main lake body, we pass through a narrow channel into a wide bay, shallow, crowded with downed timber, stickups and beaver mounds. Denis cuts the engine to paddle us through this fresh-water flat. "Here," he says softly. "We call this place 'Catch Every Cast.' Only, we must look."

Exactly: the bay's reputations has as much to do with the technique used as with the abundance of fish. In amber water we play a stalk-and-cast game.

"There. You see?"
No, I don't.
Denis has changed to Mercer's other slider, now opens the loops of his false casts. His fly slaps down six feet left of a submerged white trunk where one limb spikes the surface. Denis lets the bunny tail curl. The limb's pale reflection is underscored by a green and gold bar. Which has an eye.

It can't be possible that the pike deliberately lies along the reflection.

Denis makes two quick strips. The pike leaves the water in the arc of a throw from shortstop to first. On the way in and *down*, it spears the slider in its mouth.

Zero to 20 miles per hour in six feet.

><><>><><>—O—><><><><

And so it goes for three hours, paddling our way through the bay and afternoon. Polaroid glasses help me catch on to the sight game; when light or cover baffles vision I cast to where fish should be, on target a quarter of the time. The pike are spaced out here, seeming to occupy territories thirty or forty feet in diameter—less in heavy cover, as when two lay in ambush on opposite sides of a beaver mound. Some fish are spooky; others will cruise close or allow us to do so. When a more cautious fish follows Denis' fly, Denis demonstrates for me a figure eight retrieve right at the gunwale. The result drenches us both and threatens to put 30 inches of fresh pike in our laps. That assassin takes the fly, I'm convinced, just so we—whatever we are—can't get it.

><><>><><>—O—><><><><

Fresh fish indeed: like seven or eight others this one gets a crack on the head for the meal Denis has promised the Outpost fire crew cook. When the light starts to fade we deliver. The chef is pleased, but the assembled crew looks determined not to break their nonsmiling record until I insist Denis translate this: "Tell them the government sent us, because it's cheaper to feed them this way. Tell them that tomorrow we bring them a moose head for stew—maybe just the antlers."

Several of them smile all right, after a fashion. Sure wish I knew what those French words mean.

><><>><><>—O—><><><><

On the trek back I stop to fish the stream I'd said was my destination, in case Proctor has any questions. He does, of course, over dinner. "So you *didn't* go back to the reservoir."

"Oh. Well, yeah, I did. Just to fool around."

"How many you catch?"

I shrug. "Didn't count."

He watches me carefully. Then, slowly, he looks around the table. "By the way...these guys don't believe that brookie I took on Sunday was three pounds. *You* saw it."

I did. About 18 ounces, but I understand. "Hard to say...hell of a fish, though. Bigger than any I caught."

"Damn right," he declares.

━┼━◆━○━◆━┼━

The next day we fly out; and all I want is down to do it again.

Instead, after we land, Proctor and Sy have a heated argument over the half dozen fish we've kept. Most are Brendan's, who wants to take some home to show his Mom and sister. But by God, Proctor *will* take them back to New Jersey.

The squabble seems to last most of the three-hour drive to Quebec City Airport. It's partly the principle that galls Sy, but also Proctor's approach of "It's *my* cooler they're in now, and I won't stop *my* vehicle to buy another."

Now *there's* a tactic that's ended some stickball games. I'd almost forgotten it and hope I will again, soon.

At the airport gate we take our leave, Sy and Brendan fishless. Though Brendan's surrendered hope, Sy's not so complacent. "I can't believe this," he repeats. "An adult, acting this way." Then, to me, "Do you believe this?"

"Ah, as a matter of fact...It's time to board. Let's go."

We do, but not before Sy sends a last look Proctor's way.

I recognize that look. I've seen it so recently, so many times—the wide-eyed gaze which still seems steely and narrow, a body tense enough to vibrate. Soon I'll return home to see it on street corners—

Sy is doing a pike thing...

Women Who Fish and the Men Who Love Them

O let met go down to the stream again,
To the lonely stream and the sky.
All I need is a good long rod,
And a lass who casts a fly.

Freshman year in college and a frat party to which I'd earned an invitation with a tackle that separated several of my favorite bones from their buddies...She had red-fox hair, gray eyes and was dressed in the kind of casual clothes I would someday recognize as L.L. Bean. Amidst a beery night of 941 people asking, "So-what's-your-major?" she said, apropos of nothing, "What I'll miss most about home is a very nice smallmouth pond, though in the spring I do have to carry my pistol because of copperheads."

"Marry me," I said.

>─+◆>─O─<◆+─<

It can't be pretty, watching me watch a woman fishing. Doesn't much matter if she's 22 or 79, I stand with mouth agape and eyes askew, curious and feeling wild. Keep your *Penthouse* stories of tri-sex on horseback with twins in trains—give me a female of my species staring down a line into dark water. Give me brown neoprene and my imagination supplies black lace. I don't care what kind of angling she's up to: If she's pitched out liver for catfish my barbels start to twitch.

139

So why aren't there more of them?

This isn't a rhetorical question, and I have no answer save for the obvious: "They're not often trained to do it." We should fix that. Start a campaign with a Madison Avenue game plan: "Warm Water Ms," "NOW About Trout" and "Cosmo Girls Go Nymph." Toss in a column by Abby—"Commit your life to fishing, dear, which will have the side benefit of attracting as many men as anchovies in a school"—then a feature in *Architectural Digest*, "And for her tying room, Angie Perry picked out a plume theme, ostrich and peacock, with accents of Golden Pheasant and carpets suitable for dubbing."

Just ideas. Sincere ideas. Fishing is a sport in which women could and should excel (and sometimes do), from the timing of a precise cast to the fine motor control for tying to #24s. I personally have met women who could land a billfish in one hand and me in the other.

Give Us More, I say. To that end I've spent much of my life trying to encourage social revolution. When young I even earned a reputation for suave lines like, "Come on up to my room, I'll show you my Creek Chub," and "If you really want some wahoo, baby, let me tie you up a Bimini Twist."

Yeah, well, some sort of reputation, anyway.

There were the times when I actually did lure damsels to my boat. They almost always had a wonderful time, save for occasional discomfort over bait. One particularly good sport solved this in an ingenious fashion:

"You know," said I, admiringly, "you sure have been good about those squid tentacles. No 'yechh' noises from you, no sir."

Said companion stared at me blankly. "They're plastic," she said.

"Plastic? Ah, no. Not, ah, actually."

At that moment she held the bait knife in one hand and the tentacles in the other. Her eyes had an interesting glint. "Look, pal. We've been having a pretty good time, haven't we? Out in the middle of nature's noplace, where I've swallowed four waves, eaten a soggy, salt sandwich, and broken three nails?"

"Why…yes, we sure have!"

"Good. So listen closely while watching these eyes you've admired: *these awful things are plastic, aren't they?*"

"Absolutely. And so, you know, *life-like*, too."

>─┤◄►─◇─◄┼◄

Bait isn't the only discouraging feature about fishing for women who've had little experience. Holding fish can cause problems: the thumb-to-forefinger grip so effective with tweezers has limitations when attempted with a thrashing three-pound bass; and though it's probably as good a system as others, choosing a plug because "It's just the most darling little froggie" lacks that scientific flavor I strive for in my own selections. Sometimes even the most basic rules of obsession seem daunting, as happened on one winter steelhead trip.

"Exactly when do we stop?"

"Like I said: when your line keeps freezing in the guides."

"That's the only time?"

"Right."

Wrong, by gosh...we *would* stop if I had two hooks of a treble spinner lodged in my hiney. You bet.

><+>-O-<+>-<

Nevertheless, I remain committed to finding or developing female fishing company. I'll admit to keeping evidence of a better-fated trip under my mattress, a "fish-cake" photo in which even the crappie seems to be smiling, probably because in the battle just finished it ended up wearing half the bikini of the lucky angler who holds it. If that image doesn't silence the pervert who whines, "But I fish to get away from women," then set him in this scene.

You wake to the smell of coffee. In she comes, face flushed above her vest. "You," she hums, "were terrific last night."

"Really?"

"My, *yes*! The way you handled your rod when you laid that drift so naturally along the seam..."

"Ah, shucks. But hey, your double-haul to the far bank? And the way you high-sticked that riffle—"

"Stop it! Take me—"

"Yes!"

"Fishing! Now!"

The Grey's Ghillie

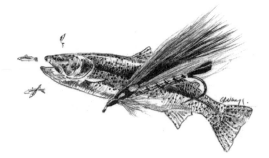

In the old days, when Mor wasn't lean but skinny and often ill, it was sometimes my place to take his father fishing. By then Mr. Goldman had been crippled by arthritis for three decades, his fingers gnarled and bent up backwards until they most resembled roots. After a fire caught him helpless in bed, the rest of Mr. Goldman also had a charred and wooden look; but his eyes would light when I lashed his wheelchair to the rail on some party boat out of San Diego. I'd tie the rod as well, then tuck the butt end into his hollow belly and fold his hands on top. "Good! Wonderful!" he'd say; and he'd choke with laughter whenever a bonito would wrench him about. After a minute he'd cry, "I've done him in, kid! You finish off." I would, then he'd tell me stories of catching marlin as a young, upright man.

>-+>-O-++-+<

Fishing with Mor was not entirely different, physically, than fishing with his father. Mor deeply loved the Boy Scout part of expeditions—I'd been cashiered from my troop for punching the scoutmaster's bully bastard—tying elaborate knots to hold down tent ropes, cooking stews, lighting fires with one match. But streamside or in a boat, Mor was pleasantly lost and ever accommodating, satisfied to hunker down with a Kleenex—he had allergies—and serve as a human rod holder. So, "Take this" I'd say, and wander off to cast fly or lure until he announced "'Something's pulling'"; then I'd return to reel in. One night in Mexico

Mor modified this procedure with a perplexed "Something's pulling me in"—a bat ray of half a hundred pounds. I made him play that beast while I waded out to grasp the great black wings. I lost the battle in the end, losing also—somehow, mysteriously—the tip-top of my left forefinger.

Mor bandaged the wound between expressions of wonder: "How could that happen? You are completely insane, by the way—-what happened?"

>-+-◆>-○-<◆-+-<

Twenty-five years later Mr. Goldman is long dead, and Mor is a psychiatrist who works out in a gym twice a week and takes enormous delight in two children who, "Demand, they *demand,* that I take them fishing. Which means *you* have to teach me how..."

This happens. Brad, third of our high school trio, came out with his son one summer for lessons on a lake. Mor has a different idea, though: the two of us will adventure out into the mountains for five days, then he'll fly his kids over.

>-+-◆>-○-<◆-+-<

On a warm August night I pick Mor up at the Oakland Airport in my tiny RV truck. Five hours of talk later—how is my mother? have I heard from Brad? how many fishing articles must I sell to make a living?—we're 4000 feet into a narrow Sierra pass. Cliff wall to the right, cliff fall to the left and in the highbeams we see a great white yacht broadside, an ocean-going yacht blocking the highway from shoulder to shoulder. "What's that?" Mor asks, naturally enough.

"Noah's Ark," I suggest.

"What?"

"I don't know, but it happens all the time."

"What?"

We both laugh. A trucker, brain-dead or drunk, took a right turn in Redding and headed east toward the wrong ocean, then tried to reverse a 60-foot-long tractor trailer on a 50-foot-wide road. A crowned road, higher in the middle than the sides; so the rear wheels of the trailer are hanging in space. We'll not go past him tonight.

No matter. I know another stream behind us and south. As we bed down in a campground, Mor in front, me over the cab, I hear him laugh again. "Noah's Ark. Does that kind of thing, do things *like* that happen often on these trips?"

I consider. "Arks not so often. But a fishing trip is always a meander. You can't quite know what will come up."

"You like that?"

"I do."

He pauses. We each have a small skylight to look through; through mine I can see an edge of cloud silvered by moonlight. Once more, Mor laughs, long, happily. "Of course. Of course you do. You've always liked that."

➤⊷➤⊷◦⊷⊷◦

In the morning I start to teach Mor the stream, reading water in a stretch near the campground. I encourage him to understand currents as a fluid weave running an infinite course of obstructions, then switch to an image of muscles surrounding systems of bone. Mor nods and practices a few casts with the spinning outfit I've given him while I stand by with my fly rod. When he can more or less direct a cast, I thread him a worm. I fish only the fly rod these days, but learning that would be well beyond his children's ability.

It's a medium size creek for these mountains, freestone, sixty or seventy feet wide. Mor casts about half that, takes a drift, then another, and another. His line twitches but there's too much slack for him to feel the bite. "Show me," he says. I do, explaining what it is I hope will happen, as it does, and I strike the fish quickly so as not to let it take the hook deep. A rainbow trout of 11 inches.

Mor's just amazed. "First cast. You did it first cast."

"That was a little lucky. Look—you see how his dorsal fin is clipped? A stocked fish, not native. There's likely to be more."

"I want to see you do that again."

I laugh. "All right. Just to show you it doesn't happen every cast."

It does though. Mor's delighted, I'm chagrined; I refuse to try again until he's caught a fish. He does, eventually. I take a photo, then walk upstream to let him practice.

I don't spend too much time with stocked trout this fresh. Right out of the hatchery, they can't recognize the bugs my flies represent. Most won't get the chance to learn on heavily fished sections of stream like this, with weekend warriors harvesting them quickly. The key for me on such water is to find an unlikely spot so removed from premium lies that other anglers won't bother. That's where I might find a holdover fish, one who's eaten enough insects to be seduced by a forgery of same.

Upstream from Mor, on the far side of a shallow riffle, I see such a place—a depression behind a stone shadowed by bankside willows. It's smaller than a sink and I miss it first cast, hit it the second. My rod flexes deep; it is a two-year-old trout, almost 17 inches. Mor scampers up to see it.

"Wow! Just wow."

I revive the fish carefully, release it. Mor watches it swim away, turns to me smiling. "You really are good at this, aren't you?"

I shrug. "Enough time trying, you have to get better. And...this is what I do."

"Yeah. Yeah, I guess that's right."

I look at him. "Not quite real to you, is it?"

He laughs. "I guess not. But you do other things, too." He mentions some investigative journalism that won awards and sent me into the mountains for three weeks after publication. Four police officers were convicted of felonies, but it wasn't retaliation I fled so much as the filth clinging to me from the cesspools I'd waded to get the story.

"All one piece," I tell him. "All part of the same thing, somehow."

He murmurs, "Hmmm. " Then "I'll have to think about that."

><+>-O-<+><

Mor tires a little in the afternoon, returns to the truck for a nap. I fish on upstream, sampling insects with a hand seine. I'm into wild trout water soon, and they will demand closer representation of the life forms on which they feed. I take several more rainbows, then two little browns on stonefly nymphs, then a stray brookie to a caddis dry fly. This section of creek is all mine, untracked save for deer trails. I hear one stumbling in the canyon above, see her humping up toward a ridge, looking from my perspective like a running rump.

By the time I return Mor has organized drawers and cabinets in the RV, extricating Jethro Tull tapes from behind my canned chili cache. "What's going on?" I demand.

"Do you realize that you have three mostly empty vodka bottles, two more of bourbon and a total of six Cokes, two that I found stashed under your rain gear?"

"Did I *realize* that?"

"Yes!"

"Yes. I semi-realized that. I forget where I put things, so I like having spares I can find."

Mor looks at me incredulously. "I just poured all the vodka into one bottle."

I sigh grandly. "Then I'll lose it soon, so I need to drink now."

I do drink, as Mor fusses happily about the stove and counter, constructing your everyday, wilderness six-course meal. "The corn will be canned, I'm afraid. Not that you'd notice."

"I can cook," I insist.

"Of course you can."

"I can so. I can cook Thai."

He smiles condescendingly. "Do the Thais know you're doing it?"

><+>-O-<+><

During dinner we talk about the research Mor's doing on schizophrenia, then about the administrative duties that divert him from this task. "It's some sort of science," he says," to get people to do what they're supposed to. And I'd rather deal with a paranoid patient than with a ward clerk who thinks someone's sat in her chair."

><+>-O-<+><

The next day we drive on to a lake and park in a crowded campground. The shore around it is wall-to-wall anglers, so I lift from its brackets my folding boat. Mor is fascinated by the craft, if a little dubious; and while I row him out, I see he's sitting in the characteristic hunch of his youth. "It floats," he says, by way of suggesting it might not soon.

"Not to worry...You do swim at your gym?"

"What?" He laughs. "Yes, I swim, but not in water of 50 degrees." He trails his hand along beside. "Or less. Speaking of which, how about tonight we find a motel? Take a shower?"

"How about a bath?"

"Even better."

"Good. Because you're floating on our tub."

"You're...kidding, right? You *are* kidding."

Just then a fish hits Mor's trolled bait; it jerks the little boat. Quite a big one, I can see from the rod's bend. In our ancient pattern, now's the time for him to hand it over.

I think that occurs to him. He waits for me to suggest it, I suspect.

I don't, and he begins to focus instead on the fish's powerful runs. Once it circles to starboard with such a strong surge it pulls the boat around. "My God," says Mor.

"Very easy, very steady pressure. Don't reel, Mor, when the line's moving out, when you hear the drag whining. Pull awhile on the left side....now, slowly, take the rod to the right and pull from that direction."

"Why?"

"Changing directions will tire him."

"How come?"

"I don't know—he loses momentum. Do it.'

"Man, is he strong."

I let Mor fight him without further tutorials, grinning as I see him lean back, pull, reel. It's a hell of a fish.

It's only a sucker of five pounds.

"Oh shoot," says Mor. "Shoot, shoot, damn."

I land the fish, hold it so Mor can examine closely the fleshy, puckered mouth, feel the smooth solidness of its body before I slide it back in. "Those aren't any good, though, are they?"

"Oh, I don't know."

"I mean, they're garbage fish, aren't they? Didn't you used to kill them?"

"Yeah. I've re-thought that a little. Suckers are native to this system; they've got some sort of place. Aesthetically, vermin...Did he give you a good fight?"

"God, yes."

"And if it was a trout, we'd have let him go anyway."

"Yeah. I get it." He looks me over, smiles. "Things change, don't they?"

⤛⬦─○─⬦⤜

Some do; but Mor's shrieks as he enters our frigid bath-lake are of the same pitch I remember from boyhood; and the giant goose bumps on his fair skin are also familiar. "Your nuts! You're crazy! I can't believe you're making me do this!" Afterwards, he sniffles happily, Kleenex in hand. "We deserve steaks for doing that. Screw *you*—*I* deserve a steak," so we indulge in dinner at the restaurant of a lakeside resort. I make grumbling noises about "roughing it," which Mor pointedly ignores. Over coffee, however, he wonders "If I weren't here....what sort of place would you be fishing? Not the same places, I take it."

No. Alone, I wouldn't be at the crowded campground to begin with, but somewhere remote. I certainly wouldn't plunge into chill water to freshen up; I'd sponge off. The bath exploit has more to do with who I am to Mor in our friendship—a role I play with other friends—to whom I seem to represent a kind of comfortable chaos: I have, they imagine, willfully traded the advantages of convention for a marginal existence, somewhat primitive, a little poor, richer in visceral adventure than allowed by their lives, wives, responsibilities. They tell exaggerated stories about my exploits with women and the time I straddled a small shark to hack off its head. Reality and illusion: Mor knows that I do not break horses on Tuesday, pull transmissions on Wednesdays, get manly the rest of the week. But he might remember that we met as he battled high school pranksters trying to "pants" him—a nasty practical joke—and that I punted somebody's testicles, by way of helping out. Mor marries, has children. I live with one woman, leave her but help raise her children, live with another. Mor commits to psychiatry, studies and works to succeed there; I take potluck as a writer, veer off into the Peace Corps, where I'm charged with sedition by Muslims, return to case-manage the criminally convicted mentally ill, continue to write, then to teach, meander the Sierra to fish, still write...but I do have an IRA.

"No," I admit to Mor, "not the same places." Then I describe for him a tiny, wild stream intricately knotted into conifers and willows, with elephant ear vines spreading over bouldery little pools where brown trout lurk beneath leaves and undercut banks. I laugh: "The wonderful thing is that few locals believe there's fish in the stream, so it's pretty much mine."

"I'd really like to go there," he says firmly.

It's not far away, but it's tough fishing—the technical challenge of casting for small, exquisitely wary prey. A stalking stream.

"I'd *really* like to go."

><+>·O·<+><

Mor's appropriately awed by the lush valley of green on brown on green, by ferns as high as his head, deep tangles of deadfall timber and live pines through which the water winds clear and shadowed. I show him scars on a sapling from a failed beaver dam; he finds on his own paw prints he recognizes from his Boy Scout handbook—"These are raccoon!"—and in an eddy I show him jewels—caddis cases constructed by pupae from grains of black iron and flakes of fools gold.

Then comes the fishing.

A wonderful thing about teaching is that you must remember what you know, frame it, provide proof on demand. We are predators here, I tell Mor; we must match our silhouettes to tree trunks, fish upstream, keep ever in mind that the trout swims always into current, calculate angles of the window through which these fish see the world. To err is to fail; but there's another chance above, a run or a pool where water tumbles into a pocket and trout wait. Crouching, knee-walking, wading with motions so careful that your prey does not sense movement through its lateral line...

It takes four hours, but at last Mor lands a fish. Five inches perhaps, bronze with vivid crimson spots and the crisply edged fins of a fish never confined in a concrete hatchery tank. Mor is proud, perhaps even moved. He holds it for a photo, gently places it back, turns to me and says simply "I get it. This is your world."

>-+•>-O-•+-+-<

Three days later and the kids are in from Chicago. I take them and Mor to a private, warm-water pond. Their mother worries about my folding boat. "You're sure about this?" she asks Mor. "You're sure?"

Mor is so certain he's cavalier. "Absolutely; it'll be great; let's get going." He notices that I bring no rod—"How come?"

"You'll see."

Mor in front, me in the middle at the oars, Brendan and his sister Megan sharing the back bench. Before I'm ten feet from the dock Mor has his line out, fishing. I've rigged the kid's rods in advance, of course: Megan, eight years old and clever, can just about cast. Brendan, however, just five, has his doubts about the whole process. By the time Mor and Megan have each caught two fish, he's sniffling.

And—it's rather incredible to me—he's clutching a Kleenex, sitting hunched over, holding his rod in an aimless attitude that stirs memories more than half my life old. I really can't quite believe how he fits the template; so I look to Mor, who's hunched over all right, but so intent that he turns only a moment to say brightly to Brendan, "Don't worry, Buddy, you'll get one in a minute," leaving to me—quite rightly—the task of baiting Brendan's hook and lobbing it out to where a bluegill takes it with conviction; and I have my hand resting gently on Brendan's little pair as he shrieks, feeling life on his line and beginning, already, to *get it* as his father and I cheer.

>-+•>-O-•+-+-<

Next June, we go to Canada.

The Siamese Avenger

No less a source than Polly Rosborough recommends cat fur as a binder for other, less tacky fibers; and I tie a nymph from Misha's, dubbed by me "The Siamese Avenger." The collection process pleases him no end, leaving him glossy and minus a few of the fleas that give my flies such an active and doggone buggy look. Misha talks as I comb—Siamese are noisy, more like dogs—purring so hard he vibrates.

Misha also expresses displeasure in no uncertain terms and was doing so quite often several months back, discussing territory with a new tom on the street. A breakdown in negotiations cost him an ear torn down to skull level and me $128. Several times they fought in the driveway behind my camper, so when I heard him scream one night I ran around to that side of the house and peered into the shadows behind the wheels. Not there.

Misha screamed again, as if he was being torn in two. Confused, I hupped back into the house and from the upstairs stairway window looked down into the neighbor's driveway to where a pair of silent pit bulls split an animal between them by head and hindquarters. They appeared to be tearing it in two.

I threw the screen at them, ran around to the front door onto the walk. The pit bulls raced by. The larger one held Misha in his mouth. In silhouette against the gray sky, I saw him toss Misha once, quickly, just the way I'd once seen a Russian wolfhound kill a woodchuck once. I ran after, roaring, or making some kind of sound that frightened them as I caught up—I did catch up—so that the big dog dropped Misha onto the sidewalk.

I stopped, stared at him. He tried to stand but his back legs buckled. I was afraid to touch him until he tried and failed again to stand, then I picked him up. He recognized me and began to purr, vibrating a little, before falling silent into shock.

>·•••·—O—·•••·<

About flyfishing: in the nature of things—in Nature, per se—it's as tough for trout in your favorite stream as for cats and people on the streets of Oakland. I mused about that while standing outside the all night veterinary hospital, watching drug deals go down on the corner of University and 6th, while waiting for Misha's x-rays to develop. I wasn't thinking about fish, initially, but about those pit bulls...so *silent*. Later investigation led me to suspect the pair are feral, but even that night I did not believe their attack was some idle pet's game, bark-bark-excited, bite something. Even as I threw the screen from the window, I was convinced they were hunting. I think they carried Misha off to eat him, though that impression may be influenced by memories of a cat-eating feral dog that stalked a cemetery outside Tel Aviv.

>·•••·—O—·•••·<

Only by way of saying that predation is a serious affair. That's what I was pondering, really, playing over and over the image of Misha's body snapping forward in the sky. In a search for balance I recalled also the look of live salamanders Misha brings home to me, dark eyes glinting in their pink heads, limbs moving feebly, as if hope is hardwired into their brains. They usually survive, because however intent Misha is on hunting, his kill instinct is dulled by Science Diet Light.

>·•••·—O—·•••·<

Trout are pit bulls, I suppose, to the creatures they consume—monsters to elegant wisps of mayfly life and midge clusters and to the bigger stonefly nymphs I've come to like because they look vicious and aren't *to us*. Trouts' own fry manifest panic in a way I understand—into which I project understanding, if you like—scattering into the air, schooling together in myriad confusion—toddlers!—as their cannibal elders strike.

So it's tough out there. No news in that, nor enlightenment. There might be a whiff of the latter, however, when we compare the nature of flyfishers to that of pit bulls. A last card to lay as context.

—◦—

Several hours before the pit bull visit, I was watching again a PBS documentary about lions and hyenas. The program should be mandatory for everyone, and those who tend to get glum about humanity should watch it every week. It's too good to describe with few words: it makes the point that, contrary to pious proclamations, animals do indulge in great nastiness, with seeming malice, and with savagery as extreme as that proposed by the pitifully endowed people I hear on radio talk shows. When all is filmed and done, lions have killed hyenas and other lions, hyenas attacked lions and other hyenas in gangs, and both species have eaten other mammals alive, starting from the anus. Which is an excellent reminder that shock such as Misha entered is not merely prudent biology but Mother's own mercy...

...And it all makes me think again, standing outside the vet's, that what is so stunning about people isn't our callous cruelty, manifest by individuals and in whole societies of Nazis and Hutus, but the fact that we so often resist chaos and cruelty, however poorly. In other words, in the rest of nature it is not interspecies savagery that's an aberration, but any attempt to do differently.

As in flyfishers, for example—predators who, like a well-fed Misha, mainly leave off the practice of killing edible creatures to instead indulge in a ritual of conscientious release. However "cruel," however "senseless," it's usually a bloodless sport these days. We settle for counting coup.

—◦—

Why? Why have we done that?

Because we've personalized fish, perhaps. Some fish, anyway. We consider them players, however unwitting and unwilling—vital, invaluable. We have entirely changed the nature of fishing, which was once the work of survival, stylizing it, rewriting the evolutionary program from "The Best Predators Eat More and Live" until it reads more like a romantic comedy. Our own motive to kill is also dulled by a "Science Diet," but like Misha, we still thrill to the chase.

>-+-+>-0-+<-+-<

Back inside the hospital—one must buzz at a window for entry off the street, by way of protection—Lisa is sobbing, insisting she wants to kill the pit bulls. "All pit bulls," whom she "hates." Having personalized them, she ascribes malice. After watching hyenas at work, I don't contradict.

The vet brings us back, describes how Misha's ribcage has been split at the sternum, how his lungs now fill with blood. The dozen punctures on his shaved skin fail to suggest the tissue damage beneath: we can see on the x-ray that, while shaking Misha, the dogs have actually injected air beneath his hide, separating skin from muscle. Still, maintained on oxygen, fed and anesthetized IV for a long time, he has a chance to live.

A chance is enough. The next day we have the ER vet transfer Misha to our own, who is far less hopeful. Misha, she insists, has one chance in five at best, and deserves a "no code": if his heart stops, as she expects it will, she wants to let him die. Unless we opt to kill him now.

I have personalized Misha. I explain to her that, peculiar as it sounds, I know him to be a particularly determined cat, as fiercely committed to living as any animal I've known. If he was a fish he'd be a steelhead on the way to spawn, hell-bent.

The vet's eyes remain opaque.

Misha lives. After a week on IVs and a month in a box, hand-fed— at first with an eyedropper—he is now whole, hearty, and loud, a mean Siamese with a wacked-out haircut and a serious dislike of dogs. At a hundred dollars a pound, he's probably the most expensive cat on the block. He acts like it.

>-+-+>-0-+<-+-<

And I'm going fishing this evening, taking thoughts of him with me. I may hook a bass I noted in a walk with Lisa yesterday. I will play him about, fascinated by the link between us. He will not appreciate it. If I win, I will stroke him back and forth, mindful of his life, careful and appreciative. He will live and, probably within an hour or two, kill something, engulfing it whole, waiting for it to die inside him, oblivious or uninterested in last movements, tiny sounds. No game for him; he has to do what he has to do.

>‑‑◦‑‑◦‑‑◦‑‑<

Me too. Shortly after we got Misha home I called Animal Control about the pit bulls. They admitted they were, all in all, pretty helpless in the situation—remember the budget, never mind the leash law. If I happened to see the dogs again, I could always call 911, though if they're moving fast, as in hunting, well...you never know. Maybe some cop would break away from greater mayhem to help out.

"I doubt it," I said.

"Me too," Animal Control replied.

"You know," I said, in a carefully measured tone, "I've got this cat, mangled still, and another one. I have a baby three weeks old. I do not wish to have feral pit bulls in my neighborhood."

"I understand."

"Then you understand, when I suggest that I have to do what I have to do."

"I understand. Completely. Yes, I do."

We both allowed a long pause to elapse, then said good-bye.

>‑‑◦‑‑◦‑‑◦‑‑<

There are no feral pit bulls in my neighborhood now. I haven't seen them in a long time. I had nothing to do with their disappearance. I'm glad they are gone, but I didn't hate them the way Lisa did. Perhaps they did indeed have hyena-malice in their brains, but more likely they were doing what they had to do; whomever or whatever removed them can claim the same. In the meantime, while I am under no illusion that any of us are generous to the animals we choose not to kill—and I'm often bewildered by the satisfaction we take both in catching and releasing— I will hesitate an instant after a fish leaves my hand, meat gone back to water, contemplating a game we have the luxury to play in a place where so many others play for keeps.

White Ducks
and Hula Poppers

For me it began at about the age of 10, when I was old enough to walk two miles home alone from school. Right outside the recess yard of Madison #2, over the fence behind the high jump pit, after a quick scoot along the third fairway—

Into the weeping willow. If I'd been spotted I would see the golf pro zipping from the clubhouse on his Cushman, leaning forward as if to lead with this forehead that blazed a wonderful red. If my Grandpa Charlie had apple carts for sport in Harlem, by God I had this Cushman at Town & Country Golf.

Sometimes. More often than not, in the heat of a Phoenix afternoon, nothing would move under the cicada's buzzy whine. That meant hand-line time at the pond and bluegill by the basket. Usually they would school around me as my bread baits dissolved, then scatter when the bass moved in.

I did get caught. Often, I got caught after an hour or so. Some golfer would tattle, alerted by my feral manner, or by an image of his Titleist lodged in my brain pan. Then the home pro would rag me, loud and red. I would stare at his forehead while he shouted, nodding, answering, "Sir, yes sir," as he swore for the fifth, eighth, 12th and 26th time "Next time, I'm gonna call the cops."

"Sir, yes sir."

"But there won't be a next time, will there, boy?"

"No sir."

"Dammit! That's what you said last time!"

"Yes sir. I remember."

➤⊹⊙⊹⊰

I was a trial for him, I really was. Fate had led him to a posh job—it seemed to me easier than sleep—on a course with a pond that was, therefore, certainly destined to be fished by me, a temptation I could no more resist than fat summer mulberries or the fatter horn toads that I would find beside red ant piles on the edges of all the desert around us. One of those absolutes: He had a pond; so I was there.

He might have figured that out, though it did frustrate him. Especially because I was such a polite nuisance. An ex-Marine, I would eventually discover, probably a spit-and-polish sort who had gone soft around the belly, he was ever disarmed by my earnest manner. Defiant only in action, never attitude or words; determined but eminently agreeable—why, I was even sympathetic, sincerely sorry that it was him I had to trouble.

Had to. As in, "Do you know how pissed off it makes me, to keep finding you here?"

"Yes sir, I do. Honest. Really."

"Then, *why do I?* Why? Can you just tell me that?"

"It's…the fish, sir. I can't help it."

➤⊹⊙⊹⊰

No, come to think of it now, I don't believe he ever did grasp the nature of an obsession that still drives me three decades later. He likely considered me slightly mad. In any case, he actually looked relieved one day when I walked in the clubhouse door, the front one, without him hanging to my ear, early autumn of my sixth grade year. Perhaps I had legitimate business.

You bet: I had a note from Mr. Simpson, my science teacher. Your proverbial innocent bystander, Simpson couldn't care less if I wanted to do my Science Fair Project on "Game Fish of Arizona." To him it didn't seem the least bit suspicious that I'd asked for a letter requesting permission to catch a few of these nearby. For science, you know.

I watched the pro's forehead as he read Simpson's note. For years he'd been trying to gets the school's help in preventing student trespasses, not the least of these mine. How would it look now, if he rejected this small favor?

Finished reading, he eyed me through eyes already bloodshot at 3:00 p.m.

"Right. Science Fair project. Right." He continued to glare. "Does this guy know about you? Me? This place?"

"Well, Mr. Simpson says all the world is a laboratory, sir. About us—"

"Not *us*. *You*. *Me*. The five hundred times…Oh, Christ."

"Sir?"

"How long is this gonna take?"

⋗—⊶•O•⊷—⋖

Two years, about. Toward the end of the second, he started getting a tad cranky again. In the eighth grade, however, I actually started playing some golf, kicking in my 50-cent green fees and whacking around before I retreated to the weeping willow to rig up. Once he said something about it, as in, "People only pay to golf here, you know." Which was fine by me: that meant the fishing was free.

⋗—⊶•O•⊷—⋖

For four more years. In high school, however, I fished strictly at night, jumping the fence, then dodging through the spray of Rain Birds. Sometimes I brought my friend Terry Breen who, after a beer, would want to eat one of the white ducks. "Look at 'em, buddy, so dumb, so trusting—worthless 'til they're deep-sixed in my Mom's Coke sauce! What kind of problem do you have with that?"

The trust of the pro, if one could call it that. The groundskeepers, also, though after an encounter or two I noticed that they looked as nervous of me as I was of them. They lived in the equipment shed among the tractors, emerging late—illegals, probably making ten or twelve bucks a night, they were wary, and too poor to refuse the beer that I'd bring them.

⋗—⊶•O•⊷—⋖

By then, of course, I'd long since graduated from hand lines and was either baiting up for the big carp some dunce had introduced or throwing a black fly rod Hula Popper for bass. Once when Terry was along, the two of us spent five minutes babbling after a brute hit the lure with such violence he hurled it four feet up a sloped bank. "Did you see that?" we said 24 times, varying the accent on each word, then on to pairs of words ""Did *you* see *that?*" *Did* you *see* that?"

Over the years, I naturally spread out my efforts. The Encanto Golf Course had not only big carp, but turtles of terrible size; and at Papago you could work bass, though it was better, if far more dangerous, to sneak into the Phoenix Zoo ponds. I also fished the Grand Canal where it traversed the grounds of a vast luxury hotel. I would dive in whenever the excited security guards arrived—in Cushmans, again—to putt alongside me on the shore road as I drifted, shouting and waving their cans of Mace. I don't believe I was quite so polite to them. Unlike my pro, they had no legitimate jurisdiction over this water; I knew that, and how to use my index finger.

It was more than ten years later that I finally found another golf course pond I could fish with permission, the Valley Country Club outside Denver, where I was tending bar at the Men's Grill. The bass that surprised me there, boiling on a little marabou streamer tied on a keel hook, remains my personal best. Even so, and despite the fact that Town and Country has long been buried beneath condominium complexes, the pro retired, it remains my home course, first in my memories. I took so much pleasure on the banks beside the 9th hole. I took Melissa there also, on the date when she caught a channel cat Terry would declare "The best fish I ever ate, though still not a duck." That night she also taught me another angle on life entirely, in the deep Bermuda grass beside the green, just in time for the Rain Birds to go on.

Talking about your red forehead.

Flying Fishing
Bora Bora

"You do the flying fishing? *Here?* in Bora Bora? No way!" Dany Leverd pulls his right hand off the steering wheel to false cast at the windshield, and the Land Rover slides sideways on the mud track. A lash of branches excites small screams from passengers in back, including a singular shriek from the American woman who's just asked Dany about his astrological sign.

"Flyfishing, right," I answer, clutching the shotgun seat's hand strap merely for emphasis.

"Too fantastic, man. You have seen *A River Runs Through It?*"

Lisa groans behind me.

"That movie is so incredible; I love that movie. Flying fishing in Bora Bora—that is special—very special. Excuse me a moment, man—People? This tree is *Hibiscus tectorus*. You know hibiscus? My ancestors make many things from this tree, let me show you…"

Dany leaps from the cab to peel bark, making twine, then shaves the cambium from this to create the white "grass" of skirts worn by Polynesian dancers. Hibiscus branches and trunks are lashed together to build outriggers for *pirogues*....

Soon we're grinding up the mountain again beneath cliffs of volcanic basalt, through forests of wild mango and guava and coconut palms: this is the afternoon leg of Tupani Tours, a four-wheel safari into Bora Bora's interior. Dany cut this track himself and rescued another from the jungle, a World War II road remembered by a relative who watched U.S. Seabees planting seven-inch guns still aimed at the ocean. Between revelations about Polynesian history and the sex life of vanilla vines, Dany peppers me with questions about flycasting and flygear.

Informed questions. Born in New Caledonia to Bora Boran parents, with a degree in economics from Paris University, Dany is both a passionate fisher and collector of American angling magazines. If I'm a long-sought resource for him, however, Dany proves more than that for me, beginning with his instant identification of the fish I'd taken already from the beach in front of our *pensione*. "This brown and white one we call *tarau*, like a grouper—they take the fly? *Wonderful*, man...The black one with blue spots is *roi*." He offers other bits and pieces about lagoon fish and their habits, and from a viewpoint a 1000 feet up the volcano slope, shows me spots to access the reef.

By the time we've toured the gardens of Eden around painter John Mason's estate, Dany and I have arranged our first expedition.

It starts with a flycasting session on the beach near Hotel Bora Bora. A white sand bottom stretches out to a deep water drop off, beyond which a pleasure yacht swings at anchor.

Like most beginners with great upper body strength, Dany overpowers the rod. So do I after twenty years, but I briefly beggar him with instructions, then metaphors. One of the latter involves a delicate reference to pleasing women. Dany gets it, laughs, and improves 100 per cent. Soon thereafter, he points to a blue and white outrigger *pirogue* sliding toward us.

"My cousin, Ke-Ke. He comes for us; now we go to the reef."

And so I meet Ke-Ke. For the second time, as it happens.

>++>O+<>++<

At the first I'd found him watching as I tried to shell a coconut on a steel bar set vertically into the ground near my *pensione*. I'd assumed I could quarter the husk like an orange rind, working pole to pole; this was awkward. As I stopped to rethink the process, I noticed Ke-Ke standing twenty feet away. An inch or two short of cousin Dany's 6'2", he had that relaxed slouch that looks good on lean, square-shouldered men; and his aquiline face was a darker, drop-dead look-alike for a boyhood friend of mine who could also laugh with just his eyes.

After a moment's mutual study, Ke-Ke said softly "You have...open coconut, that way, before?"

Which was, I realized, an infinitely gentle way of suggesting it was impossible.

"Absolutely not."

"I can show you?"

"Please."

So he did. An hour later, I noticed him flushing the engine of a lavender and pink speed boat which hung, for reasons beyond me, in a timber and rope sling set above the water twenty feet off the beach. I'd wondered then: Are those rod holders on the gunwales?

⊱┈⊰┈◯┈⊱┈⊰

Now Ke-Ke cruises up in the *pirogue*, smiling as we wade out. He speaks French to Dany, who turns to me— "You know Ke-Ke already, eh? So come, call your Lisa. We will go to the reef, to where they feed sharks."

The reef: as atolls go, Bora Bora is younger than, say, Rangiroa, older than Moorea or Tahiti. Which means the volcano that forms it has not yet sunk back into the sea, but the surrounding lagoon is mature, a mile or more offshore. Although this barrier is fissured in many places and cut deeply by a pass, the lake it creates is a distinct environment. A mile beyond and the blue waters are 10,000 feet deep.

Reef conditions today are tough for a novice flycaster, with winds gusting to 15 knots and the coral of a snatch-and-grab species with antlers, fingers and other gnarly protrusions. But Dany's game, so intent on playing through his fantasy that I soon leave him to it while Ke-Ke and I wander down the reef. We stop beside deeper water with a floor studded by giant coral heads and gray lava boulders. "Good for *tarau*," Ke-Ke says, then declines my offer of a lesson in order to watch. While stringing a Scott nine-weight, I ask about his speedboat. The mention provokes a smile.

"Yes; my *puti marara*. Flying fish boat. Before, they make like this for catching the flying fish. At night, out there." He points to the open ocean. "In the air to catch them, with nets."

"That's what you do?"

"No, no more. Now I spear the *mahi-mahi*. You know *mahi-mahi*?"

"You spear them?"

He laughs at the incredulity in my voice. "Yes. I...how you say? In the boat, I look for them."

"Chase them."

"Chase, yes, In the waves outside. I sell to hotels."

"But *mahi-mahi*....they are very fast."

He grins. "Very. But my boat, also, very fast. Very *very*." Suddenly, he looks embarrassed by his pride. "And you? You can really catch the *tarau*, with the flying fishing rod?"

I can. In fact, I soon decided the little groupers are Bora Bora's equivalent to oversized bluegill: I take two on a bead-eyed woolly bugger, lose that fly to coral antlers, then on a whim tie on a peculiar commercial lure consisting of a grizzly hackle stem sandwiched between layers of plastic—a "Frisky Fly." It has a wobbling action something like a Lazy Ike plug, and, I discover, a just-heavier than neutral density that lets me control it well in the reef's irregular structure. With a longer throw, I drop it down a dark hole amidst the aqua sea, see a blur of black dart forward, set the hook by sight. The foot-long *roi* comes quickly to hand—Ke-Ke's delighted. His appreciation grows when a I take a big *tarau* two casts later, then another large *roi*. "So good, the flying fishing!"

From down Dany's way we hear a shout. Nobody runs on razor-edged reef, so by the time we reach him he's looped in so much flyline he looks like a loosely wrapped package. But at the end of his rod tip hangs a *tarau*.

"I have *done* it! I am a flying fisher!"

><+>-○-<+><

The sharks ease in minutes later, three and four foot black-tips nosing about the shallows. "Not to worry," Dany insists, but we both step up to higher coral platforms. I tease a small one close up with a pink streamer—"Not to worry," I tell Dany—then shoot its picture with a throw-away camera. Ten minutes later I land a little *tarau*, lean over and see—upside down and between my legs—a black-tip boil at the drop-off ten inches behind my heel.

"Jesus H!"

Dany laughs. "*Now*, to worry," he says. Then, to Ke-Ke "This is the best, man! Tomorrow, you try. We get David Nakomo, eh? We will practice on the beach."

Thus begins the Bora Bora Flying Fishing Club.

><+>-○-<+><

Our *pensione* cabana has no desk, so late that evening I tie flies at one of the common tables outside, attended there by a trio of Swiss intellectuals wearing Nietzche's old face, and a middle-aged French couple with no English. The lady of the latter pair murmurs appreciation for a tinsel streamer, gold bodied, with wings of iridescent Crystal Flash and royal blue marabou; so I insist she keep it. Next morning, Lisa rushes back from the communal kitchen holding a key. "You'll never guess what happened—Nir, the desk clerk, says these French people left us a key to their motor scooter. Nir swears that French people *never* do this."

So we take a long scoot around the island before diving SCUBA with leopard rays and a Manta. The devil fish looks like a vast gray bird flying slow motion, silvered by light around the head; the great eye seems sentient. Lisa picks up a remora escort on her thigh. "He sort of, *held* me with his forehead. Like a kiss."

"Let me try," I suggest, and she punches me. Whenever Lisa turns that color I get punched.

⊱⊱─◦─⊰⊰

At five o'clock, Dany picks us up in the Land Rover; we meet David Nakomo on the beach near the hotel where he's a manager. Nakomo owns the only fly rod on the island, a Sage equipped with an old Pflueger 578—big brother to the 577 I've brought. An American raised in Hawaii, a fervent, finesse-spin fisher, Nakomo has taken to flies to try for the bonefish he often catches on octopus baits. So far, a bone on fly has eluded him; but all over the island, I will find, people associate him with his quest. "David, you have met him?" they will ask, waving an arm to mimic casting. "One day he will catch *io io* this way."

Ke-Ke joins David and Dany, as does Tommie Thomson, an American tourist from our *pensione*. I spread out amongst them the three rigs I've brought. Instruction proceeds after my caveat—I'm a notoriously ugly caster—and continues while Lisa and Tea (*Tay-a*), Dany's girlfriend, play in the sand with Tea's happy rottweiler pup, and last light settles on the yacht moored offshore, lingering a moment on the mast.

⊱⊱─◦─⊰⊰

That night I have an after dinner dinner at Ke-Ke's house across the road from our *pensione*, just beyond the long lawn where we'd met over coconut. Dany's there also, along with two more cousins and Ke-Ke's smallest daughter, Keli. I've brought over tackle and four boxes of flies. Ke-Ke produces the flyfishing magazines David Nakomo lends out when he's done.

Intent fishermen all, they examine everything, ask myriad questions. Ke-Ke, who with his father, Azim, are renowned makers of resin marlin flies, recognizes materials he has used or would like to. He especially admires the Chris Rae pin knot binding fly-line to leader. Dany's captivated by a shrimp tie, studying it minutely even as he translates a cousin's query about river currents—how do these affect fish?

Intent, yes; but in those hours there's much time to laugh. Polynesians love humor, especially a kind in which a huge lie is told straight-faced. It comes my turn to play.

"These fishes," Dany says, pointing to side-by-side photos of a Chinook salmon pair spawning in shallows with their backs exposed and a close-up of the buck's toothy and grotesquely hooked jaw. "You have taken these, flying fishing?"

"Yes."

"How big?"

"To twenty kilos."

"No way!"

"Yes," I insist with legitimate conviction. Then I carefully explain how these magnificent animals may migrate a thousand miles upstream, to the waters of their birth; how the hen salmon fans a nest with her tail while bucks hang behind the redd, ferociously defending against intruders; how these males will sometimes dash out of water to attack pedestrians…One of them, I report gravely, had eaten my dog, Spot.

Bora Boran's love their dogs. "No way," Dany breathed.

I nod once, point to the picture of the buck's mouth. Dany relays the horrible news to the French-speaking cousins. A long silence, then murmurs of awe and regret. I pass a hand down my face, then catch sight of Ke-Ke. The man who smiles with his eyes is reading mine.

"*No,*" he says suddenly.

"What?" demands Dany.

Ke-Ke's laughing now. "Never eat his dog!"

"No," I confess, and the laughter rings around. Dany shakes his head, speaks earnestly to the cousins in French. Then to me, he explains, "I am telling them, man, that we must watch you close, eh? That you look like a European, but you have Polynesian *heart.*"

Later, Ke-Ke catches me at the door as I leave. "Tomorrow, maybe the sea is not good, but you come out in my *puti marara*? We go for *mahi-mahi*, bonito. You bring the flying fishing rod, yes?"

The lavender and pink of Ke-Ke's speedboat are vivid even by early light. A boat's bright colors are as important as symbols, I will come to believe, as is the paralyzer point harpoon to the practice of this unique fishing: on Bora Bora, wheeled vehicles are seen mostly as transport— it's a man's boat that means something. None shares the reputation of a *puti marara.*

Deep-V hulled—as deep as the reef passages allow—made on-island from standard plywood—thus they must hang to dry in their slings— these craft are low slung, built for speed, 18-feet long or less. *Big,* solo outboards controlled by a joystick built into the bow. Inches aft of this stick is a "box" where the solo fisher stands braced for the chase. Behind that, where I will stand, it's open compartment clear back to the engine. Bare boats, these—no radio, no flares, no lifejackets. *Puti marara* fishers are "crazy," islanders say, always young. Cowboys. *Wild things.*

<hr>

The trip begins smoothly enough: as we fuel at a dock, Ke-Ke admires the action of an Ambassadeur reel I've brought along for the ride for trolling, if that's required. Mated to a steelhead rod, it can throw a half-ounce metal spoon well into the distance; it does, and a jackfish— *caron*—slashes twice, then bolts at the approach of another flying fish boat, brand new, with one of Ke-Ke's friends aboard. I snap a photo before we head to sea.

As during all our days in Bora Bora, the lagoon rips to breezes, tiny white caps running across pale green flats. Emerald gives way to aqua near the passage, where the sea rises to swells of eight feet. "One minute only," Ke-Ke assures me. Not so—"Dolphin!" he cries.

I think he means the fish, but it's porpoise that shoot toward us, a trio of small ones, astonishingly golden. Ke-Ke backs off the engine to allow mutual investigation. For several minutes boat and bottlenose roll side by side together; then they're gone.

So, soon, are we: a thousand yards out from the reef the bottom depth drops to a mile. The swells also fall, to five feet or so—I still cling tightly to the rail behind Ke-Ke's box. Even so, my flats boots squeal for pur-chase against the painted planks while my head bobs about like a dash-board doll. "Too calm," Ke-Ke says.

"For *what?*" I demand.

He explains: the rougher the water, the less likely that *mahi mahi* will dive as we chase. "Maybe we put out rods."

Ke-Ke's pair prove to be broomstick-stiff fiberglass. One carries a Penn reel, the other a Shimano—conventional baitcasters spooled with 180 pound test monofilament. His lures range from eight to 14 inches, epoxy or poly-resin heads trailed by feathers, plastic skirts and long strands of Mylar. I help let out a line. "You too," he insists, "little rod, for bonito."

I chose the Ambassadeur steelhead outfit to begin with, troll the silver spoon. Back braced against the rail hold, feet squeaking, I have ten minutes to develop a water-ski-style technique for keeping my balance. It's important to keep my eyes on Bora Bora's cliffs several miles distant, both by way of soaking in the grandeur and to quiet a stomach sloshing in an orbit separate from my head. I'm almost comfortable when Ke-Ke shouts "*Mahi mahi!*" and turns the world over.

Literally: it's only a dozen feet from the back of the box where I stand to the engine compartment at the stern; no sweat—I can fly that far in a second. I do, crash-land, then perform half a judo roll to starboard; I reverse the *ukemi* going back to port. Then a forward flight on a diagonal to starboard as Ke-Ke floors the engine in a portside turn. "*Mahi mahi!*" Ke-Ke shouts again as I, with great dignity, rise nearly to my knees. "*Mahi mahi!*" Ke-Ke shouts once more, and I dive headlong toward the box—sort of a dive, kind of swannish, though my honking's more goose-like. I try an upward half-gainer to my feet, then a forward foot slip back to the knees—

—as Ke-Ke will tell cousins later, "I know he still in the boat by sound of so much banging"—

—then I squat thrust toward the sky to catch a mental snapshot well worth the bruises.

Ke-Ke, naked from the waist, leans forward to the sea, left hand on the joystick as the right cocks high his harpoon, holding there to align tines of steel on the rainbow of fish planing broadside just below us. A dorsal fin throws spray as fish and boat hold fast to a parallel trajectory until the harpoon drives *down* even as the fish veers away and the harpoon line tightens for an instant, goes slack.

Ke-Ke slows the boat. "I miss," he says evenly. "One point only. He lives; he is gone."

The fish, yes. But never that moment in my mind.

"So, we see *mahi mahi*. That is good." He laughs softly. "I am so sorry, you know, about the ride. You okay, yes?"

He means the inquiry; he's concerned; so I smile. "I am half dead and very happy."

>—+—‹›—O—‹›+—‹

The world re-orders. By comparison to our chase, rocking to swells is a nap. Ke-Ke and I talk birds, cormorants, petrel and terns—what their presence suggests about the world of fish in the waves. Bonito break water behind us; we troll again. The toss-about has broken the tip-top of my steelhead rod—not a problem to fix, but I must tuck it away for the moment. We hook a *mahi mahi* on one of the big outfits. As Ke-Ke jumps from the box to play him, we see two other bull dolphin-fish following the hooked one. In a scene only wilder than the first tumble-race I pass Ke-Ke the spear, take from him the fighting rod, hold to that with one hand as I try with the other to clear the second line. Ke-Ke stabs the hooked bull, flings it into the boat. Four feet long and thrashing, it sprays blood across the deck. Ke-Ke slips in this as he hurls at a following fish. I catch him with my body, arms still full of rods; we fall together and that whomping sound is the boated *mahi mahi* splintering plywood around the engine compartment.

>—+—‹›—O—‹›+—‹

"Ke-Ke?" I ask, as we clear the tangled tackle, "is it always so crazy as this?"

He shakes his head, hands me a rod and leaps back into the box. "Oh no," he says softly. "Usually, I am alone. Then"—he hunts for the word—"is worst."

>—+—‹›—O—‹›+—‹

The pace slows for an hour. Ke-Ke suggests I try the fly rod for bonito. I do, but casting in the pitch and roll is like fishing drunk during an earthquake. The best I can manage is a swing and troll tactic, which quickly puts me into a fish. The nine-weight rod doubles over—bonito are brutal, tenacious and quick; this is a big one. Ke-Ke's infinitely amused by the light tackle battle, laughing as he brings the fish aboard; so when I immediately hook-up another I insist that he fight it out of the box. My turn to grin as it drags him about, making his bare feet scramble and veins pop out in his forearms. After the second such fight, he groans. "Flying fishing...so hard work."

Then comes the beast.

><+>·O·<+<

The frigate finds it for us. Ke-Ke points it out drifting hundreds of feet above: "Marlin bird," he says softly. "Always, that bird follow marlin. Always, alone." He edges the boat around to match its course.

We wait, the boat rocking almost at idle. Bonito begin to boil at 2 o'clock amidst the sparks of baitfish fleeing to the surface, corralled there against the barrier of air. Terns scream and a hundred feet to port the sea erupts in a blue and white gash.

"You see?" hisses Ke-Ke. "You see him?"

I am staring at a fractured swell, remains of a rise bigger than my living room.

"Big fish," Ke-Ke continues in a whisper. "*Very* big."

We rig a trolling lure on one rod, one of my bonito as bait on the other. The frigate still hangs overhead. Suddenly the bonito boils are all around—it's a circus of birds and fish stabbing from above and below until suddenly I see Ke-Ke's head snap back, and I realize that a table has turned underneath—the bonito now *flee*—and the marlin rushes up six feet off the bow.

Six feet away and its back is four feet across, its bill as long as a broadsword—a blue-gray animal of such size and seeming strength that my concept of "fish" cannot contain it, and I realize that the voice I hear shouting is mine.

><+>·O·<+<

Ke-Ke's certain he's never seen one so large. He puts its length at 20 feet and its weight at a 1000 kilos—longer than the boat, perhaps half again its weight.

For three hours we try to troll up the marlin, the first of these a silent blend of excitement and fear. Ke-Ke opens this up with a smile. "Fish of my life," he says. Then, even more softly, "This fish...he can break my *puti marara*."

"I was wondering about that."

"Maybe, if he eats, we do not go so close." Ke-Ke points out to sea several hundred yards away, then to the Penn reel with a half mile of line.

"I vote for that," I say, and Ke-Ke laughs.

"Maybe, he eat, and we wait. He dies—*comment dit-on mourir natu-rellement?*"

"A 'natural' death. Right, absolutely. Or we figure out how to poison its food—bonito *toxique*."

Ke-Ke laughs and laughs. We never see the marlin again.

>─┼─◆─○─◆─┼─<

Ke-Ke insists that I keep all the bonito, so that night Lisa sets a fish fry for the guests at our *pensione*. A German tourist sighs at the invitation and shakes her head. "Only Americans would think to do this." She brings a big bowl of potato salad; a new French couple make rice; the depressed Swiss offer their coffee; and the vacationing chef from Tahiti Airport makes a dessert of bananas *flambeau*. Dany stops by to arrange a flycasting session on the beach for the next evening. We ask him about the Polynesian dancing at the hotel nearby. "Oh yes, go. It is very special. Then, three nights from now, Tea and I carry you to see the islander's own dance contest, for Bastille Day. Different, I think. Also special."

As he speaks I notice a mischievous glint in his eyes.

The hotel dancing is...pleasant. Eight enormous women—seven middle-aged smile and sway to the plinking of one ukulele, one gui-tar. It's nearly aerobic. "Special," I am coming to understand, has as many meanings as the context in which it is spoken.

>─┼─◆─○─◆─┼─<

The next day Ke-Ke takes me as crew for a lagoon tour he must do with the *pirogue* outrigger: shark-feeding, a drift in current to skin dive coral, a spectacular meal of *mahi mahi*, two roots and six fruits on an island *motu*; then Ke-Ke off-loads the tourists in waist deep water as he, with cutting horse moves of the *pirogue*, herds toward us a stingray the size of a Cadillac hood. I drift above the ray, take its picture from three feet above, then two feet, then less—current has moved the two of us onto a sand flat so shallow that I suck up belly for fear of its spine.

>─┼─◆─○─◆─┼─<

Bastille Day lasts two months in Polynesia. Acres of Vitape are com-mitted to booths into which families weave these forests of fauna, botanical gardens from which they serve food or set up Wheels of Fortune with grand prizes of bicycles or fifty-kilo bags of rice. Dany and Tea take us to one of the flowering restaurants where we eat a pale variety of Chinese cuisine. What the food lacks in spice the meal makes up in smiles, greetings, drinks sent over... Moving through Bora Boran society with these hosts, we have found, is like keeping company with accessible royalty. Tea would turn heads in any part of the world where women consider fashion and men contemplate the beauty of women. She teaches three-year-olds to read and sing songs about conserving Bora Bora's ocean; she's also the island's most photographed model for postcards and calendars. Dany is merely some sort of collection point for good will: anyone who isn't a relative is just a best friend. Between all the hand shakes, hugs and laughing conversation, a promenade through the crowd—say two blocks—takes slightly less time than climbing K-2. Eventually, we approach the dance ground. "You remember," says Tea, in the fluted tones of her speaking voice, "the hotel dancing? This is just the same."

Lisa and I nod. Dany holds the straight face only seconds, then roars with laughter. "Just the same," he swears.

It's a white sand arena of a thousand square yards lighted by scores of smoking torches. The music begins. Dany pushes us up next to the dozen drummers and the albino beside me begins to beat his hands pink on the drumhead skin, shuddering my guts even as the transvestite troupe leader swirls his/her hibiscus bark skirt and raises a scepter so that two hundred dancers begin as one to simulate sex at 78 rpm, sweat on their bodies glistening in the flames as I wipe my own eyes and try to fathom or contain the sensory overload of sight and sound and smoke smell as Dany, laughing, grabs my shoulder and shouts "Special!" and I nod once to him, then again to the sudden image—the last time I sensed such power—of a marlin spearing up through the sea.

Urban Guerrilla Angling

Fishing in Hell might look like Albany dump at midnight, those years when they filled and burned a long peninsula out into the Bay. Vents of smoke would hiss out from tangles of rebar and broken concrete while rats moved darkly, squabbling with each other and with gulls for the rights to tear at cellophane wrappers and the rest of society's rind.

We wanted an outgoing tide. For that we'd risk the mile hike from the racecourse parking lot, long rods swinging and plugs rattling in a pouch as we picked our way farther out onto the peninsula of fill; that's when the anchovies would draw down off the mudflats, pulling back from grey shallows as humps of lost tires broke through like photos of Loch Ness. We could see the schools gathering sometimes, scattering light from halogen lamps on the petro-pier across the cove. These images mingled with reflections of pier fence, meshed steel and coiled razor wire.

Then we'd hear them—not the baitfish, but hunting splashes of stripers in a channel offshore. The anchovy hordes ran a gauntlet that hundreds of their thousands would not survive. Big as men, the pounding bass sounded. Our signal.

⊱─◈─○─◈─⊰

Not an easy beat to wade, especially with the tidal wash dragging at Red Ball waders patched solid to the knees. I remembered dropoffs only as my front foot failed to find purchase—panicking, then, falling back because it was better to splash down into known territory behind me. But wade we would, to make our casts count, put the plugs out to where our prey waited for theirs.

Futile efforts, more nights than not. Stripers were already dying out in the Bay, millions of their young sucked into pumps of Pacific Gas and Electric upstream in the delta. That was even before Fish and Game warned us away from eating striper flesh, tainted with heavy metal.

So then, never great fishing—one bass a night for two of us, if we were lucky. If not, we still had slack tide in which to drift cut-bait, maybe tentacles of squid on a slip-sinking rig. A leopard shark or ray was inevitable; there were other possibilities. Twice I was spooled here by fish I'll never identify (soupfin shark? sturgeon?), mysteries that left me gasping, actually frightened by a speed and sense of enormity beyond any other I've felt through a rod. Better than three hundred yards, took one of those fish, without ever slowing or turning his head.

Hellish, maybe, but ours alone. Mine alone, sometimes, during those years I worked p.m. shifts in a psychiatric hospital, leading a restraint team. I clocked out at 11:15 and would arrive at the race lot half an hour later. Often I'd still be riding my own tides, the swell and ebb of adrenaline rush and caffeine shakes muted by shots of cheap whiskey as I walked. Better to cast off my nerves at the dump than bring them home to sleeping children. Better to cast at the moon than lay beside their mother.

I left her about the same time as my last trip to the dump. A fruitless quest: well into a new day I took the trail back toward my car. I heard men before I saw them limned against the sky. They carried rods, so I relaxed. And tensed again, startled, when I recognized their dress as we met on a rise.

Gang "colors." Or the costumes of "wannabees," who are worse, having so much to prove. A thousand yards out onto the spit, bridge traffic coursing toward Treasure Island beyond, San Francisco lost in mist and no one within earshot of an explosion.

"Hey man, you catch somethin'? Whatch you catch?"

I stopped, waited, shook my head. There were three of them, laden with buckets and rods, surf stakes, paper bags. The middle-sized one had asked. "Nothing tonight," I answered.

"Nothin'? Whatch you mean 'nothin'? Whatch you fishin' for? What kinda bait?"

"Plugging for stripers."

"Yeah—lemme see that thing…no bait? We got bait—what we got, nigger?"

"'Chovies," said the smaller one. "Squid."

"We got worms?"

The biggest one, silent until now, snorted and shook his head. "Shee-it, man, ain't got no *worms*." Then, to me, "You know how big fish gets out here? You know how big?"

"Pretty big."

"Uh-huh…Man, I hook me a sturgeon out here 'bout like this." He put down his bucket to measure six feet between his hands. "You believe me?"

"I know they're there."

"Tha's right. Took me a *hour*. I get him up to those rocks. He come up and lay there, look at me with his *eye*. You know how they *eye* look? Little eye—mean fuckin' eye…He look at me an' I know. I *know*. So what I do?"

The big one looked to his quiet companions—they knew—then to me. "I shoot that mutha-fucker. Hell-yes. I shoot him *again*. I shoot that mother-fucker *seven times* wif a nine millimeter. You know what? He *don' die*. Mutha-fucker *don' die*, break off. Whatch you think 'bout that?"

I laughed. His companions glared at me, but the image of the sturgeon staring as this man shot him…so much for catch-and release.

The big guy laughed also, after a moment. Long, loudly. "Tha's right," he said. "Tha's *right*. You believe me. See niggers? He knows. So tonight, what I do, I come ready. Oh yes—I got three fuckin' clips. I gonna shoot out that fucker's little eye, I am, tonight."

He shook his head, grinned. "Le's go, niggers. Hey, man…Man? You have a nice night."

"Thanks. Good luck."

"Thanks. You too, you too."

⇒·┼·◆›·•·O·•·‹◆·┼·◄

I went to live with a cop who'd separated-to-divorce two weeks before. We fit his stripped bungalow well and, in one of those partnerships AA deplores, toasted our misled lives every evening. It was the absence of sleeping children that opened holes.

"Popeye," the other cops called him, not for the movie role, but because of his arms. He was just what you wanted in a peace officer;

big enough to body-slam a bad guy, sane enough not to if given a choice.

"You fish, don't you?" he asked me one night. On the way to the lake he swore me to secrecy.

Inland, a short cast from a freeway, the lake had been part of his beat for a decade. People avoided the place after sunset because of the bodies found there. Killed elsewhere, as a rule, Popeye insisted, by drug dealers and pimps; but he carried a .38 for the minutes we'd spend launching his raft. "Mostly it's just gays here at night, cruisers. You'll see them by the boathouse unless it rains." See them we did, then and in the years that followed, men approaching each other in silence, moving away together into trees or to cars. AIDS was already endemic; these fellows seemed to me as insubstantial as shadows, wraiths. "A system," said Popeye. "They have signs. Used to be scarves and keys and whatever. Now, I don't know."

It wasn't these cruisers for which Popeye loaded, however, but for those who hunted them. The gays were easy marks for robbers, and worse. "Sport, that's what it is. Guys come out just to hurt them. That's weirder than what the gays do, if you ask me. Let 'em live, let 'em die; leave them alone...Come on, let's catch fish."

⋗┄◆⋗┄○┄◁┄◆┄◁

And we would, though even Popeye had no idea about how the stripers first came into this place, or how long they had been there. All he knew was that every year they grew bigger and fewer, and that a nine-inch, broken-back Rebel would take them.

⋗┄◆⋗┄○┄◁┄◆┄◁

Astonishing, how the world around us would fade on that little lake, contract to black water and low bank even as a thousand cars an hour rushed past, their lights and the city's obscuring stars. A perpetual plume of steam from a factory nearby looked soft and cloudlike, lazy; night herons, stoop-shouldered and solitary, stood guard on docks as we passed; migrant ducks in flocks—scores, sometimes—edged away from our approach, leaving webs of intersecting wakes.

Sanctuary. To the lap of water against inflated chambers and the hum of motor we'd talk of kids and cops, of the mad and criminal "clients" Popeye and I shared. It amused us that I had no tolerance for his "thugs," and that my "lunatics" gave him willies.

Then we would lapse into silence, hands listening to the thrum of our lures along the rods.

Thisssst—the line would hiss off the water as a striper came up—always the same way—to take a plug in its jaws, breach clear of the surface and crash down like a three-meter diver. The raft would jerk back or snap around—"Jeezuz!" we'd shout, no matter how many times we'd hooked up before. One of us would scramble to cut the motor, then there'd come another crashing splash as the striper began a run which could drag us two hundred feet. "Jeezus!"—fish from seven pounds to three times that, battles of ten minutes or twenty. "Feel this! Feel this one!" one of us would say, passing over the rod. "Can you believe it? Wait a minute—is that a buoy? Look out now—"

⊱──⊰◦⊱──⊰

Releasing was difficult. A desperate striper of size will play havoc in a rubber raft, or even alongside; so we took to cutting back treble hooks to doubles, then to crushing the barbs…I remember trolling into dawn once, hunched up in wool like a warm worm, so quiet with exhaustion I was entirely happy.

⊱──⊰◦⊱──⊰

I moved into a place of my own so Popeye could keep his kids on the weekend. We still met at the lake. Steve joined us, my fishing partner of a decade, then a cop friend of Popeye's. We'd plug from shore, take turns with the raft until Steve and I spent $50 on the shell of a Sunfish sailboat, refitted the teak, relaid fiberglass.

And sometimes I'd fish there alone. On a whim, almost, after the late news.

"Careful," cautioned Popeye.

"Why? Why do you do it?" asked a new girlfriend. I neither knew the answer nor felt a need to question myself.

"Is it a thrill thing? Because you know you can get hurt there."

⊱──⊰◦⊱──⊰

True enough. On shore, this was not safe. The moon saved me one night, illuminating a man stalking me tree-to-tree. Little valor in my discretion then.

I returned again, not so lucky.

A dock extended a deep-water drop-off where Popeye and I had hooked fish from his raft. Too close to the place of gay liaisons, too well lit and exposed, I chanced it anyway.

"I want a fuckin' beer!" shouted the man as his boots hit planks behind me. Not tall, hard to say how heavy in his coat. I turned and, with my left hand, dropped the rod down between us, to let hang there the gang-hooked plug.

"You hear me, cocksucker?"

In my right-hand jacket pocket the steel of protection felt reassuringly cold. It lent me calm as he came toward me walking fast.

Perhaps he'd taken me for a cruiser, timid and easy. Perhaps he'd already had a beer too many; I think the light served me better than him. In either case, he seemed not to notice the rod and lure until I gave a shake as he closed, hooks just a yard in front of his eyes. He stopped suddenly, confused, then determined again.

"I said—"

"The waitress won't be out for a while."

It's like a nervous tick of mine, to make cracks like that. Fight, flight or quip. The habit disconcerts some; I could see him pause to inflate his frame. "Uh-huh…You think that's funny. I want money, funny guy." Then, as if the nature of his desire would be important to me, "For a beer."

That made him an amateur—no question now. If he was unarmed, then I need never thumb back the hammer. "Good luck," I said.

He stood silent for a moment while contemplating this stand-off. I saw his shoulders relax, then shrug. I kept the plug at level with his eyes.

Suddenly he laughed. And he was rueful when he spoke—"You're not going to give it to me, are you?"

I said nothing. He took a slow step back, another, then stopped. With a wide sweep of his arm he encompassed the lake, the freeway, the gay zone, even the plume of steam from the factory beyond. "Man…what the *hell* are you doing here?"

>—+—+>—0—<+—+—<

I don't remember that I said anything at all, but the question I'd ignored from others was oddly compelling from a bully-boy's mouth. "Taking what's mine," was the answer that rang in my head. Onto that I would embroider rationales and explanations, answers including my need to seek the feel of a striper coming up, the sound of waves and the sight of night herons hunched at attention. I needed these edges, of earth and land, city jungle and untamed world, extremes of solitude and companionship, solace and excitement. I needed the taut hope of a cast.

Taking what's mine and risking a little, like anchovies on the flats and a striper in the channel. Mine is the adventure, risk and pleasure as basic as hunger or the precarious urge of gay cruisers in the dark. Take nurture and nature where you find it until there's a jaw in the dark or hooks in a plug. Sometimes there's release and sometimes it ends with seven slugs. I won't defend the wisdom, but at times I still gamble the night while my children sleep.

Throwing Dace

I cut the engine and let the truck roll into a back slot of a camp-ground too overgrown for the RVs already parked. Beyond the wil-lows I had a lake view—or river, depending on where the current slowed enough to make a call on this long arm of Lake Shasta from its tributary McCloud. I set camp with a pull of the handbrake, then sat until the dust settled. After six hours on Interstate 5, I'd lost the smell of bay but not the bad taste of leaving, adding to that the sour tailings of caffeine and a crumbling cigarette from the glove box.

No question, but I'd rig the long rod, the cheap English fly with fiberglass enough to lend mercy to its graphite backbone. Weighs as much a baseball, I think, which might be why I wanted it; to weary me. I clipped off a Kispiox, tied on the biggest dace in my box, then shrugged into chest waders for a walk down the shoreline.

>-!-<>-O-<>-!-<

An old man had leveled his trailer before the gate to the path, colo-nizing a space with lawnchairs and a clothesline. I found him standing in the center of this domain staring off into some middle distance. I could not pass without disturbing his thoughts, so I waited at what I guessed was the edge of his attention.

He was so old. I know almost nothing about men so old. No man in my small family has survived his 65th year, and this fellow celebrated that age before I learned to shave, maybe before I wrote my name. His stoop seemed worn into him—the gnarling of a cypress grown vast around a stone. Though I longed to feel the rod loading in my hands, I was fascinated by his stillness, by his focus on some interior vision. I'll never reach his age. I doubt I'll ever stand so still.

He turned at last, slowly, all of a piece, to regard me from tiny eyes. "So we're off!" he said brightly. "Fishing the dusk! Double-haul a big rod like that one—I never learned how! Good luck to you, young man."

It seemed such a vehement outburst, so pleasantly intended. "Thank you, sir."

"My pleasure."

I hesitated a moment.

"Would you like a trout, if I'm lucky?"

He shook his head. "Like a trout? Like one? No one's caught trout in three days! North wind, south wind, hell. My boys fish with marshmallows and this floating pink crap." He shook his head again, then continued more softly. "There's shad schools out there, for the long cast, for somebody who'll wade out…Son, I'd sure love a trout."

⤞⊶⊙⊷⤝

It's a rocky shore for three hundred yards beyond the gate, but as the canyon bends the bank softens to mud. Still looks steep, yet most years a spit leads well out. *Well* out; I waded until another step would wet my suspender snaps.

This is a weight forward game, big water, deep and faceless save for reflected images of slate cliff and sun. Leave your tapers, your 7X tippet, that fine motor control that wraps the Cahill or dampens a dry so the circle turns. Bring gross motions, pitching muscles, the laterals left over from splitting wood and hacking out the mulberry root. Bring what's left of your back and expect it to hurt you.

Because there's shad out there sometimes, ten thousand butter-knife bodies rising to compulsions of their myriad mind, to spasms of fear for cormorant or grebe or a wolfpack of gape-mouthed bass rushing up from darker green. It's seldom the shad you see—maybe a smear of silver—but the predators that mark their hunt with sudden swirls and angled splashes, wakes of dorsals silvering a sunset mirror. Moving, moving—you've got to keep watch.

Shad and smallmouths and rainbows come up when the temperature suits them, and once in a while a great brown trout like the one that cost me a steak dinner two years back, when I bet twenty-three inches to a partner who'd said twenty. We went over or under my number, and I lost at 22 and as many eighths as wouldn't finish the inch. Jesus—his fish, too.

I smiled at the memory while snaking out a dozen feet of line, then a dozen more. The dace soaked reluctantly. When it began to sink I plucked it up and laid it out.

Pickaxe casting: up, back—keep it tight—forward. Try not to work too hard or grunt aloud if you do; hauling has another meaning with ten feet of soft rod. I worked blind for a few minutes, pulling for rhythm, then a smallmouth broke water fifty feet down the shore, and I surprised both of us with a good wye. He dove once but came up again and again until he was practically on top of me, gills flaring as I thumbed back his lip. Fast work. He was a pound, maybe.

The next was twice that and his last leap cleared my head, deep as I'd waded. He was fierce and angry; he roughed up my tippet. By the time I retied, I had light left for a half-dozen casts.

I used three, lengthening line for the longest throw of the day. The exertion pumped out of me a hard thought about a woman, then only slack saved the leader as the brown set himself and took the dace toward a far shore. Water shook off the line when he rose to my right, thrashed. Five times he ran. Twice I heard the lacquered backing knot click through my guides.

When I beached him I knew I would not lose my steak betting twenty-three inches or even twenty-five. Brassy, brightly splashed and deep as a salmon, he was such a fish that my pride embarrassed me. I determined to release him without risking his gills to the scale. Then I remembered the old man.

⤚•⟡•○•⟡•⤙

"Seven pounds seven. Maybe seven pounds ten," he said softly. His fingers were resting on the brown's side, brushing every so often against the drying scales. The big hands trembled a little except when in motion; then they looked certain and confident. By the time he'd done drawing his knife down the steel, a surgeon might admire its edge.

"Look at the colors," he murmured. "Perfect fins. What a fish."

He stood at the counter while I sat at the trailer's Formica dinette and his wife, Millie, busied herself in the back. "She's an amazing woman," he'd said when he introduced her. "Astounding, really. A child bride when I married her, as you can plainly see. And if you believe your luck," he winked "she *happens to have a sister.*"

"Ethan!" she snorted.

"Who has a *daughter.*"

"That's more like it."

"Who has a *niece—*"

"That's quite far enough, thank you . Nice to meet you, young man. Since this old one won't let me touch that fish, and since the mob will be over here soon, I'll just retreat to Agatha Christie while I have the chance. If you don't mind."

That left us with the brown, which now Ethan touched with the tip of his knife. "Like to do honors?" When I shook my head he seemed to drop the blade into the fish, pausing only as he turned his wrist to slice through the ribs. In a moment he held up a great pink slab, showed me one side, then the other. "Trout of a lifetime," he murmured.

It's a pleasing thing, I remembered, to see such appreciation.

After a sidelong glance down the trailer aisle he winked again, thumbed open a cabinet and slid out a fifth of Jim Beam. When he held up a glass I nodded and we drank an inch in silence. He filled me again, himself a half, then smiled. "A long cast?" I nodded. "Ah-hah. And if you'd waded any deeper, you'd be wetting the seat?"

"That's about it."

He clinked his drink against mine.

"My pleasure," I said.

We sat another minute in comfortable silence. Suddenly, in a softer rush of enthusiasm, he said "*Do you have any idea how old I am now?*"

There was wonder in his voice, and incredulity, and invitation, as if we'd soon share a great surprise together. "No? I am 83 years old! Can you believe that?"

I shook my head.

"Neither can I!"

I laughed. He did too, then we both shrugged together and his face lit in an expression of such gentle confusion that I thought he might hurt, that he'd swallowed wrong or felt something twist inside him. "And Christ, can you believe it? I'm *finally* dying!"

➤—◆—O—◆—◄

I could have felt betrayed, I suppose. I'd only brought him a trout, we'd shared a drink, and that was all. But there was nothing intrusive about the way he made his announcement, no demand, no plea. It was enough that I look down an instant to acknowledge what this meant.

"Sorry," he said unnecessarily. "But in this campground are four of my children. Three you'll meet, all older than you. The second boy," he tapped his chest, "lives only in here."

He stopped as suddenly as he'd started, then stared at me a long moment. "Son, your dad's dead, isn't he?"

It had happened before, when he said he'd like a trout: the word "son" resonates in me like thunder in a tympani. Now he'd put the word together with my father's death. The rod loaded.

"Yes, I can see that. But that's just *it*, do you see? None of my children have lost that something. Grown up now, with children of their own soon growing children, but they've never lost a mother or me."

Because he had never died.

I declined the dinner offer but agreed to stop in at their family campfire for another shot later on. So I did, after enjoying canned chile with enough catsup and Tabasco to make it sing on my palette. I had a discouraging moment when I tried to recall the last time I had a meal just the way I liked it, then tried to imagine such silly pleasure wasn't really self pity.

The oldest son looked like one, solid and stolid, with the neck of a fair-sized Charolais. After "good fish you caught there" he ambled off to distract a wailing child. His blousy wife was tending another, while a too-pretty teenage daughter, bored and morose, looked on. Another of Ethan's sons—the third, he could only be—sat across the fire, looking dazed as he sucked the last Bud Light of a troop he'd mustered about him. "Ethan Junior," the old man observed, "just divorced." The only daughter had Millie's humor and the old man's hands: she gave her adolescent son a Dutch rub when he moaned about pot duty, then sent him off laughing.

It was the end of a family scene, pleasant and tired, an hour after nine people fetched dinner from a grill. Grease was soaking through paper plates as coals gave out, and an earnest yellow mongrel snuffled burnt weenies from out of the pine needles—that sort of thing. Millie and the daughter did something constructive with utensils, murmuring happily across a basin of suds.

"Angina," said old Ethan shortly, with a tap at his chest. "Or reflux, I don't know. Esophageal, now *there's* a word. I learned Latin when Teddy Roosevelt went to war, just so I can pronounce the names of what hurts me today. 'Heart expulsion fraction' is my arithmetic. You heard of that?"

No other person seemed tuned to our conversation. "It's best to have a high one," I answered.

"Twenty-two percent, I'm at, says the doctor."

I looked at him hard. "Don't get up. You want anything, just ask."

He laughed and laughed. "'Don't get up,'" he repeated, shaking his head. "Oh my."

"Ethan?" Millie called, "Ethan?"

"What?" he barked.

She looked at him across the firelight.

You can talk about kisses, lips brushing past, write reams about passion and making the beast with two backs. But a look like Millie's, so full of warmth and an unspoken warning—"Don't yap at me, old man, my Life's Love, and I mean a lifetime"—that's *what it is*. When you've merged the separate nature of yourself with someone else's separate nature, survived together through a generation of great crises and ten thousand thoughtless barks sincerely regretted and forgiven; when you've managed half a century of appreciation—

—maybe you get a moment like they had in the firelight.

I like to hope so; I looked away. In flight my gaze fell first to the Charolais son beside his wife, then to their morose teenager watching them. Only when I stared toward dazed young Ethan could I quell a queer panic.

"That Millie, I tell you," whispered Ethan, his hand patting mine. "I've got to watch her, sometimes. *Lots* of times."

Whatever she'd wanted to say she'd said without sound.

"But I bet she'd let me go fishing tomorrow, late in the morning, after you've done the hard work."

>—◆◇◆—◇—◆◇◆—<

The hard work was shaking off Mr. Beam while snaking into cold waders. Just at dawn I raised another smallmouth, then two more. But these were small fish holding snug to shoreline boulders; I found no shad schools well out. When rising sun suggested a sinking line, I turned back toward the truck to dig out a spinning rod from beneath the spare tarp.

Millie sent us off with a wave and a warm thermos and, I thought, a long look at me when Old Ethan turned his back. Everybody else, he told me, had hiked up the McCloud.

We set lawnchairs in a rocky cleft and rolled nightcrawlers in the current on slip-sinking rigs. With the right tension I could feel the lead egg tapping, read the fall from stone slide onto mud. Each drift lasted half a dozen minutes; I suspected we'd do just as well leaving the baits hang.

Technique didn't worry Ethan Senior. His eyes wandered the water, the cliffs, the sky. I could see him breathe scents. "Ah, Jesus," he said.

Nonfishers often comment about how lovely it must be, to "sit around in nature all the time." I don't fish that way much. The truth is that most of what I notice is water. I don't understand that myself, but I did note that for Ethan it was all lovely. I also knew we were going to talk about death.

"Do you miss him?" he asked.

"Miss" missed the mark, but I wasn't sure what word would find it. "Yes."

"How? I mean, when? Every day? fishing? talking?"

I reeled in the end of a drift, examined my nightcrawler and cast. All that time and I still failed to frame the thought.

"Did you like him?"

"Yes. Very much. Yes, I did."

"Well, *that's* important."

In the Cascades I sometimes happened on "Seed Trees"—great monsters fallen to the moss in some enormous moment after centuries of silence. From their trunks spring new hosts, another generation of trees.

He was waiting. I shrugged. "When he died I thought I'd lost the last man of my tribe." I found a crevice to wedge the rod. "I thought I'd lost the last man who'd ever speak my language."

He waited. Then, "You loved him that way."

I looked up. "I really do."

>-+-◆>-O-<◆+-+-<

A breeze blew across the rocks, quivering our tip-tops. I wished for a bite and felt the sinker stop even as the line tightened against my finger. In free-spool I thrilled to the "flick-flick" of the running line. Then I walked the rod back.

He didn't argue; no, he grinned happily as he took it from me and watched loops of monofilament whisking out. "Now," he said, then he closed the bail and struck.

The fish was a stocked rainbow in its youth, as its dwarf dorsal fin witnessed. But that youth was long spent: it planed and dove with determination learned from two years of catch-and-kill life. Right up to the net it didn't believe it would lose.

We strung the fish and rebaited. "Two more and your brown, and we feed the whole family," he said, so we fished until we had them. "You'll come around tonight?"

>−+−◆>−O−<◆−+−<

I don't like to eat trout, which much amuses my friends. Too many summers working a fishing camp as a boy, fed there by a cranky cook whose imagination never ranged beyond a single fry tactic: "Throw them fishes in the breakfast grease." But Millie did something interesting with bacon, butter and lemon, which made me very happy.

It was rather a happy bunch, I noticed between bites. The kids had enjoyed exploring private land a mile or two upstream until rousted by a gamekeeper-with-Rottweiler. Charolais son looked a little sheepish about the encounter. "I mean, it's not like we were fishing," but he clearly relished his wife's praise for the way he'd handled man and beast. Even their teenage girl seemed impressed. I also saw her spending time with her Uncle Ethan Junior, who drank less for the attention. Daughter's son got another dutch rub and did the pans, laughing.

I was happy, they were happy, yet I felt the deference. There was thanks enough for my role in providing fish, but I realized all had determined that I was Old Ethan's select, reserved for his purpose. So the after-dinner conversation convinced me: once again it was as if he and I spoke only to each other.

"Your wife," he said slowly. "She doesn't fish."

I wasn't happy any more. "My wife goes to the club."

"No kids?"

"Two. Step kids: Lacey, eight, and William, seven."

"They don't fish?"

"They haven't time."

"No time?"

"They're in training at the club."

"Oh." He pursed his lips. "How long?"

"Three years. Or four, now."

"Oh."

〜

I thought that said it all, or most of it that mattered. For a long time we simply sat and watched his brood, troubled together.

〜

In the morning I waded deep and I worked the long rod very hard. I wanted nothing to do with shore fish. I kept working and wading the spit, seeing nothing in the water but pale sky. I only worked harder with the sun up, feeling sweat beneath my collar, sweat in my groin. I hauled and double hauled, loaded the rod until the line snapped at the drag. I raised nothing and thought nothing about it, taking more satisfaction at the grind in my shoulder where an old injury yanked ligament lines against my own spool. Twenty minutes, half an hour, forty minutes and I ached, so I cast harder and longer, setting my teeth as the running line fled out the guides, raging when a cast turned to slop on the water. I dragged it in, rolled it forward, flung it out again—

〜

"Look," said old Ethan.

Behind me, how long? Standing behind me, to my left on the spit. I was angry that I hadn't heard him come, but I followed his point to a big rise beyond a silver smear.

It was a long cast and a good one. The rainbow threw a rainbow, spraying quicksilver into low morning light. Once he speared up like a javelin in a low flight of startling speed. By the time I'd drawn him to my legs we were both panting.

The dace hung in his jaw. Old Ethan laughed as he stood at the shoreline. "I already ate mine," he said happily. "We fed the family. Two fish of a lifetime...I guess you'd best let that one go."

I did, then waded out to stand beside him and let adrenaline run out my limbs.

"Hell of a fish, son."

〜

That was it—the look on his face, that same glow my father had, taking more pleasure in my triumph than even his own. The generosity I saw in Old Ethan's family, coursing through generations—

"In the beginning," I said slowly, wading toward him through the mud, "they'll miss you moment-to-moment. The pain's so sharp it's fucking unbearable. Millie will be numb."

He gasped.

"Your oldest son will retreat to taking care of his children, who won't quite understand. Your daughter will mourn with her boy, explaining how it is to him, I'd guess. Your third son will feel like his whole life is sinking to hell."

"Wait."

"Then something happens. It's still pain but there's something welcome about it because it keeps the sense of you immediate, close by when the rest of you's gone so far away. That's when they'll learn to hold to memories of the way you laugh and bark, and the things you once said to them, strangers you brought to your campfire. Millie will stare away, sometimes, lost to everybody else. But that's all right because she'll thrive in the past as well as the present of the people who love her.

"Then—it happens so slowly, or it did to me—they'll stop waking as often to particular memories, to dreams. Then—it's gentle, this way; it's deep as bone—they'll feel you in the way they move in the world and sense who you are *in* them. The way your big son looks at his wife, the way their daughter tends to sad Ethan Junior. Your own girl sending her son off to scrub pots…They'll act in the world knowing you left them this piece of who you are. They'll just…*assume* you."

➤━┥━◆━○━◆━┝━◄

Millie came down the rocks to find us in silence. She poured coffee from the thermos, left quietly. Old Ethan cried a little when she was gone. "Yes," he said finally "Now I remember."

We sat a long time. I tried to focus on the rainbow, the way his body had broken up into light. When Ethan said "Thank you," I nodded. Then he stood and put his big hand on my neck.

"Son, I came down here to tell you something."

I waited

"Yes, well…I wasn't sure how to put it, but I guess what I wanted to say is that you deserve to be remembered."

I felt the same panic I had that first evening by the fire while look-ing around at his family.

"You're going to die too, pretty soon, and you deserve to live in memories. Just like you described it. You ought to teach somebody else that language you spoke with your dad."

A fish, perhaps the same rainbow, broke water way out. I nodded. He shook me a little, patted my shoulder again. I remembered my father's hand. He sighed. "Love and time, that's about all there is."

Another fish jumped, something enormous not a dozen feet out. It startled us both. I seemed to wake at the instant Ethan began to laugh.

I knew why. He was laughing at himself, for his bright desire, and because he'd felt my shoulder tense beneath his hand, wrist cocking, thumb pressing to cork. He laughed because we were helpless with the hope we might feel such a fish on our line and touch life strung tight. We would wonder at that, and still want to laugh and love a woman in the firelight.

"Cast!" he shouted.

Reading Water
on Rangiroa Reef

There's the *motu* of palms—a scrap of island, really, separated from other scraps in the lagoon by sandbars and coral heads—then a wide shelf of lava flat peppered by purple anemones and the occasional turquoise tail of grazing parrot fish. My Tahitian hosts have set a gill net for the latter, now spread out in a line for a family fish drive.

Out where I stand on the reef, waves break on the leading edge of a lava and coral plateau; foam drains away through crevasses into green water that turns emerald fifty feet out. "Stand" is probably too stalwart a word for what I do here. I teeter in flats boots, twisting for traction like a nervous batter in the box, testing uncertain firmament as waves surge up about my knees, sometimes to my groin. *Safe enough*, I conclude, the decision much influenced by the sight of dark shapes moving through curls. But while I snake out line from the 8-weight, a twist of mind turns hope and apprehension to bathos: *I think I can…Man, this isn't exactly a spring creek.*

><del> • O • </del><

Not quite. Rangiroa's an ancient atoll 4500 miles from home. The original volcano sank eons ago, leaving only a fringe of land and coral surrounding a vast lagoon. In truth, the lagoon *is* Rangiroa; the scant necklace of reef merely defines it from ocean. Life inside the lagoon and out, especially in the two deep passes between, attracts tourists to SCUBA. Today's outing is just a diversion for most, a boat ride and lunch on a little lagoon within the large one. But for me...I'd take a fly rod on a Saharan safari, in case there's a flash flood.

Pelagic fish (the *mahi-mahi*, bonito, and tuna found outside) rarely enter here, though sharks do in great numbers, along with leopard rays and mantas, perhaps even whales. Yesterday, divers spotted a baleen in Avatoru pass. I dove with the sharks there the day before that, wheezing into my respirator as we descended to 118 feet. There were black-tips sleeping in caves, white-tips and grays cruising depths still silver with sunlight, and schools of barracuda suspended like collections of swords. I touched a six-foot moray in its grotto, its green skin taut beneath my hand.

><+>+·0·+<+>+<

A loopy cast puts a Crazy Charlie beyond an incoming wave. The black shapes converge to charge the retrieve—triggerfish. They will take a fly, I learned on Bora Bora, though their tiny, toothy mouths accommodate only small hooks, size six, or better, an eight. Fun to fight, but they can hurt you, as my scarred fingers witness: those aren't fins near their vents, they're blades.

><+>+·0·+<+>+<

Over and over again the triggers attack Charlie, drawing in more of their kind. I switch to a small wooly bugger with brass-bead eyes, land one fish and release it, land another, then a pretty wrasse of some kind, pale green with a crimson stripe reminiscent of home-water rainbows.

I return the wrasse and consider. I'll take a fish every cast now, mostly triggers; but what I want today is something bigger, something different. I want a beast from beyond those curling waves, from the green water or the blue beyond that.

I lengthen my casts, trying to time these to incoming waves. I'm no expert at this, at any of it. I'm a trout fisher from California, catching as catch can, but if I drop the fly into ebbing water, it's drawn out a dozen feet more.

When this tactic succeeds the schooled triggers take note and adjust their position. Once I had eight or ten; now I've collected twice that, a crowd that chases and strikes from the fly's touch down 'til I roll off. Some fish swirl on the surface, others wait below. I strip faster, outrace them. A greater shape eases in from my right.

It moves so slowly, I at first think it's flora—maybe a mossy palm trunk washing up. Then I notice the eye below a grotesquely humped forehead, and scales on the bulk each the size of a half dollar. Napoleon—imagine a fat green grouper with water on the brain.

This one is probably forty pounds. He pushes through the school of triggers turning one way, then the other—What's the excitement? He sees my fly and waddles—well, lumbers—toward it. I pull it past as quickly as I can. That battle would be brief, Waterloo for leader and maybe line when he sounds.

No thanks. But I am having fun. I've got sort of a fish-circus going, with triggers and wrasse and the elephantine Napoleon all performing tricks to my ringmaster's whip. The more fish that come the more fiercely they compete, quickening to the temptation of my speedy intruder. So I strip faster, farther up, almost to my feet. The triggers dash in so close I could kick them, but the Napoleon hangs back, reluctant to commit his bulk to breaking waves and seemingly more mindful of me. He *does* see me; I catch him watching intently from one eye, then the other.

I make another long cast into ebbing water, strip madly, see a streak of blue scatter the triggers. The rod snaps forward, whips back—a tenth of a second. The hook is broken at the bend.

Caron. Crevalle jack, I believe. This is what I want.

I retie without bothering to breathe, a larger fly on stainless steel, blue and baitfish-looking. The Tahitians are shouting at my back, some word with too many vowels that I'll later learn means "moray." Never mind. The triggers explode apart from the left edge of their school. Cast, *strip strip*—

The crevalle charges in as a wave rides out. I see his blue back as he turns on the fly. The rod jerks wildly—I see him surfing out the next wave; the tippet snaps.

>—<>—O—<>—<

I manage to swear while biting off what remains of light line, tying direct to the leader. As I tighten the knot in my mouth I notice that the Napoleon no longer observes me, instead stares outward toward green water. The triggers now hug tighter to the reef. A bigger wave slaps me backward as I cast. *Strip-strip*, nothing. *Strip-strip*—

Two crevalle rush in, dorsals breaking water, snout-to-snout even with each other until one breaks right and the other engulfs my fly, doubles the rod to sprint head down to sea and string line so tight it sings.

Everything holds. The larger wave at the cast was part of a set; I use the fifth to ride the fish out on the lava plateau. The Tahitians have noticed the fight between their battles with eels for their parrot fish catch. One wades toward me to take the crevalle by the tail. "*Bon appetit,*" he says, his smile so wide it reveals both his teeth.

I release the second, smaller crevalle, a Polynesian trots up for the third, then suddenly my circus of triggers and wrasse disappear; even the Napoleon's gone. I scan the foam. Four black fins, two dorsals and two tails, cut the water twenty feet before me. When the smaller shark climbs toward my boots I step well back—he dives into a crevasse. The pair forage for a few minutes, then sweep away. When they're gone I tie on a sleek yellow popper, tease the trigger fish back to the surface, and wait for that blue rush. It comes three, four times.

>─┤◆├─◦─┤◆├─<

We lunch on breadfruit, coconut, pineapple, *poisson cru* parrot fish and barbecued crevalle served steaming on woven leaves. I eat leaning against a palm trunk and finish fast, but my hosts protest my intent to return to the reef. In vigorous pidgin and pantomime they tell me that the tide still rises, that larger morays than those they stoned now hunt the coral plateau where I stood. I concede the danger with a disappointed smile and instead fish my way out on a sandy spit near our lunch site. Beside a head of rock I take another trigger, this one a foot long, yellow and blue, then something quite like a barred perch. Meanwhile, the Polynesians set to cleaning the rest of their parrots. The offal of these attracts schools of a mullet-looking fish with wide yellow pectorals, like little gliders. Then, again, come the sharks.

I see the first as he follows my fly in, turns away. He's golden brown in this water. I cast to him. This time he follows only a foot and leaves off—no scent. I remedy that with a shred of fish flesh. He takes, and with a gentle tug, shears 20-pound test Mason.

I rerig with wire, repeat the process with one of the black-tip brethren who course the shallow water around me. He's small but fights angrily, sweeping through arcs with much of his body above the surface. The Polynesians point and laugh; on some islands, sharks are revered, but not on Rangiroa. Here they're just another fish to sell the Japanese.

The laughter turns to alarm when I land the fish by hand. I see why when I turn him over. Though less than three feet he has a maw of astonishing size—big enough to take my whole hand and filled with innumerable tiny triangles that have shredded the wire's nylon coat—not big teeth, but of a size where a mishap would require a substantial amount of sewing. I do my release work with great care, grateful for the long nose pliers.

⟩⊢⊹⟩⊷○⊶⟨⊹⊢⟨

The Polynesians finish gutting the parrot fish and hang them from a branch beneath a palm. The mullet begin to scatter, the sharks with them. I wade away into new water. Far off on a white finger of sand flat I see a bigger shark, nearly five feet. I can't believe he notices me, but no matter how quickly or cautiously I stalk him he's always moving away. After twenty minutes I lose him, so work my way back toward the lunch site. There he is—the same shark or his twin—cruising confidently in the shallows.

The take is violent, the battle thereafter extreme. His first run includes as many wild twists as a tumbler's sprint across a mat. His second tears out two hundred feet of Dacron backing. Suddenly he spears the surface, throwing spray. He holds a moment, then lunges on without me.

How's that? Ah—he's reshaped the stainless fly hook into the wide crescent of a carpet needle.

The Polynesians smile, shake their heads, begin to load the boat for our rough ride back to the bungalows. Offloading there, I'll meet one of the rare Americans I met in Rangiroa. He says almost the same words as another countryman who approached me in Bora Bora: "Is that a fly rod? Hell, I didn't even think to bring mine." So I'll offer to lend him my spare, along with a handful of flies and the story of a day on a Rangiroa reef.

Future on the Fly

etween drought and drift nets, the salmon run on our stream
wasn't a slow job this year. I feared for the fish, but it was Charlie's
mind that concerned me most.

Thirty years late, I suppose. Wiser to worry about dinosaurs—about
spilled dinosaur *milk*. The fact is that if I ever go off the Deep End, my
pal Charlie will already be there to catch me. But he *would* catch me,
don't you see? He's that kind of guy. Besides, with Charlie's imagination
and inclination, he'll have Deep End well stocked by then. I presume
I'll find him trolling, since I can't imagine false-casting from out of a
strait jacket.

Anyway, the dearth of fish had Charlie muttering to himself as he
paced the neighborhood at night. That's not so unusual ("Sleeping is for
wimps," he often says), but now I'd had reports that a cop caught him
furiously flinging streamers from the back of his boat, which was in
storage at the time, parked next to the freeway at the local "Lock and
Walk." Lucky the sergeant was also a frustrated fisherman or Charlie
might have been cited as a menace to traffic. Even so, for a week afterward he rambled on about the "Barracuda" that got away, along with an
old "Marlin" and several "Stingray" he'd seen.

So you can understand why I was concerned, and why I hurried over
one Saturday afternoon, when Charlie telephoned to insist that I witness
"The Most Stupendous Fishing Invention Since the Discovery of Fish."

Trouble: There stood Charlie in his doorway wearing a beatific smile, a pair of shredded chest waders and a vest with feather duster-sized flies taped onto the drying patch. In one hand he swung a five-weight rod while with the other he waved—was that a sturgeon net?

Either genius or madness lit his eyes. "Did you see any?" he demanded. "See any big ones on your way over here?"

"Big ones what?" I inquired, wondering why he was scanning the hills around his housing tract.

"Ha! That's just it! They're all over, but it's so few who see them for what they are! It's like the world is our fishing hole and we're the only oysters."

I mouthed that metaphor to make certain I didn't understand it. By then Charlie had hustled me back through the hallway, past the usual havoc of his styrofoam collection ("the first ever!"), out into his long strip of side yard. When he paused there he actually started to shiver, just the way he does when he's poised above a salmon pool.

"Go on, you take the first cast," he insisted, tugging at my arm. "Lord knows I love you like a brother."

I looked hard. Charlie was pointing a three-hundred-dollar fly rod toward a weary patch of oleander, so I felt grateful that this brother thing wasn't genetic. "I don't think so," I said.

His eyes misted over. "Thanks," he said huskily. Then he held up his fly for my inspection. "Recognize this?"

"Well, no offense, but that looks like a knot of dryer lint you've got there."

"Lint! So it is! Tied on a matchstick, as it happens—but what *species* of lint?"

Beg pardon? "Not to speak bluntly, but it's the same color as your awful lime green bass sweater."

"*Chartreuse*—how many times must I tell you? Now, do you see that laundry vent on the wall?"

I did indeed. Dryer exhaust was even then blowing through the grass from out of the sub-basement. Coincidentally enough, I noticed a few lime-colored lint fibers drifting about.

"Chartreuse fly? Chartreuse lint in the air? Get it? I'm *matching the swatch!*"

So saying, Charlie executed a neat little reach cast between vent and oleander.

"Structure, current, matched swatch...watch close!"

He gave the lint-lure a couple of twitches while I wondered if six half-hitches in a shooting head would hold my buddy until the white-coats arrived. "Listen, Charlie. I want you to lie down while I make a call."

"Hush! We'll get the media later!"

"I doubt it."

"Yaaaaa!" he shrieked.

"Yaaaaa!" I echoed, for the strike came so suddenly—quick as a cougar! fierce as a lion!—that I barely had time to duck as Charlie's rod bucked forward, doubled over, snapped back—

"Yaaaaa!"

—then doubled over again as Sam, Charlie's Siamese cat, seized the lime fly and leaped up the redwood fence by way of the fuse box. After a half-gainer dive he headed away toward the neighbor's live oak—

"Not that damn tree again!"

—before howling Charlie turned his feline at the last moment—"Yes! Yes!"—and back down Sam bounded, twisting like a demon, feinting toward the basement door before springing skyward five feet, losing the lint from his jaws—

"Ahhh!"

—then catching it in his claws before he hit the ground!

"Did you *see* that? *Did you see that?*" shrieked Charlie in high C. "What a *beauty*. Why, Sam must weigh eight pounds, six point four ounces!"

Probably, but we couldn't know for certain because just then Sam saw a squirrel as Charlie's basset hound barked out back and his kid ran a can opener in the kitchen—

It was all over. Poor Charlie drooped a little as he examined the remnants of his busted lint fly. "Too bad," he sighed. "Though I suppose it would be a shame to take such a magnificent creature from out of *my* home environment." He fingered his shredded waders, "Then again, Sam *is* getting touchy about the part with the net."

"Imagine that," I muttered.

Charlie nodded, looking sane for an instant. Then that light strobed in his eyes. "Sure. But I bet he'll rise to my new moth pattern tonight, just before dark. What do you say? How about right now we go get ourselves a big brown!"

We needed to talk and I told Charlie so, even as he hauled me back through the house with hands all atremble from anticipation or fever or whatever. "Charlie! Wait, Charlie," I squawked. "You've got to stop this! It's *unnatural.*"

Charlie paused at the door to give me a don't-be-silly look. "Unnatural? Of course it is, old son. We both know I stock Sam in the side yard. But hell, I just fish him catch-and-release. Now *come on.*"

I don't know quite how it happened, except that Charlie weighs 240 pounds and can bench press an elk; so I did find myself trailing him out onto the sidewalk. After pausing a moment to tie on a new fly—"Jesus, Charlie, that's a *babcock*"—he waved a moment at a nonplussed neighbor—"'Lo, Mrs. Renaldo, sorry about your roses last week!"—then raced a couple houses down. Suddenly, he jerked up short, froze, and sizzled a question from the side of his mouth. "Remember those bonefish we saw off Key West? Remember that? Well take a look beyond that Buick, in the Bermuda grass by the pine."

I'm pretty sure this cat already knew Charlie, by the glassy stare it gave him and by the way it crouched and kept still but for the lashing of its tail.

"*Tailing*, it is," Charlie insisted. "Big Birmen or Burmese—they can't help themselves, when they're in here so shallow. Here we go."

It was a reasonably good presentation, I thought, but to his credit the sly Birmen stood fast, looking stoic as the babcock twitched by him. Alas, when the lure took a slow roll down the curb the creature lost all control.

"Oho!" Charlie cried as his rod bucked again, then he madly fed line as the Birmen sped away. "Great Scot—he's into my backing! What a catch! What a...*mammal.*"

Twice more the Birmen stripped into the spool. Each time Charlie turned him, fighting from the reel. At last, the beast whipped around and charged back at cheetah speed, throwing so much slack that Charlie couldn't keep up. "Oh no! Damn, damn, this white-footed cat!"

>—⋅◆⋅—◦—⋅◆⋅—<

All right, so it wasn't exactly a "Great Moment in Sport." But it wasn't just another Saturday, either. I knew that much even then, before Charlie took me by the collar, saying firmly, "I promised you a brown, and such a brown you shall have."

Through the alley and up the hill, out into the piney canyon, Charlie propelled me, there to knot on yet another creation that he bade me examine as we dropped behind a stump. A ruff of deer hair, turkey feathers and a touch of marabou—"You bet, it's the old Dry Gulch Muddler," he announced. "Could be a sparrow, or you can work it fast like a grasshopper on steroids. Looks like a mouse if you fish it slow in the leaves. One thing's sure: no lure's taken more browns than the muddler. And there's no brown around bigger than this one I've found for you." His eyes unfocused a little.

"Charlie, exactly what kind of *brown* is this?" I asked, out of purely academic interest.

"Maine Coon, his kind is called, though this one went feral as a kit. I'll bet he's 20 pounds. North American Record, could be. I've been watching him for weeks now, but he's yours, partner, all yours. You put a cast near that culvert and keep your eyes on the shadows." He handed me the rod, then threw a crisp salute.

Charlie may be crazy, but he's a noble nut, believe it. Who could resist such an offer from such a good heart?

Me: I can. "Charlie, I won't do this. These are *cats*, for Christmas sake. I mean, I think it's *illegal*. If it isn't, I still don't even have whatever license you're supposed to—and neither does your brown, not to mention his distemper shots. I mean, this just isn't what fishing's all about, now is it?"

Charlie smiled sadly. "Do I know?" he whispered, then shrugged. "In the end, with what's left, isn't it all about fun? Pursuit and seduction, wild battles on a line? Another life vibrating through the rod…" He looked a little moist. "But that's okay, pal. It's odd. I guess I know that. I understand how you feel…"

He reached for the rod. I'm not sure how it happened, but I seemed to snatch it back—hey, that's my empty salmon river, also, *my* year without a fish. "Hang on there, buddy, hang on…Now, how big is he *really*? And what does this leader test at? I'm only trying once, you know, sort of like practice for next year. And so help me, Charlie, *if you ever tell anybody about this…*"

I'll do what? I wondered, as I brought back the loop and felt the rod load even as my belly tightened to a "scritch-scritch" sound near the pipe (was the big brown hunting?), and I double-hauled to put the muddler well out even as Charlie began the boulder-rolling sound that he claims is a laugh.

A *laugh*? "What? What's so funny?" I yelped, blushing to the roots of my grey. "Is this all some kind of trick? I *knew* it…"

Still Charlie laughed, his beady eyes disappearing into the wrinkles of his face. "I'm only thinking," he gasped at last, "that once you're hooked on this, once you're hooked…Why, next week I'll get you set up with a big tarpon rod, bonefish taper and a popper the size of your hand…"

"Yeah? So?"

"We'll stand up on my back porch, and I'll make you the second guy on the block, only the second in the world, maybe, to flyfish for—"

I groaned.

"—*bass*-et."

>-+-+>-+O-+<-+-+<

You've got to watch Charlie, you really do. You have to draw a line somewhere with him, as in "tight around his neck." No bassets for me and that's that, such short, floppy creatures, though they do jump, sometimes. But *man*, I might as well say it: a guy hasn't fished—he really *hasn't*—until he's cast a Royal Wulff to his neighbor's Great Dane.

A Lifetime of Drowning

The sea is in my blood. Got to be, I've swallowed so much; also most of a Sacramento River riffle, one cove of Lake Almanor and lots of the Colorado, on the Arizona side. Why, I've been drowning so long that by the time I get to Davy Jones Locker, I figure I'll find my bronze baby shoes and a pair of high school gym shorts.

><del>•◦•</del><

Not that I'm one to let a little drowning stop me if it's fishing I have in mind. So there I was last week, waiting for the Coast Guard beside my new bass boat, trying to look like an old salt. The old salt exercise consists mostly of squinting, though die-hards will chafe their cheeks with an emery board and, lacking rope burns for real, paint their palms with rubber cement.

"Ah me," sighed an older salt hanging nearby. "Been around boats all my life and they still shiver my timbers."

"*Da*," I answered, which is Swedish for "yes"—great men of the sea, the Swedes—and also the Indonesian abbreviation for "no." I *do* shiver, but in my case, it's fear.

He squinted at me and I at him. At least, I think it was him, since I was just about squinted shut.

"Sailing man, myself," he said. "You?"

I shook my head wisely, peeping out at what was probably the horizon. "Drowning man. From way back."

He went off to talk to a gull, dazed, no doubt, by my revelation. Scads of people sail, after all, row, paddle or roar around under power. For them the process of traveling water is a given; they presume they will proceed on top. Then comes somebody like me who can repeatedly prove that man is awfully *dense*.

It's a family thing, described best by the last words of my Great Uncle Chum. A titanic figure in our history, he spoke from the Titanic's deck while observing a shark fin cutting the wake. "Call me Is-a-meal," he said.

Da. In that tradition, with me as skipper, a canoe is a boat with a point at each end and a pond in the middle. When I brag about fish I've caught *in* a canoe, it's the *pond* I refer to. I fish the dropoff below the gunwales and always work a topwater plug across the structure of sunken seats. Never mind canoes, I have even failed as ballast in a sailboat race ("Your head's too wide, we're dragging"), capsized catamarans, and finned frantically toward shore in a float tube so deflated I looked like a frog in a tutu. Remember that cruise ship that went aground mid-Pacific? No surprise to me; dolphins had been following us for three days. They looked *worried*.

We'll get to kayaks in a minute.

><

To begin in the beginning: I began drowning at the age of eight because my father lied to me. "Wood floats," he said. So I nailed eight inches of two-by-four to a cardboard box, dragged my raft and small brother toward the canal and, much encouraged by Mom's screams of farewell—just like in the movies!—launched and went under in a single motion. I still shiver to think how much worse that spanking would have been, if bro' hadn't clung to me so tightly while I clambered ashore.

One way or another, I've been drowning ever since.

><

That kayak, for example. Mine was the pink inflatable kind with 11 chambers and 19 tiny holes. Since many of these were in the floor panel, I rode rather low, accompanied by a chorus of hisses and a cloud of tiny bubbles. Give me the Lennon Sisters and I'd be Lawrence Welk of the Lake.

Instead, I had a lemon of a fishing buddy. "What *do* you look like?" he wondered. "I know: like a weasel marooned on a piece of tropical fruit."

"Shut up and get in," I said.

He did, and for the first time in his fishing life hooked a catfish over five pounds. Pretty excited he was, managing to bang the beast on all 11 chambers when he bounced it aboard. Two pectorals and one dorsal spine per bang—

—you know why they call catfish whiskers *barbels*? Because that suggests how fast you go down with a big one in an inflatable boat.

The older salt headed back my way as the Coast Guard cutter roared toward us, with lights flashing and sirens awail.

"Wonder what's the trouble?" he muttered.

"Me," I replied. "I told you: I'm drowning."

He squinted harder. I smiled and, with a jaunty tip of my cap, stepped lightly into my new bass boat, deftly catching the plug as it shot up from its hole at the stern. The geyser that produced was as nothing to the flood soon after, when a wave broke the outboard loose—which took the transom with it.

"Abandon ship!" salt cried.

"Aye, aye," I answered gamely, already paddling a little. "But sir, remember—I have not yet begun to float!"

To the Fisher
Fishing Alone

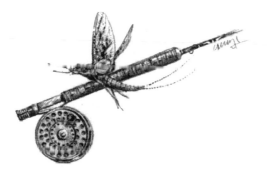

His casts have loops so tight they look pointed; I should learn
something. He doesn't pay quite enough attention to insects, by
my lights. I may bug him about this. His approach to fish in thin water
seems to me too close and erect, but he raises them anyway. He is polite
and generous in an inconspicuous way—the best way. His sense of fair
matches mine, so gas money and restaurant bills quickly become part of
an account that will settle without a hitch in a long run.

New partner. Lucky for the species it's not so difficult to find a mate
for life.

> ▷─┼◆▷──O──◁◆┼─◁

Much of the romance in flyfishing emerges from the image of a
fisher alone. Limned against a rush of moving water or tree-broken
sky, testing the elements in a game both physical and mental—no
audience is necessary or even welcome. There's only room for two at
the ends of a line.

Paradoxically enough, there's another tradition of fishers sharing on
a bank or by a fire, maybe while driving home into a night illumi-
nated by headlights and the pastel glows of the dashboard, the passion
of pursuit.

> ▷─┼◆▷──O──◁◆┼─◁

I've fished alone for tens of thousands of hours now, days, even weeks at a time. I do not remember a moment of loneliness.

I also spent 12 years fishing with the same partner and am a better angler for it. Maybe a better man; unquestionably richer by far. Part of the reason comes from the curious fact that, for me, under certain circumstances, fishing can be one of the best of partner sports.

⊱⊶⊷⊙⊶⊶⊰

I thought about that on a pond last year. It's a jealously protected place surrounded by live oaks and seven mansions. A friend's uncle became mine, by way of allowing me occasional entrance. I cruised my tube through evenings after work, playing a popper for bluegill while hoping for bass.

The kid was a surprise I discovered while first approaching the shore. Hidden in trees, he cast a conventional rig armed with a pork rind. Blonde, maybe 17 or 18, he had the shoulders of a high school tackle and the glower which might attend a grudge game. His greeting was a curt nod and short, "Hi."

"Hey."

He cast, worked his jig intently. I would foul his water when I launched, so I waited.

"You fish here much?" he asked at last.

"Once in a while," I answered. "You?"

He was silent for a moment. "Yeah. I live around here."

"Around here" did not include the proprietary mansions, I concluded.

"I catch a lot of bass."

"Do you?"

"Yeah. Six the other day. You catch many on that fly rod?"

"Not many, no."

"I didn't think so."

He still hadn't made eye contact. I had the sense that each word he spoke was an effort for him, a piece of an awkward ritual he had not mastered and maybe didn't expect he would. He was, I decided, angry. Not at me, nor about my intrusion; he was just mad.

He reeled up the pork almost to his tiptop. "Go ahead."

"Thanks," I said. "Good luck."

For the first time he looked me over. "Yeah," he answered. Then, as if he'd had to think about it, "Good luck."

I cast my little popper for bluegill, which came up beneath the branches of a giant weeping willow, out from the shelter of docks and from root tangles along the shoreline. Twice I saw the boy watching me from his shadows. He left after an hour or two.

><+>—O—<+><

When I tramped up to the house that night, pleased and easy, my new uncle was waiting. A gentle man with a wide smile, he asked if I'd seen anybody else on the pond. I told him about the blonde boy. "Yes, somebody called," he said. "I understand that the people who used to own this house let him fish. But the other neighbors disapprove."

"Has he caused problems?"

"I don't believe so. But I hear he has a reputation in the area. They seem not to want him around."

Who does? I wondered, and still wonder, two years later, remembering the morose quality of our interaction and my curious conviction that this kid didn't need, absolutely, to be this way. There seemed an enforced quality to his aloneness; I imagine him as one of those people I recall skirting the edge of adolescent society, rarely accepted, mostly avoided. His size might save him from overt harassment when it didn't provoke the same from someone wanting to make a name. On the football team I imagined he might earn respect with savage blocking, but it was hard to see him chumming around in a locker room or around a keg—he might well make a mean drunk. Yet in his conversation with an older fisher outside this difficult world, there did seem an awkward effort to connect.

Benign diagnoses, like this last, often turn malignant on closer inspection. Still, I cannot help but ponder how such a kid might, over time, fit a partnership developed along grassy banks and rocky shorelines. The kind I have known, where two fishers go separate ways on a stream, each returning at some point to check on the other, perhaps to point out a fish he can see better from his angle or to share some observation or theory. "I think the white mayflies are a masking hatch—look for the tiny green ones still in the film. Here's what's working for me…" Early on it might confuse the kid to return to the truck after a cold march up the canyon, some snowy evening, and find coffee or brandy hot in a thermos…But he'd learn.

In time, even a long time. It might take him a while to understand the fundamental contest here was not between two fishers, but between each one and a galaxy of challenges presented by water and the lives within it, current and sunlight, barometric pressure and the translucent qualities of hackle and a hundred other materials; to fathom that, facing these odds, they were allies tracing subtle patterns; that along with pride in individual effort comes a grand satisfaction in sharing these and in recognizing another fisher's clever study—"Very smart. How did you figure that?" After all, our own triumphs are finite, but the achievements of others are myriad and ever unfolding, providing for a lifetime of appreciation.

⊱━◈━○━◈━⊰

If you allow it. Some people don't. I met this blonde kid for only a moment; he might be one of those limited by the lock-step of envy, around whom the sense of *I* and *Mine* make an impermeable membrane, a cell so isolated that a partner's fish is, to him, only one he wishes he'd caught.

If so, then he would not have found such pleasure in watching my new partner raise a big brown from a slow, clear pool, throwing Joe's Hopper forty feet with a four-weight, watching, I know, without breathing as the wake swelled from the bank and the fly was tossed then taken, the rod pulling back at the butt beneath his hand and whipping forward from the tip to make of itself a longbow and a lever that, *I know*, feels alive to him, thrumming with life connected. He would not hear with pleasure my partner's pleased roar while making one of his own, or cheer him on while scrambling for the camera. His glower would not change to a grin matching somebody else's. He would not extend his hand to shake when it was over.

And he would be truly alone.

I made a guest's case for the boy with *Faux* Uncle. He listened carefully and uncomfortably; I let it rest. Probably the boy was banished.

It bothers me. I hope he's found another pond, a river. There's more than that I hope for him.

Como se llama? and the Accidental Trout

Among the important things to know about fishing this piece of the Wood River is that the browns feed on crayfish, big sculpin and stoneflies; and that when the llama skips over to inquire of your nature, he does so by blowing into your nostrils before inhaling your breath into his own. So advised, you will bring weighted wooly buggers and Dinaca, since llama breath leaves a teensy residue of alfalfa-garlic smell in the back of your throat.

>—◄—○—◄—┃—◄

Oregon: I always feel a little guilty crossing the border, contemplating California waters I'm leaving behind. With Golden State plates on the car, I also feel like fresh meat for the Oregon Highway patrol. Still, I'm pretty pleased when "The Lisa Person" has business in Klamath Falls. So much water, so many fish in so much wild land.

But there's a catch. Like other travelers of my experience, Lisa-On-the-Road is a "Let's get there" creature, one of those pitiful sorts for whom arrival is the only goal. I am quite sure this flaw can be surgically corrected; yet she resists, sacrificing the opportunity to be Mistress of Meander for the loathe title, "Madam of Deliberate Motion, Arch Enemy of Entropy." *Weeks* prior to loading the car—Ol' Viola, we sat by Your tires and wept for Thee—she called the Chamber of Commerce for a Bed and Breakfast recommendation. She has schedules and brochures labeled "Points of Interest."

None of the latter include preseason angling locales, by the way, and I, open for anything, have only vague and hopeful ideas about where I might fish. Lisa the Organized will not sully her day book with "Lost Creek, Sunday or Monday, Oregon or California side, or maybe both; unless Klamath Lake is doing well; or I decide instead to try Holy Waters…"

Off we go then, into a well-plotted Yonder, into early spring with snow on the slopes of volcanoes, pastures painfully green, through road-side forests of purple-blooming bushes. My spontaneous request to pause on the Upper Sac, I am advised, is improperly submitted: Lisa remains unmoved by both my rhapsodies about early adventures there and my observation that she has a heart the size of dime. "We," she says—note that plural pronoun—"didn't allow time for that; you *do* want to get there, don't you?" When a suggestion that "There's some interesting water" beside the highway beyond Doris receives even less attention, I make chain-rattling noises in the back of my throat. "That sounds terrible—when are you going to stop smoking?"

⊱━⊰•◦○◦•⊱━⊰

So it's still light when we reach the B & B—actually sort of a spare bedroom of a house on a cul-de-sac just outside of town—run by a wonderfully pleasant couple whose extended family has joined them here for Easter weekend. We're welcome, we really are, to join them all at the TV upstairs.

Still, our window has a view of Klamath Lakes, that great fish nursery that has not yet scummed over with summer algae. In vast shallows—a littoral zone measured in scores of square miles—landlocked steelhead graze midges and nymphs, fattening to more than 40 pounds, on occasion, before they move to the river mouths. By evening light I can see trollers trying to interrupt this feeding, brave fishers huddled in the sterns of small craft as they stare back at the sine waves of their slick-water wakes. Though I don't wish them too many fish to kill, I would-n't mind cruising out there to deliver them warm brandy.

Instead, I traipse out late to a liquor store deli to pick up supplies for tomorrow's picnic and, incidentally, to chat with four locals about fishing possibilities. Nobody pretends to grasp the Oregon fishing regulations; even so, my half-laid plans are mostly scotched. Lost River has been found by sewage spill; Holy Waters is further away than I thought; Klamath Lake would fish well from the boat I didn't bring. Now what?

Sure enough, the trollers are back out on Klamath Lake again the next morning, a sizable congregation. I almost commit to a wade, but Tourist Lisa wants to see Crater Lake, so we take a slow drive around Upper Klamath, highway to highway, passing eventually over the Wood River. I am so enamored of a green run along an oxbow that her squeak barely distracts me: "*Are those llamas?*"

"Burros," I answer. Then, "No: llamas and burros."

"It's a Bed and Breakfast! Stop!"

Everything changes. We will not see Crater Lake. It's Lisa's meander.

The Great Pyrenees at the gate has a head big enough to be a fair-sized animal all by itself, along with off-white fur that, absent polar bear, would certainly do. His Spitz buddy looks to laugh as he barks and wags his tail. Along the driveway to the plantation-styled house, several dozen rabbits munch the grass. Twice as many geese, ducks, and turkeys note our arrival along the fence of the right-side pasture, but these are soon crowded out by a chorus line of curious goats, who thrust their noses between wires and gaze fixedly though slit-pupiled eyes. "Look at all the babies!" cries Saint Francis Lisa, but I don't see any over toward the river bank—only the llamas and burros, now joined by half a dozen horses.

We've arrived at kid-feeding time, it turns out; so greetings from one of the old owners of Sun Pass Ranch, Darlene Nimmo, are somewhat distracted. She's also in the midst of instructing one of the new owners as to proper bottle protocol. Eventually, Darlene shows us one of the handsome rooms—

"—Can we stay here? Can we?"

"Gee, Lisa, I don't know, it's not part of the Grand Plan—"

—but long before that Lisa is cradling to the elbows baby goat bottles, laughing under a swarm of spindly bottle-suckers. "I'm in heaven," she announces, and because she is and will be, I realize I'll have time to steal *my* piece.

Never mind the liquor store guys—I go to the source, calling Judy Carothers at Williamson River Anglers. Judy and husband Steve own a fishing shop outside Chiloquin and, after fond hellos, I name a river that she'd sent me two years before—a venue remarkable for its lack of reputation, a population of dragonfly nymphs five times that I've discovered elsewhere, and a mix of fish species. "Now *that* river," Judy says firmly, "is open only for warm water species."

I consider this. "And bass, of course, will take a streamer."

"They will."

"Or a dragonfly nymph."

She hesitates. "It's possible."

"But if I caught a trout…"

"You'd certainly release it. Why don't you stop by the house, I'll give you directions."

⋗⊶⊷⊙⊶⊷⊰

The river is broad and swift, gray under a cloudy sky. I check: the dragonfly nymphs are so abundant that I can't imagine how any other insect species survive. I knot on a Fat Boy and a yarn indicator, then lash my way into a riffle that, on the far side of the stream, falls off a ledge into a run. I fish the water between step-in and prime lie more by way of habit than expectation; so I'm three fish to the black before I'm halfway across. Trout, doggone it—wild creatures with unusually silvery sides and backs almost black, fins so full and crisply defined they would do for Japanese prints.

Oddly enough the dropoff produces nothing, but a swing into a downstream seam creates a monstrous boil from a tail eight inches deep, along with tension too great for the tippet—not a breakoff so much as a *chop*. I stare down slack line, cursing and smiling; I will not raise the fish again.

I do, however, take half a dozen more—trout, dammit—before I exhaust my Fat Boy supply; then nothing save a small rising fish I stalk with an elk hair. I need to think deeply about this, meditate: this realization corresponds exactly with an urge to drain the morning's coffee. Halfway up the bank I hear a shout from the house perched on the opposite shore: "Come have lunch!"

Judy had introduced me to Marv earlier; he's been watching my progress from his deck. Ensconced on that perch we eat excellent leavings of a ham dinner with rice, pasta salad and beer. Marv's delighted that the fishing is so good, and together we mourn my loss of all Fat Boys—he offers to trade that pattern for a secret killer of his own—then, with wide smiles, we lament my failure to catch bass—what a pity, that all I've managed is these accidental trout. After promising to help him push a stalled jeep later that afternoon, I step back to the river to take five fish on a peacock-bodied nymph with fore-and-aft soft-hackle (the Warden's Worry of John Mckim's *Fun with Fur and Feathers)* from just below Marv's deck. He cheers.

Back at the ranch Lisa's returned from a horse ride across the Sun Pass meadow and into the state forest beyond. She's in love with a gelding named Star—and have I met the blind goat, Helen Keller, who cocks her head toward your call and licks your hand when she finds you? No? Oh, was I fishing? Which reminds her: Jean wants to learn more about fly-fishing, so will I show her the bugs in her stretch of stream?

I do, finding the Wood about as different from the morning's venue, biomass-wise, as one could possibly imagine: no dragons at all, but small pteronarcys, large goldens, tuba flex worms and a sculpin four inches long. The water's got to be ten degrees colder, and Lord, I wish it was open to angling.

It will be, in two weeks. Jean wants to know if we can return then, work a little deal, so she and husband Jerry can take some lessons. Lisa does four or five cartweels of can we? I stare out over the ranch's three-quarter mile section of Wood River, past the curious llamas…I just don't know; I must check my day book: "I'm practicing discipline. Order. The perpetual retention of spontaneous impulse. Surely you can see, Dear Lisa, how giving way to such temptation would—"

"Shut-up," she says.

I sigh. I'm trying so hard, you know.

"Shut-up shut-up shut-up, and say yes."

"Ohhh….all right. But *schedule* that, toots."

⊱┈◈┈○┈◈┈⊰

Two weeks later the Wood is open and I spend a morning with Jerry demonstrating upstream nymphing, to no avail. That night we tie the proper flies with Christopher Engel, who guides these waters and gives excellent advice, even after vodka. Jerry's one of those rare students who knows what he knows and what he doesn't and practices what he learns with an intensity that makes him quickly adept. That morning the technique is stack-mend, which he grasps well enough to hammer a brown the length of his forearm. *With* the hand.

Early that afternoon I take him to the nearby river of dragons… which have, in the meantime, hatched out for the most part. My Fat

Boys are irrelevant to them. Now the fish focus on a slow, day-long cad-dis hatch—the green rock worms, free-swimmers, coming up. Lisa has actually tagged along. Also, in the interim, she's sold her first photos to a national fishing mag, so together we've bought a new camera and planned the film mix, naturally, the proper aggregate of exposure speeds, rolls for slides and prints, black and white, color—

Well-laid plans, damn straight, and she sure would have taken some great shots if the local dolt of a dog following along hadn't chosen that day to take a porcupine tail in the snout ; so Clara Barton Lisa escorts him home, there to assist with pliers and put "needle nose" into context. After she's gone; I get a hit every cast, on average, for three and a half hours. The next morning I take a fat Wood River Brown; then, hurry-ing to meet the Carothers, get stopped by an Oregon Highway Patrol officer *who actually lets me go* with a friendly slap on the shoulder and a warning. I'm so pleased that when I do get to Williamson River Anglers, I succumb to Judy's urging that I interview Polly Rosborough…

⤙⧫◦⧫⤚

A total of three stories, I figure I've got. But better yet, I think I have Lisa looking differently at the world and its possibilities. I truly believe I've opened her mind to the host of opportunities for which you can't plan, but only accept on a moment's notice, springing forth to meet them. Yes, this is the real reward of these Oregon meanders, I'm sure; and so, on the drive home, I suggest a stop at the Upper Sac—

"You've got to be kidding. Don't even think it. Drive—I've got the evening all planned out when we get home."

A River of Child

Sophie Mariah will get no pastel-colored waders, at least not her first pair, though I may throw a Pink Lady into the mobile of flies that will circle the crib. Imagine that construction urged into motion by the nursery breeze. Better yet, imagine that among her first views of the world will be a hatch presented from the trout's point of view—how could she go wrong? It will seem completely natural, to a child so imprinted, when I explain her origins.

"Daddy sent his sperm a-spawning on the River Mom. Oh, the way was long, the journey difficult; but at last one brave sperm nestled in Mommy's redd. He shared with her a secret code, then signed a sacred pact, one clause of which requires you tie a dozen midges this morning, size 22, and please don't cheat on hackle."

Of course, Sophie will *want* to tie those midges, knowing that half are for her. She will delight to pin a few on Winnie the Pooh's little vest, crying gaily, "Oh Dad, does this mean we'll go down to the stream tonight, so I can practice my roll cast? And *please, please,* can I take the leeches to school, for Ms. Carson's show-and-tell?"

Never mind spelling and social science. I expect excellence in Entomology, Ichthyology, and Physics of Casting. By the age of five, let's say. And certainly one must read, in order to appreciate Lyons and Haig-Brown.

Balance, that's what I'll strive for.

><·>·•·O·•·<·>·<

Naturally, it's impossible not to think of Sophie exploring a stream. Images of children and water—an eddy, a riffle, an edge of pond—swell with sentiment that defies cliché; true wonder never feels cheap. Nor can a child's curiosity sit subject to ordinary judgments. In the days when I fished for food, my step-kids would demand I bring the catch home whole, so they might examine each organ I removed. "That's his heart? That's his guts—what's inside? Is that a snail? What happens when you cut open its eye?"

One stormy night, when Cathy was seven or eight, she insisted on holding the flashlight and umbrella, to watch as I cleaned live young from a viviparous perch. I worried that the sight of fry babies would appall her, but no, she was merely amazed. Her credulity, however, would only stretch so far. Neither she nor her twin Eric—not even older brother Marc—would believe the whopper I told about flounder. "Its eyes *don't* move. They can't, just because it gets older. That doesn't happen." Cynics, so doubtful; but I did catch the twins trying to adjust their own baby browns in the mirror. "See! It can't happen!"

><·>·•·O·•·<·>·<

It's possible, I know, that Sophie will have an entirely different set of reactions than Cathy, or me, or any reasonable person. Acorns may fall close to oaks, but they roll. One avid hunter friend of mine has a daughter, now a woman, who was apparently *born* vegetarian. I have plenty to worry about in Sophie's gene pool, since her mother thinks carp are "cute" and leans toward the idea that worms, while loathsome, should have the right to vote, at least in primaries. "That's not *rabbit* fur?" she will demand of me at my vise, catching the attention of Blossom, our "House Bunny." I must launch a long story about road kills, respect for resources, et al. Mom-to-be just glares; then, showing her true colors, lifts my best peacock plume for some pointless vase arrangement. Already we argue about Sophie's care and handling. "I don't care *how*

Hopis carried their babies," she snorts, "Sophie will never go anywhere zipped into the back of a fishing vest."

So much for my patented Pupae Pouch. And I bet I hear no end of objections to Sophie's first float tube, no matter how neatly I sew around the rubber duck's little head.

Still, I'm confident that Sophie will shrug off Mom's provincial attitude, educated as Sophie will be from toddler-age to casting tight loops, wasting no wraps, keeping the eye clear. She will see TV only as an excuse to sit tight at the vise, baseball as good training for overhead casting, wild dancing as practice for wading too deep. What a treat for the neighbors that first Halloween, when Sophie drifts down the street as a stonefly nymph! Neat little antenna and tail-gills out to there.

There's a more serious side to all this, of course. For one thing, I worry more about the future these days, what opportunities Sophie will have, how I might assure these. I do not like imagining the pair of us on some river or lake with me mouthing dread words like, "You wouldn't believe how good this once was." Such concern creates a curious paradox: while scaling down my life to tend to details of the home Sophie soon enters, I have also the compulsion to make larger things right. Taking notice of Sophie-Mom swelling, for example, I am suddenly reminded to write checks to a favorite conservation outfit. At times I calculate curious equations like, "If we can get 700 cubic feet of water to the Trinity River for five years, how big will the browns be when Sophie is six?'"

The future, then, means something else. But I also angle more often in memory, wandering upstream toward my own headwaters. There's gray at the edges of early images, a certain stillness. Sadness also: Sophie will never fish for porgies with Grandpa Charley, wondering about the Cossack edge to his eyes, smelling on his neck the good brown smells of beer and tobacco and sweat, or trace on his knuckles scars from that knife fight in Harlem. Nor will Sophie ever hesitate on the edge of sleep, riding home from Lake Pleasant in a '65 Ford Galaxy 500, face pressed to the bench-seat back, watching my father's eyes as he watches the road, feeling about as safe as anybody can in this life while gloating to hear, "No need to tell your mother the part about the snake…"

No, there's a limit to what we pass on, and some things just pass away. Other events wait to happen, to become memories in their own right; so suddenly I wonder—will Sophie have scars also, like Grandpa Charley? A crooked forefinger like that of Charley's daughter—what will be Sophie's Grandma Enid—the one broken by the hoof of a quarter horse? Or a white ridge of hatchet wound like the one on my thumb? Injuries fading, someday, on the very fingers that the book says are just now learning to curl inside her Mom.

Of course. *It shall be.* And I will also suffer Sophie's wounds, the way I did for Marc, Sophie's senior something-brother, when the bottle broke across his palm. Together we will know harm as well as a host of firsts, biggests, bests, even a few years of "remember when?" I'll be ready with platitudes: Fight the good fights, Sophie. Watch your shadow on the water. Listen to your mother and don't tell her about the snake. Be cool, don't drool.

I'm still practicing.

><++>-O-<+><

In the meantime, Sophie…stay limber. Flex. Because those size 22 midges? They are already hell on these excited eyes, which is just one reason I'll tie the flies of your mobile larger than life.

Destination: August

Master of Meander—it's a title I take to myself somewhere in the Central Valley, hurtling through level darkness and flinching as insects suicide against my windshield.

All right then, the bugs aren't dying by design and I'm hardly hurtling. Viola, the first vehicle I've ever named, is an ancient Toyota truck saddled with two tons of fishing castle. My darling she is, but a rattle trap with hardly enough torque to climb a curb. No matter. On 505 she hits sixty and I lean into the road, so pleased I sing along to the rattle of pans. It's a good speed, after all, since I don't know where I'm going.

It's not my job. Or it wasn't for a decade, while I had a faithful fishing partner who took great pleasure in Forest Service maps and Jim Freeman reports. Weeks in advance he'd trace lines on checkered papers and measure gaps between topographical lines. After a nod to some chapter from *Trout Fishing in California*, he'd say softly, "I think this place would be good." It fell to me to fall in and out of the truck.

Then he married. Well, twice—first to his own business as a private investigator, then to a woman who went into his business. Three years it's been now, but I think of him still as I pass the Winters exit.

We fished Putah Creek together before the Orvis onslaught, before a guy caught a nine-pound brown on a dry fly on the pool near the dam, then sent there every damn fool who bought a rod. Oh, there were browns there then, believe it, sought mostly by skulking locals baiting the beasts with shiners and nightcrawler gangs. Now the chill tailrace is a neoprene jungle.

>—+—◦+—◦—◦+—+—◦

Don't think about it; drive. It's only nine o'clock and Viola's steady shaking is settling my mind. Besides, the Aladdin's just a cup shy of full.

I-5, up the Sacramento. I could stop at Tehama, cut across to Los Molinos. I've taken shad there, from the boat of Humberto *del Rio* when he still worked the river. We'd watch otters play in a cottonwood grotto while swinging comets through the current, imagining the little quicksilver tarpon, one behind the other, stretching single file to the bay, to the sea, to the drift nets.

At night Humberto and I lay in his boat gorging on pickled shad while drinking icy tonics. What would it be like to catch the fish of your dreams and love the loveliest woman at the exact same time?

A year later Humberto called me up to write a story on squawfish. "They're killing the salmon, just killing them. Thirty or forty of them marry the hens going upstream. The bucks can't fight them all off the redd." Fish and Game told me that the squaws make a career of lying in wait behind the Red Bluff diversion dam, ambushing smolts disoriented by vertical eddies.

>—+—◦+—◦—◦+—+—◦

I wrote the story and sold it. Like everybody else, too late and too little for the salmon. Humberto of this River left it for a steady job on a lake. A minor matter of feeding his family.

No, not the Sacramento; not this time. Maybe the Feather…

>—+—◦+—◦—◦+—+—◦

At Corning I contemplate the road to Oroville. Below a bridge there, I took my first steelhead on a fly, one cold morning only minutes after landing a bright Chinook hen of nearly twenty pounds. An hour later I took a buck of nearly 50, stripping him in by hand after he ripped the handle off my reel. A head like a German Shepherd, he had, no kidding.

Then there're the odd little bass ponds nearby, fecund to stinking, and the secret population of stripers near—

But Oroville at night is a nasty gamble, the kind of place where, in the dark reaches near the dike, you want to sleep with a blued-steel companion, reminding yourself of how the safety switches off to the left. The last decision of the evening would be, "Buckshot, or slug?"

I think not.

I head east, or west, out of Red Bluff, with Viola's tiny tank full, chugging uphill either way. I could swing into Lassen, launch my tube with the Manzanita Armada, learn again not to tempt fate by fishing a #4 wooly bugger on 6X tippet. I could try a neighbor of that water where, long ago, I released my first trout longer than two feet....

Or I could turn toward Indian Creek, to test my axles in the dark while climbing reaches so windswept that Viola's shakes turn to shudders. The same has happened to me there, on those high roads, in a night that felt less solitary than full of wolves. There's wildness above Indian, truly, eerie echoes and gates with padlocks the size of a melon.

⊱─┈◈─0─◈┈─⊰

The Aladdin pours a last cup. By the cab light I search out a fine blue line. The Master of Meander has wearied now, so there slips from a synapse a better memory—

August morning, waking in a meadow, determined this time to do it right. Past a curious quartet of horses I dragged a window-screen seine, reward from a garage sale where an excited old fellow thrust it at me with a shout—"You know what it's for! At last, *somebody*. You take it free, son, so's it has good home..."

It proves its worth right off by helping me wave off the curious stallion. And in a clear little riffle it found me...what is that thing?

Ignorant I was then, even more than now, but in my box was a simple fly tied to look just like this *whatever* the screen revealed. Yellow body, black head—

I took half a dozen trout that morning. And the first fly I ever tied myself was an attempt to mimic this yellow whatever.

A tiny line on the map. Yes, that's the place I was looking for, had been, all these miles and hours; would find.
Dream and drive.

➤┤◆➤◦➤◦┤◄

Three o'clock in the morning and I'm trembling. My hands want to stay wrapped around the wheel, but there's coffee to be rid of, a moon-lit meadow at which to marvel, smells to suck into the back of my lungs. I hear the stream running over rocks I turned over so long ago. Near the fence a mare stares over the back of her foal. I return to Viola, drink to her and the morning—

—When I search Viola's cupboards for that yellow fly I once tied, finding it at last in a grey box full of "firsts"—streamers created, apparently, to imitate road kills. I fish the crude caddis and take a half-dozen rainbows, yes I do, then seine the stream again for fun. The pupae are more orange than I remember, so I cannibalize Viola's carpet for the dubbing to match, tie, return to catch *browns*. How is that?
Watching hoppers flee at noon, I laugh when I realize their legs, emerald iridescent, look just like Flashabou strands I have in my case. I sober fast when I find I've lost the gray box amidst myriad grey stones. After searching, then mourning this for hours, I find a Swiss Army knife in the dust while trudging back to the truck.

➤┤◆➤◦➤◦┤◄

And I believe that all along this was my destination. That it was mystery revealed, reward collected for risk taken—fortune favoring the ambivalent, if you're not quite so kind. And so it should happen, I think, when you set yourself free in an August, making of yourself a Master of Meander.

André Puyans: Legacy of an Emissary

The following speech was given February 4, 1995, at the induction of André Michel Puyans into the Northern California Council Federation of Fly Fishers Hall of Fame. It only suggests the contributions of the man who developed the A.P. Nymph, the hair stacker and a host of other innovations—a leader in California fisheries conservation, a national director of Trout Unlimited, 1977 Buz Buszeck Memorial Fly Tying Award winner, teacher of the first water, major player in the art and craft of this sport.

The event sold out. This tribute is included for the hundreds who would have been there and the many thousands who benefit from Andy's efforts, knowingly or not.

>-+-+>-+-0-+<-+-+-<

"I am much honored to be here, introducing André Puyans tonight, at his induction to the Fly Fishing Hall of Fame…especially pleased to have this chance to praise Master Andy a little to those who are already appreciative. It is daunting, however, to speak by proxy for so many people who think so much of him. I take courage from some things John Randolph has said. Mr. Randolph, the editor of *Fly Fisherman Magazine*, calls Andy 'Fly Fishing's Jason,' of Jason and the Argonauts. Also the Pied Piper and the Johnny Appleseed of flyfishing.

"Taken altogether, that would seem to leave to his admirers the roles of sailors, rats, and fruit trees.

><+<>+<>+<+<

"I am only sympathetic to Mr. Randolph—it's the kind of problem you run into, describing Andy. Of the many ways by which one might measure a man, none of any value will fit him into 15 minutes. It's difficult to define his importance to flyfishing, California flyfishing in particular, to list his achievements—innovations like the hair stacker or neoprene waders, his own wading boots—or to relate his life in anything less than thousands of words. I know this, because an interview with Andy that I intended to last three hours has now taken several years, filled notebooks and dozens of tapes, led to crippling cases of writer's cramp, toxic doses of caffeine…and of course, *eventually* Lisa got pregnant. Even so, all of these efforts together have produced only a footnote of the second chapter of Volume Three in the *Encyclopedia of André Puyans*, offered only an inkling of what Andy has meant to this sport and to the people in it.

"Partly because he's meant so much, partly because Andy led me to look in the wrong place and was shamelessly distracting. Arriving in an evening with some sort of agenda, waiting as Andy fended off students and friends, more friends, more students…at last he would sit down, suck his pipe and nod, looking knowing and sage, wise in the ways of trout and flies, humankind and the natural world. Then he'd lean forward and say softly, 'So then, how does Hillary Clinton tie a Humpy?' Two hours later he'd be talking about the 'world's heaviest drift boat,' built for ramming Deliverance-style pirates on a smallmouth river in Arkansas. Or describing a drunk dragging aboard a five-foot alligator gar to shoot it five times with a .357 in order to 'keep it quiet.' And, as the little rowboat sank, I presume kept it moist.

"All the stories, all the wonderful stories. Andy's a marvelous raconteur, generous with color and credit and laughter. Kind too: whenever I started running out of paper and tape, pleading with him to help me organize all this, Andy would manage an expression of great sympathy. And if I had, for just a moment, stopped vibrating, suggest that I might like another cup of coffee.

"Eventually, we did settle on a chronological structure, a linear history of Andy's life, beginning with the beginning of his fly tying and fishing, proceeding along a time line...and Andy told such stories. Of his first flies (the family doctor who urged him to try 'fishing hooks with feathers tied on'); then of his days at Wilmarth Tackle and the Anglers Roost in the Chrysler building, touching on names and personalities such as Elizabeth Greg and Jim Daren (Daren, 'who liked having me around because I remembered where he put things'), creating from memory a boy's wander around those vises; then a comedy sketch about the first professional order he tied (144 dozen Gov. Paine Boost Maine Specials, an assignment Andy accepted when he was nine years old, 'Because,' he says, 'I had no idea how many flies 144 dozen was')— he tied 100 dozen while convalescing in a hospital...the feathers kept clogging the vent of Sister Kenny's respirator vent.

➤─┼─◆➤─•─O─•─┤◆─┼─◄

"To later boyhood and Henry Newitt, whom Andy describes as, 'The most generous man I ever met.' Newitt was the one who demanded that Andy cast at a Lucky Strike pack until he hit it three times in a row from thirty feet. When Andy succeeded, Newitt gave him a Leonard rod and took him fishing, inviting him along with a triumvirate on the Beaverkill, letting Andy, the 'pesky kid,' hang around 'Watching as Jack Atherton wrote, Mead Schafer sketched, and Newitt stood around, swearing...' Andy would meet the Dettes, the Darbees, Art Flick, Ray Bergman...

➤─┼─◆➤─•─O─•─◄─┼─◄

"He speaks with great fondness about these years, even if he suspects that Newitt's original motivation was defensive. 'I'd been fishing a fly rod, all right...But *my* nymphs weren't artificial...Henry may have figured I was taking his fish.'"

➤─┼─◆➤─•─O─•─◄─┼─◄

"On to fishing in Cuba, where Puyans' family owned property 'BC—before Castro.' To a spat with a clerk at the Hardys Shop in St. James, to taking over the Great Lakes Carbon Corporation's Atlantic salmon camps in Newfoundland after Lee Wulff left. Andy was 19 then; in the same year, Al McClane wrote an article about Andy and his Portland Colonel fly for *Field and Stream*. Years later, after college, in 1958, André would turn down a job as McClane's assistant at that magazine order to set up Abercrombie and Fitchs's San Francisco store. He stayed there two years, because he promised his father he would, then quit to enter an era in which a year had three seasons: the season of fishing, then of hunting, then the season of girls.

><+>-O-<+><

"The latter eventually confused Andy, apparently, leading to marriage, settling down, a successful real estate career—but never mind all them—they can put Andy in their own hall of fame. And one day Andy and Jim Adams (Andy considers Adams one of the greatest unsung heroes of California Fisheries Conservation), stood on a bridge on Highway 299, glaring down, counting squawfish, and conceiving then the Hat Creek project that led Andy to start the first California chapter of Trout Unlimited, with Andy as president, then to the Crystal Lake spawning program. Ultimately, Andy served as National Director of TU.

><+>-O-<+><

"All this is clearly important to tonight's induction, to who Andy is in flyfishing. I wrote up much of it once and shared a draft with Richard Anderson, editor and publisher of *California Fly Fisher*, who agreed to look it over even though the article was destined for *Fly Fisherman*, because that magazine began in the back of Andy's camper one day on the Big Hole River. After nodding in a kindly fashion, Richard hesitated, then said something to the effect of, 'Flies. The man is famous for his flies. What happened to the flies?'

><+>-O-<+><

"It is really annoying when someone does that. Of course, the flies had been there all along. I just put down the history because it was fascinating and because, as you are all aware, Andy's most idle patter about flies would make a good book. What he says about deer hair is Volume III of that encyclopedia. Volume Four addresses hackle, going back to Andy stealing capes from Cuban fighting cocks, presumably the losers. Andy's theories about pattern and style, structure, about the value of identifying the nature of materials, Nature's use, that a tyer employs to create artifice (as in the classic AP nymph series, the André Puyans, as important as the 'All Purpose' AP fly sold by some national company)...

"As valuable as anything else, perhaps, is the precision Andy brings to tying, the meticulous approach that has nothing to do with picayune perfectionism, but with an exactness of understanding: that *this* is the size of *that* insect, the shape, the color—here is the quality of translucence, the way it moves or drifts at a specific stage of its life—this is, therefore, what the trout may expect.

"Books—put them together—and in the telling, inevitably, Andy will punctuate each with stories like how Jack Horner came to the Goofus, the accident of the Cosell body, and the tale about returning to a particular motel room year after year in order to clip magic fibers from an ugly orange carpet.

"There's little point in trying to describe Andy's fly tying achievements tonight, the Buszek Award speaks to his significance. The field has no greater honor.

"What might be important, however, are perspectives that emerged from these lessons: tying, teaching tying, and the history of the flies we tie are all intricately knotted together in Andy's mind. It's easier to skin alive most large mammals than to separate Andy from his sense of source. Every hackle wrapped to a hook has a history of birds and breeding: the hook has a tale of its own, so does the thread. Each element involves evolution, the innovations of a man or woman who fished a particular place and time, was influenced by water and insects and people who came before. Having lived his life flyfishing, Andy seems always cognizant of the turn of another tyer's hand on the fly that he now ties. *His memory serves as archive.*

"He brings all this to his teaching. It's safe to say that, with everything Andy has brought to this sport, that his teaching remains special. It's evident when he talks about classes he did for Vietnam vets, for Kenyans in a fly tying project there, and especially when he recalls kids in a program run by Diablo Valley Fly Fishers—years in a row, they won the top places in the national contest, the same kids Ernie Schweibert called 'Puyans' flyfishing commandos,' claiming he'd seen them 'setting up a beachhead in the park on the Madison.'

"Mel Krieger, who ought to know, wanted me to stress that it is as teacher that Andy has been, and is now, of greatest benefit to the flyfishing world.

"But there is something else, something in addition, that's vital to many people in this room and those who would like to be here. It's an element of Andy's impact that crept up on me, as obvious as it is.

"Before our interviews, during breaks when Andy did business or answered calls, afterward...people would slip in to talk in sometimes passionate terms about Andy's importance to flyfishing, insisting that, by God, it was time he got his due. One described how Andy would study and strategize on a stream, swearing that this was the zenith of the sport. Another insisted that not only had Andy taught him to fish and tie flies, but influenced him to hunt beasts for hair and fur. I believe he was learning to make his own weapons to do that, and I suspect that after another year with Andy, he'll probably be dying them using secretions from his own body.

➤┼◆➤━O━◄┼◄

"I'd write all these stories down. Tape them. Look them over later.

"I looked them over again when I was asked to give this presentation. They were important. I wanted to hear more. I asked around.

➤┼◆➤━O━◄┼◄

"Now, everybody has an Andy Puyans story. It may be funny or wild or warm, an observation of craft or skill, a moral or immoral tale. As Andy's stories are legion, so are the stories about him, almost legends ('Andy's Fables'), including fly tying bacchanals, interstate cab rides, Andy's 40-foot cast to flick a Bic, Andy showing grace in the face of the wretched English snob, Andy tying posts from the tail of the Blue Ox, Babe. Some of the best stories I heard must wait to be told, because that's the way it is with the statute of limitations, and because two people called back, worrying about libel. In the meantime, at least one person in this room should know that Andy never did hook that big, sly trout on Henry's Fork, that when he handed you the bucking rod and you felt that terrible strength, you were, in fact, fighting your first muskrat. And that's the reason, not great sportsmanship, why Andy broke him off, saying to you, 'You've got to learn that you don't need to land them all.'

➤┼◆➤━O━◄┼◄

"Now...bear with me...that story reminded me of one Andy told about Polly Rosborough, which, in the end, led me around and around again to a greater vision of Andy's role in the flyfishing world.

"But first, Andy's anecdotes about Polly Rosborough will someday fill *Hustler* magazine's first flyfishing edition, pending photos, of course. The muskrat incident had recalled another time on the Williamson, when Andy was fishing one of Polly's own flies. Toward evening he saw an enormous swirl, so he chopped down to ought-X tippet; and then, for half a frightening hour afterward, struggling desperately to break off the beaver he'd snagged. Exhausted, shaken, Andy finally returned to tell Polly all about it.

"'Man, was Polly disgusted.' First, because the beaver wasn't a 'keeper' by Andy's description, did not have a hide big enough to wrap around a Calistoga wagon rim; then, because Andy had lost one of Polly's precious, much cemented flies.

"Now, Polly's cementing style, as it happens, had appeared in several other stories, tied in with Andy's admiration of Polly's knowledge of fur, specifically the fur of aquatic mammals, and also with Andy's extending credit to Polly for bringing proper dimensions to the tying of Western nymphs. Of course, the actual stories involved an ex-wife, Polly tying in nasty boxer shorts, classical music, steelhead flies burning in the oven, cheesecake photos, Bud Lilly and a Conclave where Andy teased Polly until the Old Man glued his scissors shut and left screaming, 'You son-of-a-bitch, you son-of-a-bitch,' forgetting an entire jungle cock neck…

"You get the idea.

"Suddenly, so did I.

"André Puyans keeps in his head a tapestry of flyfishing history, woven in a thousand bright stories. From early on, he seemed to have a sense of other people's roles, how the sharing of individual visions shaped a great progression. His stories make living men and women out of names now associated with movements, styles, advances of science and art. In the telling, Andy is archivist, sometimes player, but in either role and in every incident, he strives to create a sense of inclusion, recall connections, link today to the past with a knot pulled tight from either end of time.

"If this is true, I thought, then what does it mean when the same qualities begin to appear in the stories others tell about Andy: a similar tone…an ethos…a sense of invitation that suggests that 'we are all in this together?'

>—+—•—○—•—+—<

"I had been looking, I think, for a couple of wonderful anecdotes that would grandly reveal Andy—'André on the Mount,' 'André Parts

the Madison,' 'Et Tu André'—archetypal anecdotes, symbolic. But looking back over notes, remembering conversations, reading letters, what
struck me was another kind of approach altogether, in which many
people said, one way or another, 'Gosh, I don't suppose this is that
important, but I wanted to say that I went into Andy's shop without
knowing much, with just a question or looking for a tippet, and when
I came out nine hours later, he'd changed my life.'

" 'He helped me more than he'll ever know,' read one tribute somebody sent me. Another says 'Andy shared information that some would
consider priceless.' Another: 'He's offered a million dollars worth of
knowledge to anybody who came and asked.' Two small manufacturers
I know had the same experience as I did, bringing in a product or a
prototype that Andy looked at, tried, praised or improved, and in the
process, put us on a road we're glad to travel.

"*Included* us.

>—+—•>—○—<•—+—<

"Ed Rice considers him 'The Fly Fishing Renaissance Man.' Ernie
Schweibert calls Andy the 'Unabridged Schwiebert.' John Randolph
also said, 'Andy knows more about fly tying and trout fishing than anyone who ever lived.'

>—+—•>—○—<•—+—<

"Which all suggest importance. As does this induction into the Fly
Fishing Hall of Fame. But I suggest there is another measure of Andy's
legacy, found in people who walked into Creative Sports, who took a
class or a trip with Andy and found themselves changed by a kind of
generosity, a humanity they now associate with our sport because Andy
presented it that way. And now, how many of these people carry on that
tradition—offering of themselves to other fishers, telling stories today
that weave Andy into the very history he loyally maintains and lights for
us to view? Call it charisma or kindness; consider him archivist, historian, player, innovator, teacher, but certainly he serves as emissary for a
spirit that is vital to flyfishing, well placed in this hall, here tonight
among us.

"Hear, hear."